SIGNS AND SYMBOLS
IN CHAUCER'S POETRY

SIGNS AND SYMBOLS IN

CHAUCER'S

POETRY

edited by

John P. Hermann

and

John J. Burke, Jr.

The University of Alabama Press
University, Alabama

Library of Congress Cataloging in Publication Data

Alabama Symposium on English and American Literature,
4th, University of Alabama, 1977.
Signs and symbols in Chaucer's poetry.

Bibliography: p.
Includes index.
1. Chaucer, Geoffrey, d. 1400—Allegory and
symbolism—Congresses. 2. Symbolism in literature—
Congresses. I. Hermann, John P., 1947– II. Burke,
John J., 1942– III. Title.
PR1933.A44A4 1977   821'.1   80–11064
ISBN 0-8173-0038-4
ISBN 0-8173-0042-2 (pbk.)

Perhaps as you read, you will wonder to see the meaning that was lately hidden under a rough shell brought forth now into the light—as if one were to see fresh water gushing from a globe of fire—and you will even praise yourself with a kind of mild satisfaction, that you have long been of the right opinion about poets, not, like the invidious, taking them for mere story-tellers, but rather for men of great learning, endowed with a sort of divine intelligence and skill.

BOCCACCIO

CONTENTS

SIGNS AND SYMBOLS
IN CHAUCER'S POETRY

INTRODUCTION

"No poet in the whole English literary tradition," observes John Gardner, "not even Shakespeare, is more appealing, either as a man or as an artist, than Geoffrey Chaucer."[1] What Chaucerian would wish to quarrel with such generous praise? Indeed, it might also be argued that no major figure in English literary tradition has profited more from the labors of modern literary critics. D. W. Robertson, Jr. has, in recent years, been at the center of the most fruitful critical work on Chaucer. Many scholars, whether favorably or unfavorably impressed by the so-called allegorical criticism, have found themselves confronting new aspects of Chaucer's poetry and modifying long-held critical positions after the intellectually invigorating experience of first looking into Robertson's Chaucer. *Signs and Symbols in Chaucer's Poetry* demonstrates the continuing vitality of contemporary Chaucerian literary iconography, and reveals possible directions for Chaucer studies in the future.

But first something should be said about this way of looking at the poetry of Chaucer, an approach often termed "Robertsonianism," although, as Robertson has pointed out, it might just as well be called "Huppéism." A useful way to appreciate not only what this method is but, more importantly, what it is not, is to examine a short article published almost a decade before *A Preface to Chaucer*, Robertson's most influential work. Provocatively entitled "Why the Devil Wears Green,"[2] it can serve as an epitome of the Robertsonian approach because of its brevity and simplicity; from it can be gathered the theoretical basis for much of the later work that builds upon discoveries made originally by Robertson and Huppé. The article itself, only two pages long, is devoted to providing an explanation for the green coat worn by the devil-yeoman in the Friar's Tale. Previously, the color had been discussed in connection with Celtic underworld lore, a kind of *ignotum per ignotius*. Robertson, who had for years been reading widely in medieval Latin paraliterary texts, came across an illuminating passage in the great encyclopedist Pierre Bersuire, a representative humanist of Chaucer's day and personal friend to the poets Philippe de Vitry and Petrarch. Bersuire points out that beasts are attracted to the color green because it is pleasing to them, and that hunters dress in green when in forests as camouflage, in order to appear pleasing and not to forewarn their victims. Bersuire's moralization of this characteristically medieval lore follows: "The devil is a hunter, that is to say, a hypocrite, who wears green clothing. He puts on honest conversation so that with a pretence of exterior honesty he can attract beasts (that is, the simple) to himself; and as long as they can not guard against the ambushes of his malice, he can ensnare and cheat them. Therefore, it is well said in Matthew 7: 'Look out for false prophets, who come to you in the clothing of sheep, but inwardly are ravenous wolves.'"[3] Such a scriptural explanation has none of the glamor of pagan Celtic mythology, and certain modern attitudes toward the artist as a rebel against the life-denying conventions of his age militate against our seeking an understanding of Chaucer in such a dry and dusty place. Yet Robertson's discovery in Bersuire clarifies the iconography of the devil-yeoman in a way that has great explanatory power. In terms of the thought structures of the fourteenth century, it helps account for the fact that the Yeoman's confession that he is a demon does not seem to disturb the Summoner in the tale, as well as for the Yeoman's excessively smooth conversation as he stalks his human prey in the forest. These narrative elements are closely related to his greenness, a symbolic coloration analogous in the moral sphere to a favored camouflage technique of actual hunters in the Middle Ages.

    Robertson's method of criticism, as this brief example shows, is primarily a historical one in that it makes use of source materials from the period of the text or from earlier periods when they are relevant. It is the historical impulse that leads to an emphasis on the importance of medieval iconographic habits, which to the modern eye can often seem bizarre. The thought structures of the fourteenth century differ from ours in many ways, but the most important have to do with imagery. One could well imagine a literary historian of the twenty-sixth century baffled by the following sentence in a twentieth-century text: "Because of his kindness, she gave him the green light." What sort of gift, he might wonder, is a green light? Signs have meaning only within a cultural context, and oftentimes the context for Chaucer is manifestly not our own. Green, then, clearly may be a different sign for the fourteenth century than it is for us today. Signata can be quite difficult to uncover; those of the fourteenth century are not necessarily the same as those of the twentieth, and multiple signata are also frequent. Furthermore, one of the major obstacles in understanding medieval texts is that we can easily be unaware that a sign is being used at all, so unfamiliar are we with many iconographic conventions of the age.

    A parallel to this line of argument can be found whenever the reader attempts to discover the denotation of a word, or verbal sign. The word *licour* in line three of the General Prologue does not necessarily mean the same as its modern English reflex *liquor*. Words shift referents. Processes of specialization, generalization, melioration, and pejoration occur, even when the phonology remains stable. In fact, the stability of the phonology is often the most misleading aspect of the earlier stages of one's native language. The scholar must discover not only what the word means now, but what it meant then; otherwise, it is quite easy to misinterpret even the plain grammatical sense. Just as the referents of words must be painstakingly tracked down so precise semantic limits can be grasped, so must the function of those referents themselves within the sign system of the culture be made clear, and their interrelationships mapped out, if we are to avoid misreading the text.

According to Augustine, a sign is "a thing which causes us to think of something beyond the impression the thing itself makes upon the senses." The term *symbol* can be taken as equivalent to the term *sign;* associations of the former term with the poetic techniques of modern times are not so serious that they render it useless. Iconography focuses initially on the identification of signs. While this identification is of the first importance in studying medieval texts, one would be right to bristle at the notion that the identification of signs is in and of itself a satisfactory criticism of a medieval literary work. The sign can be deployed in ways that undercut its function as a simple determiner of the meaning of a text, as when irony is present. In addition, there are polyvalued signs, some of which also have meanings *in bono* and *in malo*. Identification of the presence and meaning of signs is simply a highly important stage in coming to understand medieval literature.

In the Middle Ages many signs had referents which were suggested originally by the Bible, and consequently were reinforced by the exegetical techniques for reading the Bible common to the period. Other sources for literary signs include etymology, topology, the classics, the liturgy, everyday life, the trivium and quadrivium, the physiologus, lapidaries, herbals, the apocrypha and pseudepigrapha, and the pictorial arts, to mention only some of the more significant. An understanding of the role of the Bible is crucial for comprehending medieval literature. According to one well-known formulation, there are four levels to Scripture: the literal, or historical sense; the allegorical, referring to Christ and his Church; the tropological, concerned with moral principles and the soul of the individual believer; and the anagogical, in which the mysteries of the faith are augured. However, these levels are not always present in any given passage. Moreover, there are other useful exegetical methods, such as Hugh of St. Victor's notion of the *littera*, or grammatical and syntactical level of understanding; the *sensus*, or narrative meaning; and the *sententia*, or doctrinal content, which Hugh uncovers not only in sacred writings, but in secular ones as well. Similar notions occur frequently in medieval literature: the literal sense is called the *cortex, integumentum, involucrum,* and *pallium,* while the profound sense is referred to as the *nux, nucleus, granum,* and *medulla.* Cognates for these terms are widespread in the medieval vernaculars. A useful primary source in this regard is Peter of Riga's *Aurora,* a versified Bible with gloss which Chaucer mentions in *The Book of the Duchess.*[4] Who, if he were unfamiliar with medieval exegesis, would ever have realized that the plague of blood in Exodus is seen in the *Aurora* as dangerous poetic doctrine that dirties decent minds, and the plague of frogs as heresy that befouls true belief? Or that the decoration of the ark has a spiritual meaning for every detail, including colors, fabrics, clasps, and numbers used in measurement? We have seen similar allegorization of a seemingly insignificant color in Bersuire's moralizing interpretation of the color green. The sign system in medieval society, in large part because of the importance of the Bible and the methods used for allegorizing the Bible, is one in which green can signify as it does in the Friar's Tale without the need for any creation of an original symbol on the part of the poet. The originality of the medieval artist can usually be best seen in the use subsequently made of the traditional stock of symbols.

The historical critic, as Robertson pointed out in his English Institute essay "Historical Criticism," must attempt more than the identification of signs. He must "reconstruct the intellectual attitudes and the cultural ideals of a period in order to reach a fuller understanding of its literature."[5] This attempt at reconstruction, which parallels that of the anthropologist in significant ways, has been a lifelong enterprise for both Robertson and Huppé, and will continue to occupy large numbers of scholars for the foreseeable future. In the meantime, many of their conclusions about the intellectual attitudes and ideals of medieval culture which shocked medievalists twenty years ago are now gaining support from the findings of scholars in other fields. A recent article in *Speculum* entitled "Fourteenth-Century Religious Thought: A Premature Profile" argues:

> There is no period in the history of medieval thought which could not be presented as a new phase in the appropriation of Augustine. Yet in the third decade of the fourteenth century we encounter a revival of Augustine which may well lay claim to the much abused designation Renaissance. Its chief characteristic is that Augustine was no longer presented as only one of the four Church Fathers, but rather as the authoritative and definitive interpreter of the one *Evangelium* located in the Scriptures.[6]

Such a view of the fourteenth century is not surprising to those who have followed Huppé and Robertson into the important primary sources of the period. Because of their insistence upon the use of primary materials, they long ago recognized the key importance of Augustine and avoided the overemphasis on Thomism characteristic of much medieval intellectual history. Robertson's historicism, as we have seen, is leavened throughout by an astute iconographic awareness. The criticism that his reconstruction of the fourteenth century and its symbolic code is somewhat abstract, that *caritas* and *cupiditas* are not the only thematic particulars of interest, is one that Robertson has been willing to accept. However, it must also be recognized that *caritas* is not a reductionist concept when employed by writers of the Middle Ages. As Robertson points out, "the word *charity*, like the word *sea*, is a little misleading. In both instances a single word stands for something of infinite and continuous elaboration and variation, for something which no human mind can grasp in its entirety. For Charity, like the sea, although fundamentally a constant, changes in specific applications with time and person, with place and circumstance."[7] That the *sententia* of much medieval literature should deal with loving, and that this loving should be given a Christian orientation, are not on the surface particularly surprising conclusions. However, the iconographic approach does not necessitate an overriding concern with *caritas*. Opponents of Robertson and Robertsonians sometimes seem to assume that the claim is being made that there is no more to the poetry than what they draw attention to, surely an unwarranted assumption. Indeed, one might grant the presence of signs, yet argue that Chaucer is putting them to an artistic use quite unlike their use elsewhere in the culture, and arrive at very different conclusions. Chaucerian literary iconography, it must be remembered, can benefit from diverse critical approaches.

That the contributions of Robertson and Huppé to our knowledge of Chaucer's use of signs are incomplete should surprise no one. Their work could only be a beginning. Because iconographic work is necessarily thematically oriented, one of the directions taken in recent Chaucer criticism involves careful attention to the precise historical milieu. Is there any historical evidence in surviving records which would enable us to show in greater detail how iconographic conventions were realized in the everyday life of nobility and commons? It is in the direction of the study of the iconography of daily life that new discoveries are being made, and close attention to this area will undoubtedly continue to enrich our understanding of literary and cultural ideals of the fourteenth century.

Each of the nine essays in this collection makes a worthwhile contribution, in one way or another, to the ongoing study of Geoffrey Chaucer's poetry—our precious legacy from what were once scorned as "unenlightened" times. They share the common concern of detecting, evaluating, and interpreting the signs and symbols in Chaucer's poetry. The lead essay, by D. W. Robertson, Jr., is an examination of the meaning Chaucer may have attached to simple signs from everyday life in the later fourteenth century. That in itself is noteworthy, since it marks a shift in Robertson's critical attention. And, as we have come to expect of

him, at the same time that he makes his own telling points, he opens up
new possibilities for discussion and research by others. In earlier
work—both his own and that done in collaboration with Bernard F.
Huppé—he has pointed out the signs that place Chaucer in the Christian
tradition of the Apostle Paul, Augustine, and Boethius. Here he turns
away from those literary signs deriving from scriptural tradition and
often shared with the visual arts, and moves toward those signs rooted in
the specific historical circumstances of Chaucer's own time. His chief
interest is the rapid growth of the woolen industry in the later fourteenth century—with all that would have implied to Chaucer about the
kind of people the English might become—and how this in turn colored
Chaucer's portrait of the Wife of Bath. At the very least, the new prosperity was abetting desires for more and better worldly goods and upset-
ting the traditional sense of social hierarchy. All this, Robertson feels,
gave pungency and point to Chaucer's portrait of Dame Alice. Such
comments on his own times rather than the timeless or universal meaning, Robertson concludes, may well have been the principal interest of
Chaucer's original audience.

Edmund Reiss focuses attention on Chaucer's thematic particulars,
that is, particular signs with larger meanings. These are details, such as
the number "nyne and twenty" or the "preestes thre" attending the
Prioress, that seem to serve little or no narrative purpose. Sometimes
they are indicated by seemingly random repetition, such as a more than
ordinary number of references to the song of the nightingale or various
uses of the name Alisoun. Sometimes they are details that seem gratuitous or have no apparent point to a modern audience, such as the
characterization of Egeus in the Knight's Tale or the presence of the
"mayde child" in the Shipman's Tale. Sometimes they can be as casual as
Harry Bailey telling the Monk that he thought his contribution was "nat
worth a boterflye." Each of these, as Reiss demonstrates, has the rich
suggestiveness and complexity of meaning and purpose we should expect
from a supreme literary artist.

In earlier pieces, David Chamberlain has demonstrated the importance of musical signs and symbols in *The Parliament of Fowls* and in the
Nun's Priest's Tale.[8] Here he considers both the convention and the
originality in Chaucer's musical references by ranging through the entire Chaucerian canon. Nevertheless, he pays special attention to the role
of music in *The Canterbury Tales,* and argues that Chaucer provided *The
Canterbury Tales* with a significant musical frame. The sign of "melodye,"
he points out, is first introduced at the beginning of the General Prologue and brought to fulfillment in the Manciple's Tale, just before
Chaucer's Parson will treat divine justice in prose. Chamberlain's argument, then, assigns new importance to an easily slighted tale while offering an extraordinary range of insights into the meaning of music in the
Middle Ages.

The next two essays are concerned with Chaucer's use of signs in parts of *The Canterbury Tales*. Chauncey Wood examines the way Chaucer makes use of signs in his General Prologue portrait of the Prioress by adopting the techniques of Stanley Fish's affective stylistics. His point is that we get our best gauge on what Chaucer intended us to see in the portrait only if we understand what Chaucer's fourteenth-century audience expected a nun to be. Drawing from many sources, but particularly from the *Ancrene Riwle,* Wood argues that the signs Chaucer provides indicate that his Prioress does not measure up to first expectations. Her wimple, for instance, is pleated, not plain—an external sign of internal disorder. The unexpectedly brief and somewhat bathetic description of her conscience is an example of a descending catalogue that does not descend—another sign pointing towards the same conclusion. In short, he argues, Chaucer's use of signs forces his audience to adjust and re-evaluate their initially favorable responses to the Prioress and ultimately leads them to judge Madame Eglentyne, as a nun and because she was a nun, far more harshly than we have been led to suspect.

Gail McMurray Gibson directs our attention to what at first seems unpromising material—the bawdy Shipman's Tale—and comes up with surprising results. She finds that this tale is a sign pointing toward and beyond the Parson's Tale. She focuses on those elements in the Ship-man's Tale that make of it, beneath its frivolous surface, a deft and deliberate parody of the drama of Christ's appearance to Mary Magda-len after his Resurrection. The purpose of this parody, she argues, is to evoke the doomsday theme that we must pay for our array. The words *pay* and *array* are hauntingly echoed in the rhymes; they are illustrated in the events of a tale that reveals its characters' paying for what passes and arraying themselves in what perishes. The lack of temporal justice in the tale's conclusion, she feels, only draws attention to the nontemporal justice to come in the final reckoning when, indeed, we must all pay for our array.

The next three essays deal with signs in other works by Chaucer. The evidence of apparently conflicting signs in *The Book of the Duchess* is the problem considered by James I. Wimsatt. Many of this poem's conventions, he feels, link it firmly to a genre of secular love poems, particularly to those which stress complaint and comfort for the loss of a loved one. By making his poem a human and humane attempt to console his ducal patron in his grief, Chaucer fulfills the expectations aroused by this genre. But Wimsatt also sees the poem's biblical allusions and strategic puns as an indication that Chaucer was working within a second genre. The key pun occurs in the phrase "toun of Tewnes." It can refer to the city of Tunis, a town fabled for its riches, but it also alludes to the town of towns (the New Jerusalem of the Book of Apocalypse) and to the tune of tunes (the Song of Songs or the Canticle of Canticles). Both of these evoke the "new song" of the Incarnation. Such puns, along with numerous other echoes of the language of the Book of Apocalypse and the Canticle of Canticles, link *The Book of the Duchess* to the Eden cantos of Dante's *Purgatorio,* to the Middle English *Pearl,* and thus to a genre of religious visions rooted in the Bible. In this genre Blanche of Lancaster (Lady White) becomes associated with the Virgin and thus with the perfected soul; she becomes the promise of what lies ahead for the blessed. Wimsatt concludes that Chaucer was writing in both genres at the same time, that the poem realizes its meanings in both contexts separately and simultaneously. Chaucer left it to his audience to see one or the other or both.

V. A. Kolve directs our attention to the unfinished *Legend of Good Women.* His purpose is to find the "idea" of a poem that, like *The Canterbury Tales,* is unfinished but conceptually complete, to discover how Chaucer's arrangement of his materials might constitute a sign pointing towards his ultimate meaning. The first puzzle is the initial legend itself, that of Cleopatra, a seemingly improbable candidate for sainthood, even if it be the sainthood of love. But Chaucer made substantial alterations in the legend ordinarily associated with Cleopatra. His Cleopatra, for instance, is Antony's wife, not his mistress. Moreover, there are other indications that Chaucer departed significantly from the usual iconographic tradition for representing the death of Cleopatra, at least insofar as this can be determined from evidence available in the visual arts. The point of all these alterations, Kolve argues, was to demonstrate the inadequacy of the most noble conception of mutual erotic love the pagan world could provide. Cleopatra's tragedy and the tragedies of those who follow (and who would have followed) are tragedies of despair, of suffering without purpose, of death without redemptive meaning. But this pattern, he maintains, was to be transformed in the final legend of Alceste, a legend that figuratively possessed the very elements so conspicuously lacking in the earlier legends. The story of Alceste is the story of a lover willing to die so that another might live; it is the story of a savior rescuing a virtuous soul from hell. Thus her legend constitutes, according to Kolve, a sign pointing towards a meaning beyond fame. The idea of *The Legend of Good Women* is, he concludes, one of a progress towards the purposeful suffering of Christ's death on the cross, of a salvific act that rescues the virtuous from hell. Such an idea reveals a Chaucer questing for the most truthful poetry of all.

The essay by Bernard F. Huppé complements an earlier and famous one on Chaucer's *Troilus* by his friend and collaborator Robertson.[9] In it Robertson argued that the *Troilus* must be read as a tragedy. Huppé clearly agrees with that conclusion, but he feels obligated to account for the palpably comic tone of so much of the poem, indeed for its elements of sheer clowning. There is, moreover, much evidence of dissymmetry in the poem, particularly in the proems, that is puzzling for an age that clearly valued symmetry. Actually the *Troilus* is a triumph of subtle design, Huppé argues, once we realize how Chaucer makes use of a narrative *persona* that is deliberately unreliable. There are many indications that the narrator is not to be trusted. He pretends, for instance, to be translating a poem by Lollius when he is actually working from Boccaccio's *Filostrato*. His first three books divide the progress of Troilus's passion into three stages—the lover's hell, his purgatory, his paradise—that clearly correspond to the structure of the *Divine Comedy*. Though he parodies Dante, there is no recognition of what his gruesome inversion might mean. What becomes clear, Huppé argues, is that the narrator himself is involved only with the surface of the story. He becomes aware of its sentence, of its tragedy, only with the shock of recognition that comes when his source's Troilus laughs at his own funeral observances. At this point, Huppé concludes, the narrator himself realizes that the story he has been so carefully translating reveals the futility of earthly love and so constitutes a sign pointing upwards towards the eternal reality of heavenly love, the only thing we as human beings can really depend on.

John Gardner's essay provides a fitting conclusion to this collection, not because it summarizes them, but because it demonstrates that key issues are still open. Gardner draws attention to Chaucer's habit of poetic cancellation, whether it be canceling his signs and symbols with irony and humor, or canceling, as he does in his *Retraction,* his most successful aesthetic creations. Gardner freely admits that the signs and symbols are there in Chaucer's text—something not so freely admitted before the pioneering work of Robertson and Huppé. They are there, for instance, in abundance in the Miller's Tale. But they do not make of it, he argues, a pious meditation, because its exuberant comedy cancels an overly serious effect. On other occasions, Chaucer cancels any overly serious meaning by writing intentionally bad poems. Such, he believes, is the case with the Physician's Tale. Chaucer's real purpose in such instances, he argues, was to show how easy it is to get things wrong once one is sure that one is absolutely right. A third kind of cancellation Gardner finds more baffling. These are the cancellations of Chaucer's best work; his cancellation, for instance, of the Second Nun's Tale by the Canon's Yeoman's Tale. Such can only be explained, he maintains, by appealing to the new intellectual climate taking shape in the later fourteenth century, a climate reacting to implications in the works of earlier thinkers such as Peter Abelard, Roger Bacon, and William of Ockham. It convinced thinking men like Chaucer that we could not be certain about ultimate matters, including who would be damned and who would be saved. Thus the Second Nun's Tale demonstrates that salvation is gained by those whose vision is clear, but is canceled by the Canon's Yeoman's Tale, which demonstrates that salvation can also be gained by those whose vision is dim. God's wisdom could not be the wisdom of men. That and that alone was Chaucer's ultimate certainty.

In addition to the value of the individual essays—the contributions each one makes to an important topic in Chaucer studies—they have as a group another value. They tell us much about where we are, while also pointing to the future. That is, they open up avenues for research by others, avenues that may yet prove to be as fruitful and illuminating as anything we have discovered in the past. These essays contain, for instance, many appeals to Chaucer's audience to justify one interpretation rather than another. Yet to cite but one example of obvious contrast, Robertson and Gardner have very different views of just who the people were who most likely constituted Chaucer's audience. It would seem that more research can and should be done on those figures who can be linked with Chaucer, if for no other reason than to determine as best we can just what their responses to his poetry might have been. These essays also clearly establish our need to know more about everyday life in the late fourteenth century. We need to know more about the political, social, and economic conditions that shaped Chaucer's world. We need to know more about the piety and beliefs of the common people, of the court, and of the intellectuals. We need to know more about relationships between literature and the visual arts, between literature and music, between literature and politics. It also seems clear that we have by no means exhausted our explorations of the territory opened up long ago by Robertson: namely, that medieval sensibility, medieval psychology, medieval habits of understanding are often quite different from our own. That, for instance, the medieval response to a sign or symbol is not the same as our response in the post-romantic era; that uncertainty in the Middle Ages was not and could not be the same as uncertainty in the twentieth century. The medieval notion of hierarchy is another topic that may need further examination. The last decades of the fourteenth century saw English peasants rebelling against their feudal masters, an English priest challenging the doctrinal authority of the awesome Catholic Church, English nobles rising up to dethrone and ultimately murder an anointed king. Such events suggest at the very least that the medieval concept of hierarchy may well be more complex, more ready to shift with changing circumstances, than many of us have suspected. Our research should not neglect distinctions that need to be sharpened about the Chaucerian moment.

Finally, it is only just to acknowledge that this volume is the product of a community of effort. The work of the contributors—and perhaps that of the editors—is visible and obvious, but their work depended on the help and support of many others, not all of whom can be mentioned without hopelessly extending this introduction. The preliminary versions of the essays in this volume were read in October of 1977 at the

Fourth Alabama Symposium on English and American Literature. Richard Thigpen as acting chief executive of The University of Alabama and later David Mathews as the returning president provided important support at an early stage. The same must be said for the College of Arts and Sciences under the leadership of Dean Douglas E. Jones. The Division of Continuing Education provided invaluable help in arranging the original conference. We received special cooperation from Thomas Rabbitt, the University's Director of Creative Writing. We owe much to our colleagues in the English Department, and we thank them through our chairpersons, Dwight L. Eddins and Carol McGinnis Kay. As always in cases like this, we depended upon the patience and support of our wives, Jean and Mary. Finally, we acknowledge the financial assistance provided by the Research Grants Committee of The University of Alabama that helped make the preparation of this volume possible.

JOHN P. HERMANN
JOHN J. BURKE, JR.

SIMPLE SIGNS
FROM EVERYDAY LIFE
IN CHAUCER

D. W. ROBERTSON, JR.

Perhaps it would be helpful at the outset if I explained my title or "theme," somewhat in the fashion of a good medieval preacher, although I have never, in spite of my reputation, sought to rival a good preacher. The title, "Simple Signs from Everyday Life in Chaucer," falls into three parts: "Signs," "Everyday Life," and "Chaucer," which I shall discuss in that order, including under "Chaucer" some brief observations about the poet, his audience, and his work. I regret that I do not have time for more *exempla,* since these, as any good preacher knows, are more entertaining than anything else. But to begin with the word *sign,* I should like to say at the outset that I do not care much for disputes about terminology, which strike me as being pedantic. However, I think that Chaucerians should use as much medieval terminology as possible, recognizing the fact that medieval authors except for scholastic theologians tended to use terms rather loosely. But modern terms tend to carry with them connotations in a universe of discourse alien to that of the Middle Ages. The term *sign* has the advantage of being current in the Middle Ages and being very loose at the same time, allowing me considerable freedom, since a *sign* is simply something that signifies something else. *Signs,* as Saint Augustine tells us,[1] may be either words or things, or even actions, some of which are literal and some of which are figurative. The word *iconography,* borrowed from art history, implies the identification of objects represented, or the study of literal signs, whereas *iconology,* borrowed from the same discipline, is concerned with meanings.[2] Many persons, myself included, use *iconography* to mean both, a simple and convenient stratagem. The word *symbol* has the disadvantage of bearing connotations in modern art and literature consistent with an expressionistic style, so that it can sometimes be misleading when used in connection with styles different from expressionism, and I think that C. S. Lewis was wrong in adducing such symbols in the Middle Ages.[3] Finally, although medieval writers used the terms *types* and *antitypes,* the word *typology* is late and not generally current in the Middle Ages. As I have sought to show elsewhere,[4] the juxtaposition of types and antitypes in accordance with what was called *allegoria* in scriptural exposition usually implied a moral or "tropological" meaning, so that the mere juxtaposition of Old and New Testament events or even fictional or current events with scriptural events carried out for its own sake, without further implication, was not a common medieval practice, in spite of some observations in a recent book.[5] Altogether the word *sign* thus has distinct advantages, although I have no wish to be pedantic about this, nor to condemn anyone for using the other terms mentioned, especially since I have used all of them myself.

A sign, like a word, may mean one thing to one individual and something else to another, for no two of us have exactly the same experience. But members of a given culture often employ figurative signs that mean roughly the same things to many other individuals in that culture, although a sign may have a more profound or more emotionally charged meaning to some than to others, depending on differences in experience, education, and intelligence; and there may be some who fail to perceive some figurative signs, or who take them literally.[6] "Meanings" do not exist in words, events, or things, but in the individuals who perceive them, where they have a certain regularity because of custom. Since people are constantly changing, both within generations and from one generation to the next, "meanings" change constantly. It is also true that the meaning of a sign may be very different from that of its referent. For example, the printed word *tiger,* even burning brightly in the forests of the night, does not alarm me, but an actual untethered tiger in my vicinity would suggest immediate evasive action. Similarly, a broiled lobster on a plate before me might produce one kind of meaning if I were hungry and quite another meaning if I had just eaten three of them. To put this in another way, the universe of discourse is made up of arbitrary signs, and these are not identical with the universe itself. Both shift with time and circumstance. The study of signs is thus difficult and poses many problems.

In recent years many scholars have become occupied with the study of figurative signs. Not all of them, incidentally, are "Robertsonians," since such studies, especially in the visual arts,[7] long antedate my own efforts, and students of Renaissance literature, some of whom have never heard of me, now sometimes pursue the subject with avidity. Signs from scriptural texts and their commentaries, from classical texts and their commentaries, or from mythographic writers, from astrology, from music, from early medieval texts, like the *Psychomachia* of Prudentius, from texts widely used in schools, like the *De nuptiis* of Martianus Capella, or the *De planctu Naturae* of Alanus, from popular vernacular texts like the *Roman de la Rose*, and from representational conventions in the visual arts, including the drama, have all been studied, and their presence traced in Chaucer's poetry. There is still a great deal of this sort of thing to be done. In many instances we do not understand earlier texts very well, and in others we lack readily available primary sources since many commentaries both on the Scriptures and on the classics remain unpublished, and others, especially from the late Middle Ages, have been lost. Moreover, much evidence from the visual arts has been destroyed by religious or rationalist zeal, or simply by the ravages of time. We are thus often forced to adduce traditions rather than sources, but in any event it is necessary to exercise extreme care to become familiar with available primary sources and to avoid speculation as much as possible. Rosalie Green of the Index of Christian Art has recently issued a very stern warning concerning undisciplined iconological studies,[8] and it would not be difficult to compile a long list of highly dubious interpretations of figurative signs in Chaucer studies, some of them ostensibly relying on primary materials.

Turning now to my second topic, "Everyday Life," I should like to assert first of all that this was Chaucer's primary concern and that he hoped that his work would be beneficial in a practical way. But this hope was probably tempered somewhat by a realization that passionate zeal is not productive and involves an undesirable submission to Fortune. That is, for the most part he seems to have taken his own advice in "Truth":

> Tempest thee noght al croked to redresse,
> In trust of hir that turneth as a bal.

He did not usually employ figurative signs and other forms of indirect language for merely decorative or what we might call "literary" purposes, but to comment, frequently in a humorous way, on the mores of his own time. Throughout the Middle Ages, but especially after the middle of the twelfth century, figurative devices of all kinds, combined with other devices like specious argument and irony,[9] were often used for humorous moral comment. Since we cannot hear Chaucer reading, we probably miss a great deal of his humor, especially various kinds of ironic intonation. However, we can probably rely on the advice of Boncompagno of Signa quoted by John F. Benton: "Irony is the unadorned and gentle use of words to convey disdain and ridicule. If he who expresses irony may be seen, the intention of the speaker may be understood through his gestures. In the absence of the speaker, manifest evil and impure belief indict the subject. . . . It is nothing but vituperation to commend the evil deeds of someone through their opposite, or to relate them wittily."[10] To the modern mind a basic moral stance and humor, like Ovid's majesty and love, do not readily go together; but in the Middle Ages even scriptural materials could be used humorously since they afforded a background of rationality or "pure belief" that could be used to comment on ludicrous speech or behavior,[11] a fact that has misled certain staid and serious readers of more recent times to invent such things as "the religion of courtly love," or to find "pagan values" (whatever they are) in medieval texts presented before reasonably orthodox audiences. Where Chaucer is concerned, the monitory raised finger and the prayer beads in the Hoccleve portrait, combined with his early reputation as a "philosopher," are probably sufficient indications of the basic attitude we should expect from him.

Chaucer's moral comment, although based on certain Christian principles that are not difficult to recover, even though literary scholars are sometimes reluctant to pursue their implications, was directed toward specific fourteenth-century English problems, and I think that it is time we paid more attention to these problems. Chaucer did not write "for all humanity," or "for all time," but for a specific audience that had immediate everyday concerns. The indirection he employed lent his comments a certain incisiveness, making them more entertaining and hence more effective than the more direct criticisms of his friend Gower. The evidence of the visual arts, music, and literature itself, not to mention overt statements by writers like Boccaccio and Petrarch, suggest strongly that sophisticated medieval audiences were not, like modern audiences, passive, awaiting technical operations on their feelings and vicarious thrills, but active and alert, perceiving the activities of the poet before them (who was often beneath them in rank) with a certain detachment, and demanding that he supply substantial food for thought in a diverting manner. I think that we often fail to realize the rather curious effects of mass culture in modern times and to discount those effects when we study earlier literature. The earlier attitude is well described by Erasmus, who wrote in a letter to a friend, "Horace thought that advice given jocularly had no less effect than that given seriously. 'What forbids,' he exclaims, 'that anyone speak the truth with a smile?' This fact has not been overlooked by the wisest men of antiquity who have preferred to express the most salutary principles of conduct in the form of laughable and childish fables, because the truth, a little austere in itself, adorned with the attraction of pleasure penetrates more easily into the minds of mortals." Erasmus goes on to cite Saint Augustine's *De doctrina Christiana* for the appearance of similar principles in the Scriptures.[12] Chaucer was thus fulfilling an ancient tradition when he read his Tales with a certain subtle indirection. But he also had in mind the immediate interests of his audience.

Much of Chaucer's figurative language was readily available, however, in "everyday" sources and was not in itself very obscure. The visual arts offer some fairly simple examples. Thus the significance of the Marriage at Cana, the implications of which are so blatantly disregarded by the

Wife of Bath, were explained in part in an inscription on a stained glass window at Canterbury,[13] a "gat-tothed" wife appears in an illustration for the *Roman de la Rose*,[14] cloistered monks leaving their cloisters to signify inconstancy appear in Gothic statuary,[15] wrestlers were used in marginalia to signify discord,[16] and so on. Since Chaucer was once appointed Clerk of the King's Works, an office that involved the maintenance of royal buildings and their decorations as well as the arrangement of pageantry, we can assume that he was familiar with a wide variety of representations in the visual arts. But it is also possible to find figurative signs in everyday sources that are neither "literary," exegetical, nor visually representative. For example, the pilgrimage of the spirit, now often adduced in connection with the larger thematic structure of *The Canterbury Tales,* appears vividly represented in an early fourteenth-century legal document, a charter written for the foundation of a chapel, which begins as follows: "How many and how great are the tempests of the inner man, the foes of peace, wherein the exile of this world abounds, experience, the effective revealer of doubts, daily makes manifest. I, therefore, Roger de Martivallis, archdeacon of Leycestre, and lord of Nouesle, wishing, with the Lord's consent, to make ready for myself in the desert of this world, a straight path, whereby under the guidance of divine grace, amid the powers of darkness, I may more easily be able to come to that place where I may deserve after toil to receive the wages of true recompense . . ." and so on concerning the chapel first planned by Roger's father, Sir Anketin de Martivallis, knight.[17]

Here are the storms of the inner man that Chaucer urges us to calm in "Truth" by avoiding trust in Fortune, the "exile" of Boethius at the beginning of the *Consolation,* the desert or "wilderness" of this world in Chaucer's *House of Fame,* elaborately and competently explained by B. G. Koonce,[18] and reflected in other ways as the realm of the Fox in the Nun's Priest's Tale or as the "wilderness" that is no home in "Truth," the straight path that is the alternative of the "croked wey" recommended by the Old Man in the Pardoner's Tale, and, finally, the movement toward the Celestial Jerusalem that the Parson urges us to follow through penance at the close of *The Canterbury Tales.* I call attention to these things simply to indicate that a great deal of material we so laboriously seek out in learned and literary sources is actually a part of the everyday language of the time, at least among the literate. Chaucer was not always obscure to his contemporaries when he is obscure to us. Meanwhile, I think we should also notice that the archdeacon refers to experience as the revealer of those tempests that disturb the inner man and destroy his peace. Within the terms of their own means of describing human nature medieval people were very practical, and we do them a disservice when we substitute our own "psychological" terminology for theirs. Not only is the practicality of that terminology rather dubious, but it is out of context in their very different society.[19]

Turning now to the third division of my theme I should like to discuss Chaucer, his audience, and his work, and, finally, to illustrate the importance of simple signs from everyday life to our understanding of what he wrote. First of all, it is now clear that Chaucer was a gentleman and, as the positions he held reveal, something of a clerk, and not, as is frequently said, a "bourgeois," except in the sense that he lived for a long period in London, which might be called a "bourg."[20] He was also a "court man" who served the king and certain members of the royal family in a variety of ways. He was a royal squire and not a knight, probably because he was insufficiently wealthy or unwilling, for many persons sought to avoid knighthood and its obligations. He was thought sufficiently distinguished to be named on peace commissions, but this fact does not indicate that he ever actually sat as a Justice, and there is no record that he ever received any pay for that office, although it is true that Justices of the Peace often served without payment. He served once in Parliament, although this was not a great distinction, and frequently on government commissions, often for the Chamber, with which he seems to have been closely associated. He was Controller of the Customs in London, an office that brought him in close contact with the Exchequer, and he held the important office of Clerk of the King's Works for a reasonable period. His son, Thomas, also a squire, received numerous grants from John of Gaunt and the king, and in the year of his father's death became sheriff of Oxfordshire and Berkshire. He married the daughter of a knight, and his daughter, Alice, was married in succession to two earls.

Chaucer's audience, as Derek Pearsall has recently suggested, probably consisted of "household knights and officials, career diplomats and civil servants," men like "Clifford, Clanvowe, Scogan, Hoccleve, Usk, Gower, Strode."[21] This rather miscellaneous list could easily be expanded to include chamber knights like William Neville, who was Clanvowe's close friend, Peter Courtenay, Richard Stury, Philip la Vache, William Beauchamp, and John Montagu, who became Earl of Salisbury in 1397. We know something about some of these men, and since, as I suggested earlier, meanings exist in people rather than in words, it should be helpful to Chaucerians to learn all they can about them. For Chaucer was a successful poet whose skills as an entertainer probably account for the respect paid him by both supporters of Richard II and supporters of Henry IV. It would be absurd to attribute attitudes to Chaucer that would have been either offensive or incomprehensible to his audience. In the first place, a number of these men were lords of manors, thoroughly familiar both with problems of manorial administration and with the rapid changes in manorial economy and society in many areas after the first outbreak of the Black Death. They had considerable experience with yeomen, reeves, millers, plowmen, dairy maids, franklins, and poor cottagers like the widow in the Friar's Tale or Griselda before her marriage. They knew knights and merchants in variety, sergeants at law, both royal and ordinary, physicians, clothiers like the Wife of Bath, clerks, and a wide variety of ecclesiastics. Some had seen extensive military service, and a number had obvious literary or cultural interests. Gower was a successful poet in three languages; Clanvowe was the author of a graceful Chaucerian poem and of a stern moral treatise; Usk, secretary to London's controversial reforming mayor, John of Northampton, wrote a Boethian treatise on love; and Montagu was praised for his verse (which does not survive) by Christine de Pisan. Strode was not only a distinguished Oxford logician but probably also the author of a poem, now lost. He undoubtedly appreciated keenly the amusingly specious arguments advanced by some of Chaucer's characters. Stury owned a copy of the *Roman de la Rose;* Beauchamp had a university education; and there were probably a number of well-educated clerks and ecclesiastics in the audience.

Some of these men were keenly interested in social and ecclesiastical reform, and, in fact, have been accused, falsely I think, except for a temporary lapse on the part of Usk, of being Lollards.[22] Let me consider some examples.[23] Sir Lewis Clifford, after an early military career, was made squire of the Black Prince in 1364 with an annuity of £40, increased to a hundred marks in 1368 and to £100 when he was knighted. I might observe in passing that the Black Prince was on the whole an efficient and charitable administrator of his landed estates.[24] Clifford fought in Spain in 1367, in France in 1377, and in Brittany in 1378. John of Gaunt, who led this last unsuccessful venture, made him one of his executors. Between 1370 and 1372 he married Eleanor, daughter of John, Lord Mowbray of Axholme and Joan of Lancaster. Their daughter later married Philip la Vache. Clifford was made Knight of the Garter in 1377 and became a royal knight in 1381. Joan of Kent granted him custody of Cardigan Castle in 1378. He served her faithfully until her death and was made one of her executors. In about 1385 or a little later he joined the Order of the Passion founded by Philippe de Mézières, who had been chancellor to the famous crusading leader Peter of Lusignan and who, in his later years, dedicated himself to the moral reform of European chivalry and the establishment of peace between France and England, preferably through a royal marriage, for which Sir Lewis conducted negotiations between 1391 and 1396, after 1392 as a member of the Royal Council. Literary scholars will remember Philippe as the author of the liturgical drama, "Figurative Representation of the Presentation of the Virgin Mary in the Temple."[25] Clifford befriended Eustache Deschamps during a mission to France in 1385 and 1386, and brought back with him that author's little poem in praise of Chaucer. He and Stury were among the executors of the Duchess of York, who left him, in 1392, her book of Vices and Virtues. This has been a very brief sketch, but enough to show that Clifford was among the most trusted and reliable members of the court, a distinguished knight in the field in his youth and a wise and discreet counsellor in his maturity, sufficiently pious to be deeply interested in the Order of the Passion and rigorous enough in his views to be branded with the unsavory epithet "Lollard."

Among his friends were Sir John Clanvowe and Sir William Neville. Clanvowe had begun his career as a knight bachelor serving under Humphrey de Bohun V of Hereford between 1363 and the earl's death in 1373. During this period he fought under Sir John Chandos, who was one of the great exemplars of English chivalry, wise as well as worthy. Together with Neville, Stury, and Philip la Vache he commanded a group of 120 men during Gaunt's Breton campaign of 1378. The king made him a knight of the Chamber in 1382. Like Clifford, he was one of the executors of Joan of Kent, who seems to have gathered around her a group of men interested in reform. When England seemed certain to be invaded by the French in 1386, he and Neville went to Essex and Sussex to prepare defenses. In his later years he served on the Council. On 17 October 1391 he died near Constantinople. He and Neville had participated in a crusade in Tunisia during the previous year. Neville, who was with him in his last days, died of grief two days later.

Neville was a Chamber knight after 1381, and served on the Council. His later reputation for "Lollardry" stems from the fact that he sought the custody of the heretic Nicholas Hereford at his castle of Nottingham "because of the honesty of his person." Others apparently agreed with this estimate, however, for Nicholas recanted and became, during 1395–96, Chancellor of St. Paul's Cathedral. We may remember that Cecily Champain's release of Chaucer for all claims of rape or other actions against him filed before Bishop Sudbury in the Chancery was witnessed not only by William Beauchamp, the royal Chamberlain, but by Clanvowe and Neville as well. Considering the character of these witnesses, we can be fairly sure that Cecily had no real claims.[26]

The most distinguished members of Chaucer's audience were probably men like these. Perhaps we should occasionally ask ourselves rather simple questions like the following: What would Clanvowe have thought of Neville if, while arranging the defenses of the southern coast in 1386, he had become infatuated with a widow simply by looking at her, had shown immediate suicidal tendencies, had forgotten his obligations to the kingdom, and had feared nothing except the possible reluctance of the lady? Those who think that Troilus is an admirable character should recall that Englishmen regarded themselves as inhabitants of New Troy[27] and that their realm was in serious danger of foreign invasion at the time Chaucer completed his poem. French incursions on the south coast had caused unrest for many years and had given rise to serious doubts about English chivalry, concerning which Peter de la Mare complained bitterly in Parliament in 1377, alleging that chivalry and other virtues were being neglected in favor of vice. It has even been suggested that a failure to defend the coast properly was one of the causes of the revolt of 1381.[28] The idea that Chaucer's audience could have regarded Troilus with any real sympathy borders on the absurd; it is most probable that the character was intended as an exemplary warning to the men of New Troy. Certainly, no one in Chaucer's audience would have sought to excuse Troilus on the ground that he was a "courtly lover." There is absolutely no evidence to show that either Chaucer or any member of his audience had ever heard of "courtly love"; and we might say exactly the same thing about "psychological realism." The figurative signs in the poem, insofar as we can identify them, its classical mythography, its scriptural and doctrinal echoes, and its reflections of Boethian philosophy all suggest that Troilus is an example to be avoided. And the historical circumstances under which the poem was written strongly reinforce this impression. Chaucer's good reputation both as a man and as a literary craftsman was probably not achieved by sentimental or "sophisticated" endorsements of human weakness. Rather, he could be counted upon to ridicule foolishness with good-natured philosophical detachment wherever it might appear in his society, although, except for Harry Bailey and perhaps Hodge of Ware,[29] he generally refrained from attacking individuals.

And this observation brings me to *The Canterbury Tales*. Chaucer's technique of portraiture in the General Prologue reflects a medieval tendency to identify individuals in terms of attributes. That is, for example, we identify Saint Peter as he stands among other saints in sculpture or illumination by the fact that he carries keys; we can recognize Saint Paul as a miller grinding the grain of the Old Law to produce the flour of the New; John the Baptist is dressed in the garments of the wilderness; and so on. Similar techniques had been used by both Ovid and Prudentius, and by their imitators. We can observe a similar tendency in everyday life. Thus a bailiff attending a manorial court might be fined for not carrying his rod, the attribute of his office, or a hayward for not carrying his horn.[30] Trespassers placed in the stocks were often adorned with objects to show the nature of their crimes, a whetstone being placed around the neck of a slanderer or a liar, for example, to show that he was like the deceitful "sharp razor" of Psalm 51.[31] Or a trespasser might be paraded through the streets, like the false physician, who, it is said, in 1382 rode backward through London carrying not only a whetstone but two urinals, fore and aft.[32] There is a strong element of humor in these punishments, for trespassers were thought to find the ridicule of the community discouraging. A number of the characters in the Prologue and the subsequent Tales are, legally speaking, trespassers; others are guilty of extremely dubious practices. Are their portraits literal and "realistic," or does Chaucer gather together his little collections of attributes to create figures very like grotesques? Are the characters actually "typical"? The same questions apply to many of the figures in the Tales, especially since the Tales often elaborate the significance of the attributes mentioned in the Prologue, serving, in effect, as additional attributes of the speakers.

There is only one way in which we can reasonably answer these questions, and that is by a careful study of everyday life in the later fourteenth century. Before illustrating this point, however, I should like to discuss briefly Chaucer's technique. At the beginning of the Prologue to the Tales he says that he will tell us who his characters were, indicate their "degree" in society, and describe their "array," a subject that includes their horses and their trappings. In practice, he includes direct observations about virtues or vices, significant attributes of complexion or physiognomy, significant actions, like the Miller's wrestling, and observations about what the various figures love. The "ideal" characters—the Knight, the Clerk, the Parson, and the Plowman—love intangibles, whereas the others love more tangible goods, ranging from little dogs and fancy dress to lands, robes, expensive foods, jolly wenches, and money. Chaucer is especially hard on figures who pretend to higher station or greater wisdom than they actually have. Thus his Sergeant of the Law, who seems wise, apparently knows all the cases since the Conquest and all the statutes by heart, a manifest impossibility, which means that he pompously refers to nonexistent authorities. Similarly, the list of authorities known to the Physician probably indicates simply that he overawed his patients with what sounded like authoritative citations in connection with his ministrations. Henry Fielding was by no means the first author to discover that vanity and hypocrisy are excellent sources of the ridiculous. It is true that Chaucer assumes a good-natured and self-effacing attitude, and does not hesitate to make fun of himself as he does, for example, in the Prologue to Sir Thopas or in his dream visions, a fact that has, I think, misled some readers into sentimentalizing or "humanizing" his characters and to oversimplifying the idea that he presents himself as a naive persona. The group for which Chaucer probably wrote was a tightly knit community in which everyone knew everyone else, and in which, as we have seen, many were above Chaucer in degree. They were thoroughly familiar with the poet's actual attitudes, so that remarks like the mild comment on the Monk's desire to abandon his cloister, "I seyde his opinion was good," are actually examples of antiphrasis, or explicit irony, reinforced in this instance by the subsequent comments, including, "How shal the world be served?" But this is more than antiphrasis, or saying the opposite of what is meant; it probably provoked laughter from Chaucer's friends. If instead Chaucer had made a directly pejorative comment he would have sounded much more like his friend moral Gower, and his audience might well have been bored rather than amused. The criticism of inconstant monks was still there, and Chaucer's humor does not either temper it or diminish it in any way; if anything, it makes it more incisive. Our bold lover of fat swans, as well as of other kinds of flesh, riding on an ostentatiously decorated horse, represents an increasingly common kind of monastic weakness in the later fourteenth century. One historian has observed that after 1350 the relaxation of the Benedictine Rule in matters of occupation and diet had become common, so that many monks liked luxurious dress, kept greyhounds, and were frequently outside the cloister.[33] But this situation represents a considerable decline from conditions earlier in the century,[34] largely due to economic factors that resulted in a reduction in monastic population,[35] and a general decline in mores. But some monks were poorly fed, not all monks were degenerate, and it would be unfair to say that Chaucer's monk is "typical." He is, rather, an exaggerated picture indicating a trend that was evident during Chaucer's lifetime and that eventually led to monastic dissolution. Here, as elsewhere, Chaucer was deeply interested in and genuinely concerned about developments that were taking place in his own society.

One other feature of Chaucer's technique is, I think, sometimes neglected. Most of the Tales, the exceptions being the Clerk's Tale, the Second Nun's Tale, the Parson's Tale, and, possibly, the Knight's Tale,[36] are adorned with learned allusions like those in the Wife's Prologue, reflections of doctrine, and various kinds of eloquence that would have been completely beyond actual persons in the degrees of the fictional speakers. In other words, the Tales represent Chaucer still talking to his audience about his fictional narrators, and this is also true of his more worthy characters, whom he treats with approval. I do not think that anyone in the audience would have missed this point as Chaucer stood before them, taking advantage of opportunities to imitate local dialects, as in the Reeve's Tale, or to render speeches or descriptions with humorous emphasis. The fact that both he and his audience had first-hand knowledge of the groups represented by the various characters, as well as of the pressing issues of the day, probably lent his oral delivery an effectiveness we cannot now recover. The audience knew, for example, with reference to the Miller, how dangerous contentiousness could be in local communities, and something about the steps taken to control it.[37] A more detailed knowledge of daily life should not only help us to understand what Chaucer was saying but also afford us some helpful clues about how he probably said it.

I should like to use one pilgrim as an example—the Wife of Bath—

who has frequently been seen as a champion of women and their rights, although it is doubtful that Chaucer's audience would have seen her in this way. Rather, like the Monk, she represents a new and distinctive feature of fourteenth-century life, again treated with humorous exaggeration. Chaucer tells us that she was a clothier or cloth-maker:

> Of clooth-makyng she hadde swich an haunt,
> She passed hem of Ypres and of Gaunt.

This business, in which the English had indeed begun to surpass the Low Countries, has made her very wealthy. In church, we are told with humorous exaggeration, she wears almost ten pounds of expensive coverchiefs. Kerchiefs were among a woman's most prized possessions, as we learn from their careful distribution in wills.[38] Her hose were made of the most expensive of all woolens, scarlet, dyed with kermes.[39] Pilgrimages to Jerusalem were extremely expensive, available only to the wealthy,[40] but the Wife has been three times, as well as to Boulogne, which was not very far, Cologne, St. James of Compostella, and Rome. Her "wandering by the way" confirms our suspicion that these journeys, like the present one to Canterbury, have not been undertaken with much penitential fervor. Pilgrimage was sometimes enjoined as penance for adultery,[41] a fact that lends a certain irony to the Wife's peregrinations.

To return to the cloth industry,[42] the manufacturer of woolens, as distinct from linens, worsteds, or local coarse cloth, began to flourish in the north of England in the late thirteenth century, and by the fourteenth century fulling mills and dyeing vats became common features of manors in the area. Dyeing, which required considerable skill in the mixing of dyes and the application of mordants, as well as a tolerance for strong odors, which sometimes moved communities to restrict dyers to isolated spots, was usually undertaken by men. The wool was sorted, beaten, and washed. It was then carded and spun. After spinning, warp threads were sized and wound to make them about thirty yards long, and the wool was spooled on a bobbin. After it was woven, the cloth was fulled, either by being trodden in a tub with fuller's earth by three strong men (known variously as fullers, walkers, or tuckers), or by being treated in a fulling mill operated by water power. The cloth was then tentered, or stretched to exact size on a frame to which it was attached by tenterhooks. Once dried, it was teaseled, or brushed with the dried heads of *dipsacus fullonum,* which have hooked barbs, to raise the knap. It was then sheared, a delicate process, with long flat shears before being brushed, folded, and tacked for shipment. Except for dyeing, fulling, and shearing, this work was ordinarily done by women. In the course of time, many women became masters of the trade, supervising the work of others. We should imagine the Wife of Bath as the master of a shop, becoming wealthy through the labors of other women, employed either in the shop itself or in the countryside, dealing effectively at the same time with dyers, fullers, or shearers to whom her products were sent for processing. She was hardly a liberator of women, although some women eagerly sought higher income in industrial employment, even though it meant long hours of hard work. The prosperity of female masters, the quality of whose products was sometimes said to be questionable, caused some uneasiness among male masters of the trade, who sought to restrain their activities by guild regulations at the close of the century.

After the Black Death various industries were attracting workers from agricultural manors, bringing about a demand for hired agricultural labor that in turn created a demand for higher wages by the day.[43] Workers wanted not only better pay but better food, and were naturally not much interested in the closely knit organizations of the manorial communities in which they worked or in the customary laws by which they were governed. A new spirit of enterprise was abroad in the realm, a fact that has led one historian to characterize the later fourteenth century as an "age of ambition."[44] Among the growing industries the cloth industry was especially spectacular. After an interruption brought about by the Black Death it recovered in about 1353, so that between that time and 1369 exports of woolen cloths rose from less than 2,000 cloths a year to 16,000. There was a lull in the industry between 1369 and 1379, reflecting a general depression in English trade, but after that, except for another lull during the period of widespread panic and confusion resulting from threats of invasion between 1385 and 1388, the industry expanded rapidly. By the early nineties England was exporting 40,000 cloths, or half as much wool in the form of cloth as in the form of raw wool. Prosperity encouraged shady practices, however, and in 1390 clothiers from the west country, which had become the new center of the industry, became notorious for selling poorly dyed and sheared cloths, folded and tacked so that their defects were not visible. English merchants who sold them abroad were sometimes subjected to violent treatment.[45] Bristol became the chief port for the export of cloth. The Wife thus represents a new kind of wealth in a new area whose prosperity was accompanied, incidentally, by a spread of heresy.

It is not surprising that Chaucer, who admired those who loved "common profit" and who remembered the relatively tranquil, closely knit communities of his youth, should have devoted considerable attention to a clothier, and, to make his point more trenchant, chosen a female clothier for illustration. No one in the audience would have failed to recognize the Wife as a greedy exploiter of female labor who could be expected to enjoy a sense of mastery over men as well as over women. If Chaucer had been a modern realist he might well have given us a detailed picture of the cloth industry, but he was instead a medieval moralist who could reasonably expect his audience to know a great deal about that subject. Instead, therefore, he developed the implications of the activities of the Wife and those like her, using for his purpose the theme of marriage suggested in the General Prologue and the parallel between the Wife's five husbands and the five false husbands of the unconverted Samaritan woman, who were understood to represent the senses.[46]

However, as a general framework he employed a variation of another late medieval development, a practice M. M. Postan is said to have described as "the marriage fugue,"[47] which was becoming fairly common in the countryside. That is, landless young men eagerly sought out relatively wealthy widows to marry. After marriage the young men naturally awaited the demise of their wives so that they could obtain younger ones, "fressh abedde." But they often had to wait until they were themselves advanced in age before their unsatisfactory spouses died, so that when they did marry the position was reversed, and it was the women's turn to seek wealthy husbands. Women are said to have sometimes run through two or three husbands in this manner, and this is exactly what the Wife has done. In effect, like the wife in the Cook's Tale, she "swyved for her sustenaunce" in youth, albeit under the cover of marriage. Thus she wore out three "good" old wealthy husbands before succumbing to a young man who presented difficulties because he was unfaithful. But he too passed when she was old. Even then, she overcame her fifth wise husband, a clerk who should have known better,[48] in an amusing echo of the Fall of Man. Marriages of this kind were naturally not conducive either to domestic tranquility or to genuine sexual satisfaction, which was considered especially desirable among women (who had not yet learned any curious nineteenth-century attitudes toward the subject),[49] although, as Henry of Lancaster tells us, women of lower station were more desirable in this respect than others, being less restrained.[50] It is not surprising that the Wife displays sexual uneasiness and a keen appetite indicative of frustration.

In a general way, the Wife represents a humorous caricature of the pursuit of worldly satisfaction in defiance of traditional values that was growing in fourteenth-century society. To make the point as vividly as possible, Chaucer creates what might be called a "Babylonian" situation. To illustrate this point I might quote a passage from the most influential late medieval commentary on the *Aeneid,* describing Carthage: "In this city [Aeneas] found women ruling and Penos serving, for in the world there is such confusion that libido reigns and virtues, which we understand by Penos, strong and stern men, are suppressed; and thus the man serves and the woman rules. Thus in the divine books the world is called 'Babylon,' that is, confusion."[51] The Wife, deaf to spiritual understanding, becomes a fairly obvious figure of the flesh rampant, with overtones recalling the unconverted Samaritan, the Old Whore in the *Roman de la Rose*, Ovid's Dipsas, and the Synagogue. She neglects the sacramental implications of the Marriage at Cana, glosses the New Law with the Old, turns Saint Paul upside down by reading him "carnally," turns so-called antifeminist clichés, actually attacks directed against venereal inclinations in men, against her old husbands, and in her tale promises that those who allow the flesh, or the wife, to rule will find satisfaction for their "worldly appetite" in an essentially illusory earthly paradise.[52] Her tale is followed by two vivid illustrations in which those "children of wrath"[53] the Friar and the Summoner humorously illustrate the corruption of spiritual offices for money. As we learn from the Clerk, a great many persons, failing to follow Griselda in obedience to the operation of Providence, belong to the Wife's "sect,"[54] and it is to them that we owe the confusion or "Babylon" of the world.

The basic moral ideas are, of course, not new with Chaucer. But the scriptural and doctrinal materials in the portrait of the Wife add considerably to its humor and sharpen its satiric point. She is neither a "personality," a "realistic portrait," nor a "typical example" of the female clothier. She typifies instead a new spirit of self-aggrandizement and a new kind of wealth that were disrupting traditional values cherished by Chaucer and by most of his audience, and, at the same time, destroying traditional communities based on a concern for the "common profit." Conditions in the cloth industry afforded an especially vivid illustration, but the same sort of thing was evident elsewhere, if on a smaller scale.[55] I suggest that it was this situation, not the literary portrait for its own sake, that was the focus of Chaucer's attention and the principal interest of his audience. Further, I think that unless we learn to understand the immediate relevance of Chaucer's work to the everyday life of his times, we shall run the risk not only of formulating undisciplined interpretations, but also of failing to appreciate his real craftsmanship in making what he has to say vivid and entertaining. If it is objected that everyday life is not the true subject of literary study, which should concern itself with aesthetics, I can only reply that in the humanities there may be some virtue in the study of humanity itself.

CHAUCER'S THEMATIC PARTICULARS

EDMUND REISS

Whereas many of the details in Chaucer's narratives are obviously symbolic, not many function solely as symbols. Details that stand apart from the narrative—like Saint Cecilia's name, which is explicated outside the story of the Second Nun's Tale—are unusual in Chaucer. At the same time, likewise unusual are details—at least noteworthy details—that have meaning only in terms of the developing narrative. Whatever their literal or symbolic purposes, the particulars of Chaucer's narratives frequently have a thematic significance, and function as Chaucer's way of commenting on, or of providing a perspective for, what is at hand. The five different etymologies of Cecilia's name, for instance, though not properly part of the story at hand, serve to bring out the range of meaning of "faire Cecilie the white" (G 115)[1] and to provide a context or thematic grounding for the subsequent story.

The reason for the existence of such details is primarily one of theme and only secondarily one of narrative. That is, Chaucer's main concern is less with the developing narrative than with the developing theme; and for all his storytelling artistry, he will readily sacrifice narrative consistency for thematic sense. Details that may appear out of place or inconsistent on the narrative level may function effectively on a thematic level. I would argue, for instance, that the much-commented-on reference to "preestes thre" in the General Prologue (A 164), far from being an error, demonstrates vividly Chaucer's preference of theme over narrative. Functioning immediately as part of the Prioress' entourage, the three priests are the final touch in a portrait dominated by an imitation of the courtly; they, superfluous in number, comprise the incongruous retinue of a great lady who is making what seems to be more a progress than a pilgrimage. Later, when Chaucer needs a "neutral" tale-teller, one we have not prejudged, he employs *the* Nun's Priest; and it is doubtful that either he or his audience worried about the earlier reference to three priests. The point is not that they might likely have forgotten the detail but rather that it functioned one way in the General Prologue and

another way after the Monk's Tale; number here would have been regarded as an accidental quality, not a substantial one.

I would likewise argue that a number like "nyne and twenty" is less a
realistic detail than a thematic particular. Offered as the number of
pilgrims gathered at the Tabard Inn (A 24) and also as the number of
degrees the sun has descended when the Parson is called upon to tell his
tale that will "knytte up" *The Canterbury Tales* (I 4), "nyne and twenty" has
a significance that goes beyond the actual number of pilgrims or the
actual time of day. As a numerological equivalent to the approach to
salvation and/or perfection, it gives a spiritual dimension, even a cosmic
sense, to the journey at hand. Appearing at the beginning and end of the
Canterbury pilgrimage, encompassing, as it were, the entire work, it calls
up the ideal of Pilgrimage that is the ultimate point of the comic version
of pilgrimage, organized by Harry Bailly and encompassed by Miller and
Reeve, that is Chaucer's narrative. The issue of how to reconcile "nyne
and twenty" with the actual number of pilgrims—whatever this number
may be—is a false issue created by those for whom Chaucer's details have
primary significance on the narrative level.[2]

What I am calling thematic particulars are those details that serve as
more than means of supporting the narrative. In one sense they are the
literary equivalent of those parts of speech that have lexical significance—nouns, verbs, adjectives, and adverbs—as opposed to such linguistic elements as prepositions, conjunctions, and articles which help
the utterance along but which lack meaning in their own right. At the
same time, thematic particulars are more than merely meaningful terms
and likewise more than allegorical details whose meaning is brought to
the work by the audience and not created by the writer. With the spring
setting at the beginning of the General Prologue, the garden created by
January in the Merchant's Tale, and the rocks complained about by
Dorigen in the Franklin's Tale, for example, Chaucer does more than
merely employ traditional symbolic significance. The *Natureingang* is juxtaposed against the sense of pilgrimage; the garden blends traditions of
the earthly paradise, the *jardin de deduit,* and the *hortus conclusus;* and the
rocks become a vehicle for investigating the reality and purpose of *Natura naturata.*

It should be understood, however, that thematic particulars do not
have to be details that are first symbolic and then developed further.
Ordinary descriptive terms may come to be thematic particulars when
they are made to stand out from their context. For instance, when
Chaucer uses the word *worthy* in one form or another five times in the
description of the pilgrim Knight and then repeats it in the description
of such unworthies as the Friar, the Merchant, and the Wife of Bath, it is
not only to make us aware of the ironic application of an ordinarily
complimentary term. We should also see that *worthy* refers to a quality

which Chaucer wants us to be concerned with in the subsequent tales, and, furthermore, that real worthiness may be a quality not easily defined or recognized. Similarly *conscience,* a key term in its own right, noticeably changes meaning in its various applications in the General Prologue to the Prioress, the Shipman, and the Parson and becomes a major issue in understanding the essential *condicioun* of the pilgrims and the action of later tales.

The creation of meaning through repetition is not limited to single words, as may be seen with that particularly favorite Chaucerian line, "pitee renneth soone in gentil herte." While the association of pity and true nobility has a long history from antiquity to the Renaissance, and while the concept of the *cor gentile* especially dominated Italian poetry of the thirteenth and fourteenth centuries, we need not think that Chaucer was merely employing a convention in order to speak of what was *gentil.*[3] His first use of the phrase, "pitee renneth soone in gentil herte," in the Knight's Tale, purportedly describes the nobility of Theseus, revealed in his change of mind after he comes upon Palamon and Arcite fighting and does not put them to death as he had rashly said he would (A 1761). The second occurrence is an ironic comment on the secret illicit longing of May in the Merchant's Tale after she is attracted to the squire Damian (E 1986). And a third use of the phrase occurs when the lovesick, deserted falcon in the Squire's Tale awakens from her swoon (F 479). Whatever the incongruities revealed when the term is applied to Theseus and May, something is surely lacking in this appeal to the dignity of *edele herzen* when it comes from the beak of a bird. And whatever Chaucer meant by the phrase in its first appearance, subsequent repetitions necessitate subsequent reevaluation.

Other instances of line repetition, while perhaps less obvious than this, are no less meaningful. In the Knight's Tale, when the dying Arcite refers to the transiency of life and to man as a helpless creature, here today, gone tomorrow, he says, "Now with his love, now in his colde grave / Allone, withouten any compaignye" (A 2778–79). The juxtaposition makes us aware of the fragility of both life and love and of the pathos of the human condition. But when in the very next tale, the un-pathetic fabliau told by the Miller, we hear that *hende* Nicholas, knowledgeable in matters of *deerne love* and *solas,* along with being "sleigh and ful privee," lives in his chamber "allone, withouten any compaignye" (A 3201–04), the echo reveals additional connotations of the phrase. We may even be shocked at the irreverence of linking the serious, dying lover, Arcite, with the frivolous seducer, Nicholas. Whereas the phrase "allone, withouten any compaignye," functions poignantly in relation to Arcite and to man alone in his grave, it is largely irrelevant to Nicholas and his chamber, unless, that is, we are aware of the link to the previous tale. Although it may be too much to expect that Chaucer's

audience would recall the phrase from the Knight's Tale—and it apparently is not a stock phrase in medieval poetry—at least Chaucer himself
may have enjoyed the irony of linking grave and bedroom, and of providing in the Miller's Tale a comment on the love seen earlier in the
Knight's Tale.

At the same time, Chaucer's poetry is full of ironic echoes of and
allusions to earlier details. Sometimes his procedure is to join together
elements previously unrelated. As part of the portrait of Alisoun in the
Miller's Tale, for instance, Chaucer includes the detail of her brooch: "A
brooch she baar upon hir lowe coler, / As brood as is the boos of a
bokeler" (A 3265–66). Compared to the vivid barnyard and orchard
images that fill this portrait, the brooch may seem a rather insignificant
detail. Situated low on Alisoun's collar, it may be linked to details like the
apron on her loins and the shoes laced high on her legs that call attention
to the flesh beneath. But beyond this, the brooch may function to call up
the significant brooch of the Prioress (A 160), as well as the Wife of Bath's
hat, which was described as "brood as is a bokeler" (A 471). The combination of these two attributes in one detail may serve to link Alisoun with
Chaucer's two notable female pilgrims. Not only are their attributes
combined in her, but the two pilgrims, who seemed initially to be quite
different, are themselves joined unexpectedly. The *condicioun* of Alisoun
might be regarded as an ironic synthesis of the essential natures of the
two previously mentioned women.

In this context we might consider a detail from the Wife of Bath's
Prologue. Speaking of her fifth husband, she tells how he had been a
clerk of Oxford and had boarded at the home of her gossip, whose name
was Alisoun (D 527–32). As readers have long realized, the Wife would
seem to be referring to the situation at the beginning of the Miller's Tale;
and it is as though Alisoun in this tale is a young version of the Wife of
Bath, whose name is, not accidentally, Alisoun. Whereas this connection
seems to be intentional, the point of Chaucer's making it may not be
clear. In linking Alisoun of Bath with Alisoun of Oxford, Chaucer is
doing more than relating two female characters. He is recalling and
reevaluating a situation as directly as when he recalls the Wife of Bath's
name in the allusions to her made in the Clerk's Tale and the Merchant's
Tale (E 1170, 1685). Such recalling functions, at least on one level, as
does the repetition and echoing of lines and words. Focusing attention
on particulars, it in fact demands that they be reexamined and reas-
sessed in terms of their new context; and, at the same time, our awareness of the repetition gives additional meaning to what is at hand.

The portrait of the Wife of Bath in the General Prologue offers a
wealth of details that, for all their vivid realism, function primarily as
thematic particulars. For instance, her deafness—even before we know
its actual cause—provides a basis for judging her distorted views; and

her skill at clothmaking links her with the Virgin (notable for weaving the cloth without a seam, namely Christ), though, of course, the Wife is hardly Virgin or virgin. A comparable detail is the hat whose description—"As brood as is a bokeler or a targe" (A 471)—we have already noted. In conjunction with particulars like the "foot-mantel aboute hir hipes large" and the "paire of spores sharpe" (A 472–73), the broad hat would seem to be one more detail in a developing picture of grossness, echoing, as it were, the ten pounds of kerchiefs, referred to a few lines earlier, that she sometimes wore upon her head (A 454). Joined to kerchiefs, "fyn scarlet reed" hose, and "shoes ful moyste and newe" (A 456–57), the hat may reflect her interest in clothing and more particularly her concern with new fashions. Moreover, the simile, "As brood as is a bokeler or a targe," in association with the sharp spurs, may serve to make the Wife resemble a knight dressed for adventure, though here it would more accurately be a knight *manqué* comically armed for a battle of what the Clerk later calls "crabbed eloquence" (E 1203). But beyond these suggestions, the broad hat may also parody a well-known iconographical detail, the cardinal's hat of Saint Jerome.

Though obviously an anachronism, this hat was the most familiar attribute of one of the favorite saints in the Middle Ages. Acting to justify and reinforce Jerome's reputation as the most learned and eloquent of all the Latin Fathers of the Church, the cardinal's hat, supposedly given to the saint by the Virgin Mary, also called up his reputation as defender of chastity.[4] Indeed, in Ricardian England, Jerome was best known for his famous letter against Jovinian, in which he celebrated the virtues of chastity.[5] This is the work used by Chaucer to provide the Wife of Bath with her arguments against virginity in the Prologue to her Tale. But here the point of Jerome's work is reversed, and the Wife uses the specious arguments of his opponent, Jovinian, to beat down those of the saint. In effect, she takes the role of the saint; but just as her words function as a parody of those of Jerome, so she herself, dressed in her broad hat, may act as a parody of the learned cardinal. Although we are not told the color of her hat, we do know that red is the Wife's dominant color, covering her, as it were, from head to foot—from her face "reed of hewe," to her hose "of fyn scarlet reed" (A 456, 458). Notwithstanding the Ellesmere artist's depiction of the hat as black, it may not be too far-fetched to think that Chaucer meant for the color red to extend to her broad hat.

If this interpretation is accepted, the hat then changes from being an innocuous detail, or one providing only a satiric comment on the Wife's physical grossness and interest in clothing, and becomes a key detail for understanding her as a ludicrous *auctoritas* who jangles while she thinks she is being eloquent, who is not only knight *manqué* but also clerk *manqué*.[6]

Still other details in Chaucer's narratives come to be thematically
meaningful not because of explication, repetition, or their own symbolic
suggestiveness, but because of their incongruity or inappropriateness to
the given situation. When in the Shipman's Tale the monk and the merchant's wife meet in the garden, Chaucer includes a strange detail that
most readers today are apt to pass over. Accompanying the wife is a
child: "A mayde child cam in hire compaignye, / Which as hir list she
may governe and gye, / For yet under the yerde was the mayde" (B^2
1285–87). Nothing more is said of this "mayde child" in the entire tale,
but during the subsequent action in the garden, when the wife complains
about her husband, and when she and the monk arrange their assigna-
tion, culminating in the monk's parting gesture of affection—"And with
that word he caughte hire by the flankes, / And hire embraceth harde,
and kiste hire ofte" (B^2 1392–93)—the child is apparently an onlooker.
Although it may be convenient to think that Chaucer forgot the presence
of this child, we might wonder at his including her in the tale in the first
place. Without precedent or equivalent in any of the analogues, she is
found in all manuscripts of the Shipman's Tale.

Most immediately, the child's presence both reveals strikingly the
wife's indifference to the example she is setting, and provides a comment
on her fitness as instructor and guide. Abrogating her role of guide, she
is oblivious to any moral responsibility. That Chaucer avoids stating that
the girl is the wife's child may make the wife's inadequate guidance all
the more serious in the light of medieval attitudes toward the responsi-
bilities of guardians to their charges. In the Physician's Tale, when the
narrator speaks of the responsibility of governesses, as well as of fathers
and mothers, he admonishes them that they should be aware while children are under their guidance that the "ensample" of their "lyvynge" be
such as to keep the child from perishing (C 97). The corruption of the
wife in the Shipman's Tale is made even more blatant by her oblivious-
ness to her duty. The silent witness of her action, the "mayde child," may
be seen providing a before-the-fact comment on her immorality and an
indication of serious consequences beyond the comic happy ending of
the tale. Though at first glance merely a narrative detail, interesting only
because of the scene of which it is a part, the reference to the "mayde
child" comes to be a meaningful contribution to the developing theme of
proper "governaunce," of self and others, so important in *The Canterbury
Tales.*

A likewise incongruous detail is included in the Squire's Tale. When
Canacee is out walking in her garden one morning, she comes upon a
strange scene:

Amydde a tree, for drye as whit as chalk,
As Canacee was pleyyng in hir walk,

Ther sat a faucon over hire heed ful hye,
That with a pitous voys so gan to crye
That all the wode resouned of hire cry.
Ybeten hadde she hirself so pitously
With bothe hir wynges, til the rede blood
Ran endelong the tree ther-as she stood.
And evere in oon she cryde alwey and shrighte,
And with hir beek hirselven so she prighte.

(F 409–18)

Although the figures of the dry tree and the bird that makes itself bleed
are familiar mystical symbols, they seem completely out of place in this
courtly narrative that is concerned with magic, marked by romance conventions such as the garden of love, and permeated with the rhetorical
prolixity of the Squire. According to medieval tradition, the bird that
pricks its own breast is the pelican, thought to demonstrate the greatest
love of all creatures since it pierces its breast to feed its offspring with its
own blood. In Christian tradition, from at least the second-century
Physiologus to and beyond Dante's *Paradiso,* this bird and its action were
seen to symbolize Christ and His sacrifice for mankind. Moreover, the
dry tree on which it nested, stemming from Apocryphal accounts of the
fall of man and appearing throughout medieval narratives, was frequently depicted as the cross. Both images had scriptural authority also:
In Ezekiel 17:24 the Lord says that He will "dry up the green tree and
make the dry tree flourish"; and in Psalm 101:7 (Vulgate) the Psalmist
cries in despair, "I am like a pelican in the wilderness." As the Psalm was
commonly interpreted, the bird suggested Christ abandoned, particularly Christ on the Mount of Olives before his Passion.[7]

Regardless of Chaucer's source for these images, their presence in the
Squire's Tale provides a basic sense that gives meaning to Chaucer's
parody. They serve not to suggest a spiritual sense for the rather silly
story of Canacee and the falcon but rather to provide a detail that with its
fullness of meaning contrasts with the vacuousness of the other particulars employed in this tale. At the same time, ironically, nothing is done
with these symbols. The dry tree is never mentioned again, and the
falcon that sits in it, trying to commit suicide because of her grief, is but a
poor imitation of the self-sacrificing pelican. Similarly, the story the falcon tells of her desertion in love is a poor imitation of the account of
Christ's desolation and solitude, and Canacee at the foot of the tree
looking up "pitously" (F 400) is a poor imitation of the Virgin at the foot
of the cross.[8]

Whereas the pelican illustrated self-sacrificing love, the falcon, a traditional symbol of wealth, was commonly linked—as in courtly lyrics—to
the vanity of earthly love. As Peter of Blois noted, a hair shirt and a hawk

do not go well together. Associated with avarice, as in John Gower's *Mirour de l'Omme,* and regarded through its Latin name *accipiter* as essentially related to robbing, it was seen, as Isidore notes in his *Etymologiae,* as snatching greedily from other birds. Furthermore, in a tradition going back at least as far as Ambrose's *Hexaemeron,* the hawk is singled out for its harsh treatment of its young. When it feels they should be able to fly, it gives them no food, beats them with its wings, and pushes them out of the nest.[9] Such actions would make the falcon seem diametrically opposed to the pelican, consistently portrayed as concerned about tending to its young. In fact, as the late fourteenth-century *Plowman's Tale* suggests, the two birds are essentially opposites, the pelican being juxtaposed against those fowls of ravine "that flyeth up in the ayr, / and liveth by birdes that ben meke," an action understood as paralleling that of Lucifer, who flew high in his pride and who preys on "sely soules." And the pelican's constant caring may be opposed to the ways of the hawk, which in *Piers Plowman* B and C is linked to the figure Sloth.[10]

Such traditions and identifications would seem to make the bloody falcon in the dry tree a ludicrous image. Neither a reflection of the traditional harbinger of spring singing in a tree nor of the symbolic pelican, the falcon is out of place in this image in the Squire's Tale. More accurately, it is the dry tree and the self-sacrificing bird that are out of place. But calling up a love which is completely beyond the courtly affair—and the *pitee*—of the narrative, both bird and tree suggest a renewal of life and contrast with the intended suicide that will destroy not nourish, and with the sterility of courtly love. They thus allow Chaucer's audience to assess the action of the tale and offer a corrective to what is at hand.

Elsewhere Chaucer uses such symbolic details not only to provide a comment on an action or a scene but to develop a pattern that marks an entire narrative. At the beginning of Book 2 of *Troilus and Criseyde,* as Pandarus is preparing to go to Criseyde on Troilus's behalf, he is overcome by a green sickness and finds it necessary to return to bed. At this point Chaucer writes as follows:

> The swalowe Proigne, with a sorowful lay,
> Whan morwen com, gan make hire waymentynge,
> Whi she forshapen was; and ever lay
> Pandare abedde, half in a slomberynge,
> Til she so neigh hym made hire cheterynge
> How Tereus gan forth hire suster take,
> That with the noyse of hire he gan awake,
>
> And gan to calle, and dresse hym up to ryse,
> Remembryng hym his erand was to doone
> From Troilus, and ek his grete emprise.
>
> (2.64–73)

Although the swallow was viewed from antiquity as a harbinger of spring, suggesting by extension the renewal of life, and as such may seem relevant here as an expression of Troilus's newly awakened love, the reference explicitly made is to the classical story of Procne and her sister Philomela, who, as Chaucer knew from the account in Ovid's *Metamorphoses*, were turned into swallow and nightingale after Philomela was raped by Procne's husband, Tereus.[11] The significance of the myth, however, is not brought out in the *Troilus*, for the swallow's song functions for Pandarus as an alarm clock and as a reminder of his imminent errand.

Later in Book 2, Chaucer appears to allude to the legend once again in a lengthy scene not in Boccaccio's *Filostrato*. Criseyde, after musing about Pandarus's message that Troilus is in love with her, and after debating within herself concerning the merits of this love, listens to her niece's song about how wonderful love is and then goes to bed, where she remains awake thinking: "When al was hust, than lay she stille and thoughte / Of al this thing" (2.915–16). At this moment a sound from outside catches her attention:

> A nyghtyngale, upon a cedir grene,
> Under the chambre wal ther as she ley,
> Ful loude song ayein the moone shene,
> Peraunter, in his briddes wise, a lay
> Of love, that made hire herte fressh and gay.
> That herkned she so longe in good entente,
> Til at the laste the dede slep hire hente.
>
> (2.918–24)

Apparently reinforcing the song of love Criseyde has just heard from her niece, the bird's song that "made hire herte fressh and gay" leads to her dream of the eagle who tears out her heart and replaces it with his own. Although the act in her dream is violent, she is neither afraid of nor hurt by it.

On the one hand, the nightingale may function here as a symbol of spiritual joy, calling up the soul's love for God, in accord with interpretations like that of Bonaventure or, more particularly, Pierre de Beauvais, who, in his thirteenth-century bestiary, interprets the nightingale as the image of the holy soul which in the night of this life awaits the Lord, and when she feels that He has come into her heart, her joy is such that she cannot keep silent.[12] On the other hand, the nightingale may represent a deliberately comic sexual allusion, as in the Fourth Story of the Fifth Day in Boccaccio's *Decameron*, where the nightingale is referred to several times as a humorous sexual euphemism and where the lovers who spend the night together are said to "make the nightingale sing many times."[13]

Without negating the possibility of such significance—in fact, of both

significances—the nightingale in the *Troilus*, though not explicitly linked
to the classical legend, may most properly be viewed in conjunction with
the swallow whose song began Book 2. The point is not only that these
two birds and their singing act as structuring devices in this book of
Chaucer's poem, but that they provide signs, even prophecies, of things
to come. Although the characters in the narrative are not able to perceive or to read these signs, the audience still has a responsibility for
interpretation. In terms of the classical myth it is ironic that the song of
the swallow should cause Pandarus to awaken and to recall his errand of
love, and that the song of the nightingale should reassure Criseyde and
permit her to fall asleep. Each character misses the obvious symbolic
significance of these details; each is unable to use the special sign that is
offered.

We may use Chaucer's version of the Procne-Philomela story in *The
Legend of Good Women*, a narrative of 165 lines apparently written soon
after the *Troilus*, to get a sense of how he viewed the legend. There he
explicitly emphasizes that it is to be regarded as an instance of foul lust
and false love. Dominant in his treatment is sorrow—"the wo, the com-
pleynt, and the mone" (2379) caused by Tereus's lust. And this interpretation is in agreement with that offered by other late medieval poets. In
John Gower's *Confessio amantis* the story is ostensibly told by Genius to
illustrate the danger of lust's leading to rape. Moreover, in the vision the
narrator has at the end of the *Confessio*, where he sees the company of
famous lovers, he hears "the pleignte of Progne and Philomene" and the
"untrouthe" of Tereus and feels "that was routhe."[14]

Chaucer's references to the songs of swallow and nightingale may also
be related to Boccaccio's ironic references in the fourth book of the
Teseida. The happiness of Pentheus in love is compared, incredibly, to the
joy of Tereus when he finds that his sister-in-law Philomela—whom he
has already planned to rape—is permitted to go with him back to
Thrace. Further, in Boccaccio's poem, after falling asleep, exhausted
from his love-longing for Emilia, Arcita hears "Philomela sing as she
makes merry over dead Tereus."[15] Chaucer's allusions to the birds would
also seem to be related to the passage in canto 9 of the *Purgatorio*, where,
after falling asleep in the valley of negligent rulers, Dante dreams of the
eagle who swoops down and catches him up. The context for the dream
is, Dante writes, "the hour near morning when the swallow begins her
sad songs, perhaps in memory of her previous woes."[16] Here the swallow's sad song provides a basis for the notion that the mind may be a
pilgrim from the flesh, no longer captive to it; and the song thus leads to
the purgation that follows. In the *Troilus*, on the other hand, the bird's
sad song suggests ironically the movement from the mind to the flesh.

As Petrarch alludes to the myth, it is to link the birds with the return of
spring to the world. In his 310th song, "Zefiro torna, e'l bel tempo

rimena," we find that along with the beautiful weather and flowers come the sad songs of these birds: "Procne laments and Filomena weeps."[17] Although our first impression may be that Procne and Filomena function here as innocuous symbols of spring and renewal, Petrarch goes on to contrast his narrator's feelings with the world of nature. Although air, earth, and water are full of love, the narrator feels only the heaviest sighs as though his loving has pulled them from his heart and has flown away with its keys. The final sense is that small birds which sing, along with flowers and beautiful women, create for him only a desert (12–14). Moreover, Petrarch's next sonnet, "Quel rosignuol che sí soave piagne" (no. 311), reinforces this association of swallow, nightingale, and unhappiness. The tender weeping of the nightingale, sweet as it may seem, fills the earth with notes piteous and poignant. The lament leads the narrator to the understanding stated in the last line of the poem, that nothing can please and endure, a theme related to that expressed by late medieval mythographies, such as the French *Ovide moralisé*, which sees Philomena as signifying false love, more specifically the disruptive and deceptive love of things of this world.[18]

Regardless of the particular use Chaucer is making of the legend in the *Troilus*, it would seem to provide an ironic comment on the imminent love of Troilus and Criseyde. As the detail immediately preceding Pandarus's endeavor on Troilus's behalf, the song of the swallow would seem to presage disaster; as a climaxing detail of Criseyde's psychomachia, the song of the nightingale may likewise be regarded as calling up unhappy love. As the Nightingale explains in the Middle English debate, *The Owl and the Nightingale,* her song is designed to teach that earthly love does not last for long.[19] Although such is hardly the lesson that Criseyde draws from the song, Chaucer's audience might well be aware of the incongruity of these birds' songs preceding the love, and view them as indeed symbolically suggesting the disaster to come and as developing the pattern of unhappy love that ultimately dominates the narrative.

Another figure from classical mythology used as a thematic particular in Chaucer's poetry is Egeus in the Knight's Tale. First mentioned after the death of Arcite—when the tale is almost two thousand lines old—he appears as a corrective of sorts to the excessive grief and weeping of Duke Theseus and the Athenians over the death of the Theban knight:

> No man myghte gladen Theseus,
> Savynge his olde fader Egeus,
> That knew this worldes transmutacioun,
> As he hadde seyn it chaunge bothe up and doun,
> Joye after wo, and wo after gladnesse,
> And shewed hem ensamples and liknesse.
> "Right as ther dyed nevere man," quod he,

"That he ne lyvede in erthe in some degree,
Right so ther lyvede never man," he seyde,
"In al this world, that som tyme he ne deyde.
This world nys but a thurghfare ful of wo,
And we been pilgrymes, passynge to and fro.
Deeth is an ende of every worldly soore."
And over al this yet seyde he muchel moore
To this effect, ful wisely to enhorte
The peple that they sholde hem reconforte.

(A 2837–52)

Whereas Egeus may seem like a voice anticipating Prudence's reprimand of Melibee for his "outrageous wepyng" (B[2] 2180), his words are noticeably ignored and the weeping does not stop. The episode would seem to have little place in the narrative at hand, but strangely it represents Chaucer's conscious alteration of his source. The *Teseida* of Boccaccio says that no one could console either Theseus, who had loved Arcite so perfectly, or Egeus, whose white beard was all wet with his sorrow. It is later in Boccaccio's poem, when proposing the marriage of Palamon and Emilia, that Theseus expresses the sentiments here put in the mouth of his father.[20] Chaucer, on the other hand, alters things so that Theseus later utters the famous Boethian speech on the chain of love—which is not in the *Teseida*.

One of the effects of Chaucer's change is to make Egeus into a Polonius-like character, uttering obvious truisms. Although readers today might find effective his statement that this world is but a thoroughfare full of woe, with man a pilgrim passing to and fro, the idea of life's being a *peregrinatio animae* would hardly have seemed new to Chaucer's audience. But more than this, we should look carefully at what other "wisdom" Egeus is revealing. His grandiloquent words about life and death state that for a man to have died he had to live, and that for a man to live he would have to die. This great truth, taking four lines and several rhetorical devices to reveal, would hardly have made Chaucer's audience pause and ponder. Though couched in the form of an intricate simile, it and the pilgrimage metaphor that follows can hardly be termed wisdom or, for that matter, effective argument. And, to repeat, nobody seems to pay any attention to Egeus's words, neither to these two apparently pithy utterances nor to the "muchel more" that he says—which we are happily spared. The weeping continues; in fact, it goes on until "by lengthe of certeyn yeres" (2967) it ceases. What then, we might well wonder, is the function of this episode? What has been the point of giving such a speech to a character who has not even been mentioned earlier in the tale and who does not say anything—much less anything about the meaning or mutability of life—in Chaucer's source?

The answer may come with understanding the medieval view of Aegeus. As his story was told in antiquity, Aegeus, King of Athens, is forced to send periodic sacrificial victims to King Minos of Crete, to be offered to the Minotaur. When Aegeus discovers, on the occasion of the third offering, that his son Theseus is one of those chosen by lot, he is distraught. Seeing, however, that Theseus is confident that the gods are on his side, Aegeus gives him a white sail to hoist in place of the ship's black one in the event that he should be able to return, as a sign of his success. On his return, Theseus, though successful, forgets to replace the black sail. When Aegeus, who has been watching daily, sees this sail, he in despair hurls himself into the sea, which thereafter bears his name. What is emphasized in this account is the great grief and rash action of Aegeus. As Plutarch phrases it, citing Simonides, Aegeus in despair threw himself from the rock and was dashed into pieces; as Catullus describes it, Aegeus, with eyes wasted by tears, hurled himself from the summit.[21]

In the Middle Ages the story of Aegeus was widespread, and as told in the *Genealogiae deorum gentilium* of Boccaccio, for instance, it stresses the great grief, both when the king watches his son leave for Crete and later when he sees the black sail.[22] Although not spelled out by medieval commentators, Aegeus's overwhelming grief and rash action would have made him the antithesis of wisdom and certainly an inappropriate counselor of moderation. Unable to control his own emotions—as Chaucer's audience would have realized—Egeus as spokesman against grief in the Knight's Tale must have seemed incongruous if not ludicrous. And both Chaucer and his audience must have enjoyed the inconsistency between this speaker and his words.

The function of Egeus and his words, however, is not merely to inject a note of humor into the scene following Arcite's death—a scene, it should be noted, marked by several blatant and purposeful incongruities. The function is rather to suggest something of the folly of the entire episode and to undercut the apparent seriousness of the Athenians' response to the death of this knight, who had for years endured a living death in their prison. And, depending on how one finally interprets the Knight's Tale, the words of Egeus may be seen either as contrasting with the wisdom later offered by Theseus in his speech on the chain of love, or as providing a basis for understanding the inadequacy of Theseus's wisdom.

Occasionally the thematic particular in *The Canterbury Tales* functions as an ironic commentary giving new meaning to a tale that has just been told. After the Monk is interrupted by the Knight who can no longer listen to his gloomy tragedies, recounting man's fall and loss of hope, Harry Bailly in his own inimitable way agrees with the Knight's objections and comments on the Monk's Tale:

                           pardee, no remedie
It is for to biwaille ne compleyne
That that is doon, and als it is a peyne,
As ye han seyd, to heere of hevynesse.
   Sire Monk, namoore of this, so God yow blesse!
Youre tale anoyeth al this compaignye.
Swich talkyng is nat worth a boterflye,
For therinne is ther no desport ne game.
Wherfore, sire Monk, or daun Piers by youre name,
I pray yow hertely telle us somwhat elles;
For sikerly, nere clynkyng of youre belles,
That on youre bridel hange on every syde,
By hevene kyng, that for us alle dyde,
I sholde er this han fallen doun for sleep,
Althogh the slough had never been so deep;
Thanne hadde your tale al be toold in veyn.

                                              (B^2 3974–89)

The Host's "no remedie" echoes the "no remedie" that is at the heart of
the Monk's view of tragedy: the fall of those who stood in high degree so
that "ther nas no remedie / To brynge hem out of hir adversitee" (B^2
3183–84). In the context of this echo, Harry Bailly's interjection, "so God
yow blesse!" casual as it is, may not be without ironic significance, for it is
diametrically opposed to the Fall of man and to the human "adversitee"
that the Monk has been describing in his tale. The interjection also offers
what is, in effect, the "remedie" the Monk is not aware of; for the phrase
"so God yow blesse" calls up the grace of God that Chaucer's audience
would realize is what, according to medieval Christianity, can release
man from perdition and bring him to salvation, even when man himself
is unable to see any hope.
   The Host's reference to the butterfly may likewise call up the possible
redemption of man, for the butterfly was a rich symbol in medieval art
and literature. Although in its *significatio in malo* the butterfly was regarded as suggesting idleness and triviality, in its *in bono* meaning it was
widely viewed as suggesting resurrection and rebirth, an association apparently stemming from the Greek term *psyche,* meaning both butterfly
and soul. In changing from caterpillar to chrysalis to butterfly, it was
seen implying the movement from life to death to rebirth; it appeared
frequently carved on tombstones, indicating the flight of the soul from
the body, and in paintings of the Christ child it depicted the Resurrection
and the redemption of man effected by Christ.[23]
   It is precisely the idea of rebirth that the Monk has in effect denied in
his various "tragedies," and although the Knight objected to his unre-
lenting insistence on the Fall, the Knight's suggested substitute—to hear
how man rises on the Wheel of Fortune and "there abideth in

prosperitee" (B^2 3967)—hardly indicates any more understanding of the issues at hand. The real solution, the real "remedie" that the Monk apparently cannot see, is found incongruously and unexpectedly, in Harry Bailly's humorous response to the tale—though, of course, the Host is no more aware of its implications than the Monk is aware of his own inadequate view of life. But Chaucer seems to have provided in the comic commentary a proper *moralitas* to the problem being raised by the Monk's insistence on the fall of man into "myserie," where he "endeth wrecchedly" (B^2 3167). The casual "so God yow blesse," along with the allusion to the butterfly, hint at what is missing in the tale and in the discussion of it.

This conversation on the road to Canterbury clearly provides a comic episode, with the Host's words functioning far beyond his intention. And Chaucer, with obvious delight in the irony and incongruity of the Host's corrective, extends the play, also adding further to the point. Continuing to press the Monk to tell another tale, Harry Bailly says that if it had not been for the bells on the Monk's bridle, he should have fallen asleep and from his horse. The irony is not only that the Monk's words would seem on the verge of bringing about a fall—which, of course, is the very subject of his words—but also that the Host's interjection, "By hevene kyng, that for us alle dyde," provides in plain language the Christian solution to the Fall of man. Christ's death was designed to bring about man's return to Paradise, and the Harrowing of Hell, occurring between the Crucifixion and the Resurrection, was the immediate sign of the salvation to come for the world. Although the "slough" referred to by Harry Bailly is not so deep as hell, if the Monk's words had caused the Host to fall into it, the tale would ironically have been in vain, as though it were not already in vain in failing to indicate the "remedie" for man's "adversitee." The irony of these words following the tale underscores the Monk's denial of grace and salvation and, moreover, the inability of this contemplative to realize the meaning of the Crucifixion and Resurrection.

Although the details discussed here represent only a few of Chaucer's thematic particulars and illustrate only a few of the ways he employs them in his narratives, they may indicate something of what I mean by the term itself and something of the extensiveness and complexity of Chaucer's blend of symbol and irony. Sometimes representing a symbolic detail and calling up an ideal, the thematic particular is most frequently a necessary part of the narrative, functioning to provide a contrast between itself and what is at hand. Although Chaucer will sometimes employ such ready-made symbols as butterfly, swallow, nightingale, and dry tree, he uses these to do more than give an allegorical sense to his narrative. In fact, I have purposely avoided using the term *allegory* because I have found that in modern criticism it too frequently clouds

issues. Sometimes apparently ordinary details take on a symbolic or extraordinary sense through being repeated or through being juxtaposed
against other details; sometimes the symbolic sense stems from or leads
to our awareness of incongruity and irony as well as our awareness of
pervasive or overriding themes. By understanding the working of
Chaucer's thematic particulars, we may understand an essential ingre-
dient in his literary artistry.

MUSICAL SIGNS AND SYMBOLS IN CHAUCER: CONVENTION AND ORIGINALITY

DAVID CHAMBERLAIN

I feel some trepidation, a discord in *musica humana,* at the thought of my presumption. Among my fellow contributors to this volume is the very founder of the "olde daunce"—or more aptly, the very founder of musical iconography in Chaucer studies, D. W. Robertson, Jr. Other contributors include an expert on bells, both pious and phallic; another expert on the "most solempne service" or songs of Lauds; and experts on erotic birdsong and dancing; on roundels, ballades, and the *lay de comfort;* and on the court entertainment of Chaucer's kings. I am referring, respectively, to Edmund Reiss, Bernard Huppé, Chauncey Wood, James I. Wimsatt, and John Gardner.[1] Their interpretations of music left me, like Chaucer's Man of Lawe, feeling similar "To Muses that men clepe Pierides"—a musical sign for foolish pride, from mythology.[2] I seemed to be left only with old chestnuts such as the Miller's bagpipe, a simple sign for lechery from daily life; or the Wife of Bath's nightingale song, another sign for lechery from mythology and natural history; or the familiar duet of the Pardoner and Summoner, with its gross punning sign:

> Ful loude he soong "Com hider, love, to me!"
> This Somonour bar to hym a stif burdoun;
> Was nevere trompe of half so greet a soun.[3]

So I spent time considering, "without noote, withoute song"—which is a sign for the "synne of Accidie" or "worldly sorwe" in *The Book of the Duchess*[4]—what material might be left to me. I could make a close study of musical signs in one work, say, in *Troilus,* from Thesiphone, a Fury of discord in stanza one, to the final melody of the spheres, but I wanted to be more comprehensive. The same objection existed to a close study of just one musical image, such as Chaucer's superb symbol, "melodye," in *The Canterbury Tales.* Something new would be a careful semiotics of

Chaucer's music, covering pragmatics, syntactics, and semantics, but this required more space and also seemed too much like deliberate "newefangelnesse." Then I examined the old chestnuts again. They showed significant differences. Two were thoroughly conventional in medieval iconography—bagpipe and nightingale—but one was more original, the Summoner's "stif burdoun" and "trompe." Other signs show the same contrast. At old January's marriage, the dancing of Venus (even without "hire fyrbrond") is a conventional sign of prurience; but the "songes that the Muses song" at the wedding of "Philologie and hym Mercurie" is an original and subtle allusion or sign of wisdom or divinity.[5] Chaucer's combination of the two sources is the heart of his artistry. He is a learned poet imbued with conventional materials; he is also a genius who originates his own striking signs and symbols. This, then, will be my focus: convention and originality in Chaucer's musical signs and symbols.

By *sign* I will mean any word, thing, or action that signifies something other than its literal referent. This is Augustine's definition for figurative signs in *On Christian Doctrine* (2.15). Only rarely, I would suggest, is Chaucer's musical imagery mainly literal and not a sign of anything except sweet sound, as with Arcite: "And if he herde song or instrument / Thanne wolde he wepe, he myghte nat be stent" (A 1367–68), but even here the sweet sound is a sign of joy, which Arcite lacks. Conversely, some of Chaucer's musical signs have no literal meaning but are wholly moral or allegorical, or both; such is the "olde daunce." I use *allegorical* here in the specific, religious sense, "Quid credas" (What one may believe—in terms of Christian faith). Most of Chaucer's musical signs are moral, but not strictly allegorical in this sense, as we see in the "murye note" of the Friar (A 235) and Theseus's return to Athens "with victorie and with melodye" (A 872). Of course, literary allusions can be such moral musical signs, as shown already with the Pierides and Philology. Moreover, in keeping with medieval conventions, some of Chaucer's musical signs have both favorable ("in bono") and unfavorable ("in malo") senses. Such is the nightingale's song, which Chaucer uses almost always in a mildly unfavorable erotic sense, but once importantly in a favorable sense, as I will suggest later for the first time; and such also is general birdsong, which is wholly "in bono" in *The Book of the Duchess* (291–320) but obviously "in malo" in Sir Thopas (766–75) and, yes, in the opening of the General Prologue (9–11). Other musical signs have only a favorable meaning, such as the "hevenyssh melodie" of the spheres in *Troilus* (5.1811–13) and *The Parliament* (59–63). Finally, some of Chaucer's signs are highly conventional and some are largely original, as we shall see in detail, but all of them are traditional in a broad sense. They do not revolutionize ideas and techniques, but they vary and improve ideas within traditional limits.

A "symbol" in Chaucer is not, I think, qualitatively different from a "sign." But when a musical sign becomes unusually complex through its abundance, its variety of meaning, and its originality, I will call it a "symbol." About the only such musical symbols, I think, are "melodye" in *The Canterbury Tales,* "accord" in *The Parliament,* and perhaps "singing" in the Nun's Priest's Tale.

Musical signs provide one useful means of comparing convention and originality in Chaucer. The tradition of ideas about music offers a firm external control of meaning because it is widespread and clear in medieval culture. Its control is strengthened because it overlaps with other bodies of conventional signs—scriptural, philosophic, mythologic, social—although not with physiognomic, except when Minerva threw away the flute because it distorted her features.[6] We know that Chaucer was thoroughly familiar with works that created or used musical tradition, works such as Boethius's *Consolation,* Macrobius's *Commentary,* Alan's *Complaint,* the *Roman de la Rose,* Dante's *Commedia,* and Boccaccio's *Teseida.* We can assume that he was familiar with the Psalter, which abounds in musical imagery, as well as with Apocalypse and Song of Songs, and other works in which music is significant.[7] Moreover, Chaucer's musical imagery is abundant enough to offer considerable control of its meaning from inside his own work. For example, although he says simply that the Wife of Bath knows "the olde daunce" (A 476) of love, elsewhere he links that dance clearly with "freletee" and the "devel."[8] Again, after Troilus and Criseyde arrive in bed, they begin "th'amoureuse daunce" (4.1431), which finally makes clear Pandarus's earlier invitations to Criseyde to "lat us daunce" (2. 111, 221).[9] Chaucer's musical imagery as a whole is not as abundant, of course, as in the most "musical" of medieval poetry, such as Dante's *Commedia,* Boccaccio's *Ameto,* Middle French allegories such as Machaut's *Dit de la Harpe* and Froissart's *Paradys d'Amours,* and perhaps Alan of Lille's philosophical poems, but in some works he equals or surpasses their density and subtlety, as in *The Parliament of Fowls* and the Miller's Tale.

External tradition and Chaucer's own abundant imagery also are the necessary means of revealing his originality. Without tradition, his originality would be difficult to detect, and without abundance, his originality could only be narrow. This originality seems to fall into five main categories, ranging in complexity from single signs to overall musical structures or frames. A fairly original single sign is the divine service of the Prioress, "Entuned in her nose ful semely" (A 123)—but not, implicitly, in her heart. An elaborate combination of signs of unusual originality appears at the fall of Chauntecleer when the music of mermaids, angels, "Boece," Chauntecleer's father, "Daun Burnel the Asse," and "seinte charitee" dominate about fifty lines. Vivid contrasts of signs exist within single works—for instance, in *The Book of the Duchess* between the

"mery . . . soun so swete entewnes" (309) of the birds and the "maner
song . . . withoute note" (471) of the Knight—but especially these contrasts exist between contiguous works, such as the Prioress' Tale and Sir
Thopas. A complex recurring sign, or symbolism, appears in the
polysemous "melodye" of *The Canterbury Tales;* and overall musical structures or frames appear, for instance, in *The Parliament of Fowls,* the
Knight's Tale, and, I will suggest for the first time, in *The Canterbury Tales*
as a whole.

These, then, are the five main areas of Chaucer's originality with musical signs: single signs, elaborate combinations, vivid contrasts, recurring symbolism, and overall structures. *The Canterbury Tales* best illustrates Chaucer's originality, although it is firmly rooted in convention;
The Parliament of Fowls best illustrates his use of convention, although it
shows much originality. In their overall effect, these musical signs serve
mainly to enrich and vivify the meaning, or moral nature, of setting and
character, rather than to control or identify that meaning. But in some
instances, musical signs become a crucial determinant of meaning, as in
the birdsong of *The Book of the Duchess,* the "welle of musik" in *The
Parliament of Fowls,* the voice of Chauntecleer "murier than the murie
organ," and, perhaps, the music that Chaucer adds in the Manciple's
Tale.

Medieval conventions about music derive from four traditions, or
strands, of intellectual culture: philosophical, scriptural, mythological,
and poetic tradition; and from a fifth strand, social tradition or everyday
life. The five strands are interwoven, but in general the philosophic and
scriptural strands dominate the whole cloth. John of Salisbury shows
more graphically than anyone the general contribution of four of these
major strands. Philosophy defines, classifies, and explains music, he tells
us. Scripture teaches the right use and abuse of music. Mythology illustrates vividly that use and abuse. Society, or everyday life, either imitates
or rejects the other three, as in the "effeminate dalliance of wanton
tones" that John finds defiling "the very service of the Church."[10] Finally,
it should be added to John's discussion that major poetry, such as
Dante's, Chaucer's, or Machaut's, combines material from the other four
traditions. Visual art represents a sixth tradition, of course, but its musical iconography draws inspiration mainly from the five traditions just
described. Visual art creates its own body of conventions, but it does not
seem to have directly influenced medieval poetry or Chaucer to a large
extent. Visual iconography confirms vividly, but does not usually create,
the signs of music in poetry.[11] Many authors could be used to illustrate
these five traditions, but for their proximity I will use mainly four from
Chaucer's own century, Jacques de Liège for philosophic, Richard Rolle
(who translated Peter Lombard on the Psalms) for scriptural, Pierre
Bersuire (who commented on Ovid) for mythological, and Dante for
poetic tradition.

The philosophical strand is formed mainly in the Patristic Age by Augustine, Macrobius, Chalcidius, Martianus Capella, and Boethius. Although considerable differences exist among them, especially between Augustine and the other four (who pass on the ideas of Plato's *Timaeus*), they all embody the same general ideas.[12] Music embraces all numerical proportioning. It pervades creation from God and the celestial spheres to man, the four elements, and other relationships. Man's moral behavior is a kind of music that should imitate the harmony of spheres or, in Augustine, imitate the eternal "rhythms" or "numbers" of God.[13] And instrumental music too should imitate the harmony of creation in order to foster virtuous humans. These ideas are passed on from the sixth to the fourteenth centuries, with many minor variations, in numerous encyclopedias, classifications of the arts, and treatises on music.[14] In general aesthetic terms, the most influential of these writers is Augustine, but in specific ideas about music, the most influential is Boethius.[15]

The Boethian philosophic tradition reaches a zenith in Chaucer's own century in the immense *Speculum musicae* of Boethius's great admirer, Jacques of Liège. Jacques defines music as "the harmonic modulation of all things related to each other by any measure," and further defines "harmonic modulation" ("armonica modulatio") as any condition of "proportion, concord, order or connection" among all things "sonorous, human, terrestrial, corporeal or spiritual, celestial or supercelestial."[16] Subjectively, music is the rational knowledge of these objective proportions. On the other side of the Alps, and of A.D. 1400, Ugolino of Orvieto confirms Jacques' broad definition of music in his own long treatise, *Declaratio musicae disciplinae* (ca. 1430).[17]

Chaucer shows some familiarity with the sources of philosophic tradition and with its broad definition of music. He refers easily to Macrobius, "Marcian," and "Boece" on music.[18] With most originality, he uses "Boece" tersely as a sign of rational music in the Nun's Priest's Tale. When the fox tells Chauntecleer,

Therwith ye han in musyk moore feelynge
Than hadde Boece, or any that kan synge.

(B[2] 4483–84)

the amusing point is that Boethius disparaged the use of feeling or the senses in judging music, and urged the use of reason, as I have suggested elsewhere.[19] Also with originality, in *The Parliament of Fowls*, Chaucer adapts from Boethius's *Consolation* the broad term *accord* as a sign for universal music. He uses *accord* to describe the harmony of instruments (197), of wind and birds (203, 675), of hearts or persons (371, 668), of the elements (381), and implicitly of the spheres (60). In terms of Boethian tradition, *accord (concordia)* is a conventional sign, but Chaucer's thematic use of it is original.[20]

The first branch of music in Jacques de Liège is *divina musica,* which is his own logical addition to Boethius's classification *(mundana, humana, instrumentalis).* Divine music is explicit and implicit in some earlier writers on music, but never before had it been added to Boethius's other three branches.[21] Divine music includes God's being, where exist "omnis melodia, omnis concordia, omnis consonantia." It extends to all relations of "substance and accident, unity and multiplicity, potency and act, the same and diverse." It includes the Trinity, the exemplary forms, and the "order and concord" of all other natures with God. The divine mind is "the most excellent modulation and the most perfect music." But divine also includes the "celestial music" of saints and angels, both subjectively and objectively. Music abounds, says Jacques, in their "continual nuptials and perpetual feasting." One song is common to all, but distinct songs signify different merits. The "citharoeda David" knew this "heavenly melody" when he urged his people to sing the "canticum novum." Here too is found "omnis melodia, omnis harmonia," and here "all things are referred to God, whom they enjoy." This music is available to travelers ("nos viatores") on earth through "Scripture and sound doctrine and philosophy."[22] Jacques thus blends much scriptural tradition with his philosophical material. He reflects the coherence among philosophy, musicology, and theology in high medieval culture.

Chaucer uses several conventions of divine music in minor, straightforward ways. In the Parson's Tale Christ "deyde for to make concord" (641) and the "trompe [of doom] sowneth" in the ear of St. Jerome (159); and in the Physician's Tale Nature and God are "ful of oon accord" (25). The celestial "Osanne" of angels appears in two tales, and the "song al newe" of the Lamb will be sung by the Prioress' "litel clergeoun," but with some subtle suggestion that women like herself may not be singing it.[23] With more originality, but drawing from scriptural and poetic tradition—especially Dante's earthly paradise *(Purgatorio,* 28.7–18)—Chaucer uses "birdsong" as a sign of heaven. In *The Parliament* it is combined with strings (suggesting Apocalypse 14:2) and other paradisaic details:

> On every bow the bryddes herde I synge,
> With voys of aungel in here armonye;
> . . . .
> Of instruments of strenges in acord
> Herde I so pleye a ravyshyng swetnesse,
> That God, that makere is of al and Lord,
> Ne herde nevere beter, as I gesse.

(190–200)

These details help to make clear that Chaucer divides his walled park into three distinct regions that embody the "hevene and helle and erthe"

(32) of Scipio's dream. The melodious wood signifies heaven ("ay cler day"), the Temple of Venus (with the well of Cupid) signifies hell in late medieval humanistic terms, and the "launde" of Nature represents earth, where the "choosing" occurs that leads to bliss or pain hereafter. Recent scholarship on Boccaccio, one of Chaucer's sources, strengthens such a reading.[24]

In *The Book of the Duchess* elaborate birdsong is a sign for heaven itself as well as for creation's praise of God at dawn (as in Lauds):

> And, as me mette, they sate among
> . . . .
> And songen, everych in hys wyse,
> The moste solempne servise
> By noote, that ever man, y trowe,
> Had herd; for som of hem song lowe,
> Som high, and al of oon accord.
> To telle shortly, att oo word.
> Was never herd so swete a steven,—
> But hyt had be a thyng of heven,—
> So mery a soun, so swete entewnes,
> That certes, for the toun of Tewnes
> I nolde but I had herd hem synge;
> For al my chambre gan to rynge
> Thurgh syngynge of her armonye.
> For instrument nor melodye
> Was nowhere herd yet half so swete,
> Nor of acord half so mete.
>
> (298–316)

The brilliant claim of a pun in "toun of Tewnes" (town of towns, tune of tunes, Song of Songs, or heavenly grace), advanced by Huppé and Robertson, is strongly suggested by the convention of birds as souls, or saints, and by the phrases "thyng of heven," and "al of oon accord."[25]

More original than these signs in *The Parliament* and *Duchess*, however, is *The House of Fame*'s inverted or ironic sign of heavenly music, the eternal praise of the Muses:

> And, Lord! the hevenyssh melodye
> Of songes, ful of armonye,
> I herde aboute her trone ysonge,
> That al the paleys-walles ronge!
> So song the myghty Muse, she
> That cleped ys Caliope,
> And hir eighte sustren eke,
> That in her face semen meke;
> And ever mo, eternally,
> They songe of Fame, as thoo herd y:

"Heryed be thou and thy name,
Goddesse of Renoun or of Fame!"

(1395–1406)

As B. G. Koonce has argued convincingly, the content and the details
leave no doubt that this is a ridiculous imitation of heavenly praise,
probably inspired by Dante.[26] We would add that these nine Muses are
similar to the poetical muses of Boethius, the "comune strompettis" or
"mermaydenes" who "destroyen the fruytes of resoun" and serve Fortune (book 1, prose 1). In *The House of Fame,* they invert ironically the
nine orders of angels. Earlier the long catalogue (1193–1250) of musicians, harpers, pipers, trumpeters, "Many thousand tymes twelve, / That
maden lowde mynstralcies," that includes Orpheus, Marsyas, and Joab
(but not David, Apollo, and Gabriel) is a longer amusing inversion of the
singing souls (rather than angels) of heaven. Less obvious and more
controversial is Chaucer's subtle suggestion of divine melody at Sarpedon's feast in *Troilus and Criseyde:*

Nor in this world ther is non instrument
Delicious, thorugh wynd or touche of corde,
As fer as any wight hath evere ywent,
That tonge telle or herte may recorde,
That at that feste it nas wel herd acorde;
Ne of ladys ek so fair a compaignie
On daunce, er tho, was nevere iseye with ië.

(5.442–48)

The scriptural echo in "tonge telle or herte may recorde" suggests
strongly that this musical "feste" is another false heaven to which Pandarus is trying to lead Troilus.[27]

Jacques of Liège goes on to elaborate carefully Boethius's three famous branches of music. *Mundana musica* consists in the "proportion and
concord" of the *spheres,* of the *elements,* and of *times* ("days, months, and
seasons"), with other minor subdivisions. This music results from an
"innate condition of love and concord" instilled by God, which Jacques
derives in part from the "alternus amor" and "concordia" of Boethius'
Consolation.[28] Like Chaucer, Jacques reflects a general revival of the *Consolation* and Boethius in the fourteenth century.

In Chaucer, the melody of spheres is the most obvious and significant
aspect of world music. In *The Parliament of Fowls* it is a conventional sign
of the "hevene blisse" (48, 72, 77) that rewards those who love the common profit (47, 75), but Chaucer makes it vividly influential:

And after shewede he hym the nyne speres,
And after that the melodye herde he

That cometh of thilke speres thryes thre,
That welle is of musik and melodye
In this world here, and cause of armonye.

(59–63)

Although this borrowing from Cicero or Macrobius is conventional, including the strong emphasis on the spheres as the "welle" of all other
music, Chaucer's use of it is highly original. In the poem, this "melodye"
is implicitly both the *source* for the other world music in the poem (of the
Edenic paradise, four elements, seasons, and rondel at the end), and a
model that the discordant Temple of Venus and the parliament do not
imitate. In its seven tones, this melody of spheres is also the source or
rationale for Chaucer's seven-line stanza and seven-hundred-line poem,
as I have contended elsewhere.[29] Thus the music of the spheres is a sign
of an all-pervasive harmony, from the bliss of heaven to the form of
poetry, and a norm for judging the discord or "noyse" created by "liker-
ous folk" (79).

In two other poems, the music of the spheres is a less organic but still
important sign. Troilus's ascent to "the holughnesse of the eighthe
spere" is well-known and conventional:

And ther he saugh, with ful avysement,
The erratik sterres, herkenyng armonye
With sownes ful of hevenyssh melodie.

(5.1811–13)

It is less obvious that this sign of "the pleyn felicite / That is in hevene
above" (5.1818) also offers a useful control or norm for all the earlier
music in the poem that does not accord with "pleyn felicite." This earlier
music includes Troilus's first "Canticus" of complaint (1.400–34); An-
tigone's seductive "Troian song" (2.827–75); Troilus's inverted Dantean
song in bed, "O Love, O Charite" (3.1254–74); his edited Boethian song
to Love (3.1744–71); Sarpedon's feast (5.442–48); and the second "Canticus Troili" of woe (5.636–44).

In *The House of Fame* the melody of the spheres does not appear
literally as a sign, but it does appear implicitly as a contrast to the discord
of Fame and Rumor. Jeffrey himself implies it while in the eagle's claws:

And than thoughte y on Marcian,
And eke on Anticlaudian,
That sooth was her descripsioun
Of alle the hevenes region.

(985–88)

In both "Marcian" and "Anticlaudian," the melody of the spheres is an

unforgettable aspect of "the hevenes."[30] The reader is reminded of this
music, therefore, in *The House of Fame* shortly before he hears the "grete
soun . . . that rumbleth up and down" (1025), a fearful "soun . . . lyke
betynge of the see . . . ayen the rockes holowe" (1034) outside Fame's
house. Later, he may think again of that music, which is usually a sign of
true heavenly bliss, when he sees the whirling House of Rumor, as John
Gardner suggests:[31]

> And ever mo, as swyft as thought,
> This queynte hous aboute wente,
> That never mo hyt stille stente.
> And therout com so gret a noyse
> . . . .
> For al the world, ryght so hyt ferde,
> As dooth the rowtynge of the ston
> That from th'engyn ys leten gon.
>
> (1924–34)

Even when Chaucer cannot introduce the spheres' music literally as a
sign because it would not cohere with the ironic mode of his poem, he
still subtly implies it as a norm.

Chaucer's translation of *Boece* shows which words and phrases are signs
of other world music, mostly that of the four elements and seasons. Most
vivid are the following: the "accordable chaungynges," "accordaunce of
thynges bound with love," and "accordable feyth by fayre moevynges" of
book 2, meter 8; the "nombres proporcionables" of the elements and
"membrys accordynge" of the world soul of book 3, meter 9; and the
"ryghtful alliaunce" of the stars, the "accordaunce" that "atempryth by
evenelyke maneres the elementz" of book 4, meter 6. Chaucer uses these
conventional signs of music of the elements—"accordaunce . . . by
evenelyk maneres" and "nombres proporcionables"—straightforwardly
in the *Parliament:*

> Nature, the vicaire of the almyghty Lord,
> That hot, cold, hevy, lyght, moyst, and dreye
> Hath knyt by *evene noumbres of acord,*
> In esy voys began to speke and seye.
>
> (379–81, my
> emphasis)

With this reminder, Chaucer reemphasizes the theme of universal harmony that appears earlier in the melody of the spheres and the
paradisaic wood. In the Knight's Tale the "faire cheyne of love" does not
include explicit musical signs, but the music of elements is implied when
the First Mover "bond / The fyr, the eyr, the water, and the lond / In
certeyn boundes, that they may nat flee" (2991–93).

In Jacques de Liège, *humana musica* reposes *in the body* (its "disposition" for receiving the soul, its "complexion" for operation of the senses, and its blending of the four elements), *between the body and soul* (physiologically in their natural life and theologically in their great love and ultimate beatitude), and *in the soul* itself (its operations, its hierarchy of rational and irrational powers, and its reception of grace through memory, intellect, and will).[32] Most important here is the idea of an inner moral music. It is a commonplace of medieval tradition. Augustine conceives the three chief vices ("voluptas," "superbia," and "curiositas") and the cardinal virtues as "numbers," or rhythms, or music of the soul. To Chalcidius, the "optima symphonia" is justice, when *ratio* rules, *iracundia* executes, and *cupiditas* obeys. Macrobius's musical motions of the soul include "the love of virtues and the lust of vices." In Cassiodorus, Rabanus, and Roger Bacon, virtue is music, but vice is not.[33] Other well-known scholars speak of "ethicam consonantiam," "modulamen morum," "moralis musica," "concors mentis et oris et operis harmonia."[34] To Hugh of St. Victor and his disciples, the music of the soul consists "in the virtues such as justice, piety, and temperance; and in the powers, that is, reason, anger, and desire."[35] We shall see that scriptural tradition identifies moral behaviour and music even more closely. This tradition of moral music is especially important for literature because it means that the song or music of every character may be a sign of his virtue or vice. Since this inner moral music overlaps widely, and often ambiguously, with external sonorous music, however, and also overlaps with the scriptural and mythological traditions, only a few instances of moral music in Chaucer will be suggested now.

Although the Parson's Tale belongs to scriptural tradition, its occasional terms "concord" and "discord" are borrowed partly from philosophic tradition. These and other musical terms are conventional signs for virtues and vices. They are wholly figurative. Sin overturns "every manere of ordre or ordinaunce" creating "disordinaunces" (260–66). Wickedness is "discordaunce" (274), envy makes "discord" (510), wrath is "discord" (562, 642), forgiveness is "accord" (991), and lechery is "desordeynee moevynges" (915), implicitly unlike the "accordable . . . moevynges" (book 2, meter 8) of *Boece*. Griselda banishes "discord" for "commune profit" (E 431) echoing the *Parliament;* and because of her patience she and Walter live many a year in "concord and in reste" (E 1129), which is an echo of true bliss from *Boece*. These terms are most abundant in *Melibee,* and their implication of traditional inner moral music is strengthened by explicitly musical uses of *accord* in other tales of fragment B². Melibee's counsel should "accorde" to reason (2395, 2568); "discord" is cured by its contrary, "accord" (2478–80); and "accord" is vividly a synonym for peace, as *concordia* is in musical passages of the *Consolation.*[36] In the context of Chaucer's works, especially the *Parliament,* then, "accorde" in *Melibee,* without any accompaniment of outer sonorous music, mildly suggests inner moral music. Here as elsewhere, however, one must be cautious not to overstate the implications of terms that have musical connotations.

Most of Chaucer's musical signs of vices and virtues, however, do involve sonorous music. With most originality, the Miller's Tale shows amusingly the subtle mutation of a seemingly virtuous literal sign, "melodye," to a wholly erotic figurative sign. At the outset Nicholas would have his literal music seem wholly pious:

> And al above ther lay a gay sautrie,
> On which he made a-nyghtes melodie
> So swetely that all the chambre rong
> And *Angelus ad virginem* he song.
>
> (3213–16)

The next time he sings he has just "accorded" (3301) with Alisoun about adultery, and the erotic nature of his literal music becomes obvious:

> He kiste hire sweete and taketh his sawtrie,
> And pleyeth faste, and maketh melodie.
>
> (3305–06)

In the third stage his music is wholly figurative, but still seemingly concordant:

> Withouten wordes mo they goon to bedde,
> Ther as the carpenter is wong to lye.
> Ther was the revel and the melodye.
>
> (3650–52)

Only near the end of the tale is the true discord of Nicholas' music revealed in the "thonder-dent" from the perverse instrument of his "toute" (3812, 3853), with perhaps a musical pun. This is only a sketch of the subtlety of the tale.[37] Another musical sign of more grisly eroticism is the singing of old January after his wedding night:

> And after that he sang ful loude and cleere,
> And kiste his wyf, and made wantown cheere.
> . . . .
> The slakke skyn aboute his nekke shaketh,
> Whil that he sang, so chaunteth he and craketh.
>
> (E 1845–50)

And in the Pardoner's Tale (and the Cook's fragment) music is a conventional but vivid sign of riot or debauchery:

In Flaundres whilom was a compaignye
Of yonge folk that haunteden folye,
As riot, hasard, stywes, and tavernes
Where as with harpes, lutes, and gyternes,
They daunce and pleyen at dees bothe day and nyght.

(c 463–67)

Finally, in the General Prologue an abundance of musical details of varying originality are all signs for inner folly or vice.[38] The nature of music in the whole Prologue is established tersely by the opening image of birdsong:

And smale foweles maken melodye,
That slepen al the nyght with open ye
(So priketh hem nature in hir corages).

(9–11)

Here is a music only of physical nature, or "corage," which is implicitly contrasted a few lines later to spiritual nature, or "ful devout corage" (22). It is implicitly the singing of nightingales (because nocturnal), and its eroticism is confirmed by the pun in the last line. With varying degrees of obviousness, all other music in the Prologue is a sign of the fleshly rather than the spiritual orientation of the pilgrims. Most obviously, the Pardoner sings in church only for greed, and on the pilgrimage, for lechery. Quite obviously, the Monk's bells on his bridle signify pride and lechery; the Friar's "mury note" and "yeddynges" his hypocrisy; and the Squire's "syngynge," "floytinge," and dancing quite conventionally signify his frivolity and eroticism. The more original "entewning" of the Prioress in her nose and the "stif burdoun" of the Summoner have been mentioned already. The Miller's bagpipe, like the melody of the little birds, is a sign that tends to characterize the music of the pilgrims as a whole:

A baggepipe wel koude he blowe and sowne,
And therwithal he broghte us out of towne.[39]

In every instance, we find implicit the "modulamen morum" of philosophic tradition: virtues and vices are music, but here we have only figures for vices.

The last branch of music in Boethian tradition is *instrumentalis*, or literal sonorous music. Jacques divides it in two ways that are relevant to literature, in both cases following Boethius. *Modesta musica* is ordinate and virtuous; *lascivia* is the effeminizing music of Roman theatricals, "today filling the churches, replacing plainsong indiscriminately."[40] A second division of sonorous music, into *theorica* and *practica*, is based on a famous distinction of Boethius' (*De musica*, 1.34). Theoretical concerns knowledge, while practical treats the actual execution of music. Theoretical is superior because soul is superior to body. Only the theorist can be called *musicus* because he judges by reason, and only the theorist can give the delight of discovering subtle truth after hard thought. Finally, only theoretical satisfies man's "innate desire for the true and the good," Jacques says, again quoting from the *Consolation*, and only theoretical speculates about the relation of instrumental music to its source, divine music.[41] The same general ideas can be found in numerous treatises. They are the dominant medieval view.

Since these two kinds of sonorous music are relevant, implicitly, to nearly all Chaucer's music, only two new points will be made at present. Chaucer knows clearly the distinction between *lascivia* and *modesta* music from his translation of *Boece*. *Lascivia* is the music of the "poetical Muses" or strumpets who "wolden fedyn and noryssen hym with sweete venym" (book 1, prose 1). Most of the characters in Chaucer's poetry are inspired implicitly by these muses that serve Fortune rather than Philosophy. In contrast, *modesta* music is the rational and delighting verse of "Musice, a damoysele of [Philosophy's] hous, that syngeth now lightere moedes or prolacions, now hevyere" (book 2, prose 1).[42] She is really an aspect of Philosophy herself, since it is Lady Philosophy who nourishes Boethius "with the weyghte of [her] sentences and with delyt of [her] syngynge" (book 3, prose 1) and who accompanies her "subtil soong, with slakke and delytable sown of strenges" (book 3, meter 2). Her songs, the meters of the *Consolation*, are refreshing and delighting. They vary from terse to elaborate, direct to oblique, metaphysical to ethical, philosophic, or mythological. By the definitions of Boethius and Jacques, Lady Philosophy is the complete *musicus* who embodies both *theoria* and *practica:* she composes, she performs, and she judges music by reason. With some originality, Chaucer uses signs of the true *musicus* in his own poetry. The *musik of Boece* in the Nun's Priest's Tale (B[2] 4484) has been mentioned already. With more originality, perhaps, Chaucer uses an elaborate sign of rational music in *The Book of the Duchess*. The Black Knight admits that he could not make songs as well as Tubal:

> That found out first the art of songe;
> For as hys brothres hamers ronge,
> Upon hys anvelt up and doun
> Thereof he took the firste soun,—
> But Grekes seyn Pictagoras,
> That he the firste fynder was
> Of the art, Aurora telleth so,—
> But therof no fors, of hem two.

                                                                         (1163–70)

The real point here is not who discovered music, as the Knight implies it is, but the implicit contrast between the rational music of tradition based on arithmetical proportions, whether discovered by Tubal or Pythagoras, and the irrational songs of the Black Knight himself.[43] He makes songs "of my felynge, myn herte to glade" (1172), just as Chauntecleer's foolish singing is all "felyng" and "herte" (B² 4483–93). The amusing insufficiency of the Black Knight's "firste song" is suggested also by its brevity and childishness in contrast to the elaborate lyrics in French love allegories.[44]

The second great strand of medieval ideas and signs of music is the scriptural strand. It originates in the Bible, of course. It is elaborated at great length in exegesis, the most abundant of all medieval genres, especially in exegesis of the Psalms, and in prefaces to the Song of Songs.[45] It was disseminated through the liturgy, especially the Canonical Hours (widely attended by laity as well as clergy) but also the Mass, and through psalters and treatises on the liturgy. The role of music in Scripture and the meaning of that music, therefore, were thoroughly familiar to the educated. Musical imagery and signs were also prominent in the mystical works that multiplied in Chaucer's century, such as Richard Rolle's *Canticum amoris* and Walter Hilton's *Of Angel Song,* and they were also prominent in England in the thirteenth century in the long devotional and mystical Latin poems of John of Howden *(Philomena, Quinquaginta cantica, Cythara)* and John Pecham *(Philomena).* In contrast to the abundance of these authors' musical signs from scripture, Chaucer's are somewhat thin, though graphic.

In its substance, scriptural tradition confirms and extends the ideas and signs of music in philosophic tradition. Whenever possible, I will draw signs from Chaucer's countryman, Richard Rolle, in his partial translation of Peter Lombard's commentary on Psalms.[46] The levels of exegesis cohere with the music of philosophic tradition. Literal sonorous music is the source of all the signs. Tropology develops moral music; allegory and anagogy develop two kinds of divine music. The literal divine music of heaven appears tersely in Scripture itself (Apoc. 14:2–3, 15:2–3) and elaborately in exegesis of Apocalypse and Psalm 150. We have treated it already with the divine music of philosophic tradition. More unusual kinds of divine music also appear in exegesis. In Jacques de Liège we find that the Trinity, the exemplary forms in God's mind, and divine charity are music. To Augustine, the Redemption itself is a musical octave; to others, Christ is the "summus musicus" who "made our peace by a double proportion" (the octave, 2:1), and His "song of love" for His mother is the Song of Songs. In Peter Lombard He is the "praecentor" who leads the "chorus"; to Bersuire, He is the "teacher of spiritual music" who "begins low and ends high"; His miracles are a *psalterium* and His sufferings a *cithara* in Lombard and many others, with numerous variations. His beatitudes and two testaments are a *cithara, consonantia, concordia,* and melodies.[47] In exegesis of psalms, many other musical details are signs of Christ. Chaucer undoubtedly knew many of these aspects of tradition, but he uses them only glancingly, as in the "concord" that Christ created by his death (I 642). A more original figurative divine music (of a saint) appears in one of Chaucer's additions to his source in his "A B C," or Prayer to the Virgin:

> We han noon oother melodye or glee
> Us to rejoyse in oure adversitee.

> (100–01)

The Blessed Virgin is a true *melody* or joy, who will take our part in adversity, a sign and reminder for numerous Chaucerian lovers who lament their "maladye" without a thought of spiritual remedy (or "melodye").

The world music of philosophy understandably appears very little in scriptural tradition, but it is supported by the "concentum caeli" in Job (38:37) and by passages in which God is said to "number" creation. The most important of these is the famous text from Sapientia, "Sed omnia in mensura et numero et pondere disposuisti" (11:21). It has been called the key to the medieval view of the world, but in scriptural exegesis it does not give rise to much musical imagery.

Most musical signs in scripture are aspects of human moral or spiritual music. Nearly every musical phrase, and certainly every instrument, is interpreted in exegesis as virtue or vice, usually virtue. Only the briefest sketch can be attempted here. Through exegesis and liturgy these signs were widely known. Though Chaucer may use a few of them explicitly, he would have taken for granted their metaphoric principle: music is virtue or vice. The metaphor appears in the Bible itself in Paul's famous passages: "singing and psalming in your hearts to God" (Eph. 5:19), "in grace singing in your hearts to God" (Col. 3:16), and "I psalm in spirit, I psalm also in mind" (1 Cor. 14:15). In exegesis universally "to sing" is to praise God with a devout heart, and "to psalm" is to praise Him through good works; similarly, a *psalmus* signifies "good work" and a *canticum,* "joy over eternal things."[48] Among musical instruments in Rolle and scriptural dictionaries, the *tympanum* is "mortification of flesh," *cymbala* are harmonious human lips or "the concords of the faithful," the *tuba* is a preacher or one perfected by tribulation (hammering), the *tibia* is one preaching in charity, the *cithara* (sounding from below) signifies service in "worldly" matters and the *psalterium* (sounding from above) service in "eternal" matters, or the *cithara* is "mortifying concupiscence" and *psalterium* is observing the decalogue or preserving charity. A chorus is charity or concord; charity is a "suavis melodia" and truth a melody in Augustine.[49] Several specific songs are figures or signs for faith, charity, and grace: the "canticum Domini," "canticum Sion," and "canticum graduum," or Song of Ascent, the "canticum novum," and the "canticum canticorum," which is often the highest grace in heaven, as in the "song al newe" of the Prioress' Tale (B² 1774).[50]

Music as a figure for vice is much less abundant in exegesis, but still vivid. The Song of Babylon, or vice, is contrasted to the Song of Sion, or piety, the Old Song to the New Song, from Augustine to Rolle. We find the song of "delights of the world" in Jerome; the "song of the devil" and "song of man," or pleasure, in Bersuire. *Melodia* and *carmen* can signify the sound of tyrants, hypocrites, and lechers.[51]

The fourth kind of music in scriptural tradition, instrumental or sonorous or literal music, is the foundation of all the foregoing allegorical and moral signs. At the literal level, we find two vivid kinds of music, one serving the Lord and one serving the appetites. In keeping with exegesis, we can call them the Song of the Lord and the Song of Man, or the New Song and the Old Song. The Song of the Lord appears in two main forms. One form is the many occasional songs of thanks from the Songs of Moses, Debbora, and Judith to the Songs of Zacharias, Mary, and Simeon, with many others between.[52] The other form is the ritual song or psalms established by David before the Ark of the Covenant in Chronicles (23, 25) under the direction of Asaph, Heman, Idithum, and Ethan. Its purpose is obvious—to serve God and increase piety. The Song of Man appears in numerous brief passages, mostly of the Old Testament, but also in Apocalypse, and sometimes vividly juxtaposed to the Song of the Lord. It falls into four main kinds, songs of pleasure, hypocrisy, vicious abuse, and Babylon ("canticum meretricis").[53] Chaucer would have found several instances of it in the treatise he translated from Innocent III, the "Wreched Engendrynge of Mankynde" (*Legend of Good Women*, G 413). There we find "the timbrel and the harp . . . and the organ" that "go down to hell" (Job 12–13) and "the harp and the lyre and the timbrel and the pipe" of those who follow drunkenness (Is. 5:11–12), suggesting the rioters of the Pardoner's and Cook's Tales. The contrast is vivid in Amos (6) between the instruments of luxurious feasts and the instruments of David; and in Isaiah (24, 26) between the *cantus falsus* of worldly joy, as Bersuire says, and the praise of God.[54] Examples could be multiplied.

Chaucer uses the Song of the Lord explicitly as a sign of faith or grace in a few minor and mostly conventional ways. His "A B C" to the Virgin is a "carmen" and, therefore, a Song of the Lord. The Prioress considers her tale a "song" in honor of God and Mary (B² 1677), a true Song of the Lord, but it does not seem to be "entewned" in her nose, or in her spirit, as sweetly as the Song of her little "clergeoun" and martyr:

> Ful myrily than wolde he synge and crie
> *O Alma redemptoris* everemo.
> The swetnesse hath his herte perced so
> Of Cristes mooder that, to hire to preye,
> He kan nat stynte of syngyng by the weye.
>
> (1743–47)

His singing is a conventional sign of true love and innocence developed with some originality and vividness, "acordynge with the note" (1737), "loude and cleere" (1845). More original is the amusing contrast to this music of piety that Chaucer develops in the very next tale, Sir Thopas. Here we find birdsong, also "loude and cleere," as an amusing sign of foolish erotic love:

> The briddes synge, it is no nay,
> The sparhauk and the papejay,
>   That joye it was to heere;
> The thrustelcok made eek his lay,
> The wodedowve upon the spray,
>   She sang ful loude and cleere.
>
> Sire Thopas fil in love-longynge
> Al whan he herde the thrustel synge,
>   And pryked as he were wood.
>
> (1956–63)

This sign is an elaborate version of the birdsong in the General Prologue, where simply the "smale foweles maken melodye / So priketh hem nature in hir corages." The "thrustelcok" is especially erotic and amusing.[55] The amusing contrast of Thopas himself to the clergeoun of the Prioress is also partly musical because he too is a "child" ravished by love for a queen who fosters music:

> Heere is the queene of Fayerye,
> With harpe and pipe and symphonye,
>   Dwellynge in this place.
>
> (2004–06)

Although music does not control meaning in these two tales, it enriches meaning. Music is a sign of true and false innocence, of pious love and foolish eroticism. One love is directed toward the "song al newe" of heaven (B² 1774) and the other subtly toward the "harpe and pipe" of "Fayerye" or mischievous devils.

Chaucer uses the sonorous Song of the Lord in a variety of other ways. In the Second Nun's portrait of St. Cecilia, he vividly subordinates the

sonorous Song of the Lord to Paul's spiritual inner song, another conventional sign, in order to emphasize the depth of her charity:

> And whil the organs maden melodie,
> To God allone in herte thus sang she
> "O Lord, my soule and eek my body gye
> Unwemmed, lest that it confounded be."
>
> (134–37)

In the Nun's Priest's Tale the same sonorous Song of the Lord is contrasted to erotic song. Although the "voys" of Chauntecleer is "murier
than the murie orgon / On messe-dayes that in the chirche gon" (4041),
that organ music is a sign of the love that human Chauntecleers should
be cultivating. It contrasts vividly with the erotic duet he and Pertelote
celebrate at dawn (an hour of prayer in the Parson's Tale):

> But swich a joye was it to here hem synge,
> Whan that the brighte sonne gan to sprynge,
> In sweete accorde, "My lief is faren in londe!"
>
> (4067–69)

The sweetness of their erotic harmony is what really deceives Chauntecleer, of course, into forgetting the warning of his dream: "For whan I se
the beautee of youre face ... / It maketh al my drede for to dyen"
(4350–52).

In other tales an abuse of the Song of the Lord is a sign of vice rather
than folly. Such abuse is obvious in the Summoner's Tale, where the friar
first claims that his house honors the "divine servyce" (1719), but then
praises singing thirty masses ("trentals") in one day (1723–28) and lies
about singing a *Te Deum* for Thomas's dead child, "withouten noyse or
clatterynge of belles" (1867), which is an amusing disparagement of the
sign for prayer. In the Miller's Tale both Nicholas and Absolon abuse the
Song of the Lord, but especially Absolon, a "parissh clerk" who should be
doing his chanting (3367) to his Lord rather than "brokkynge lyk a
nyghtyngale" (3376) to Alisoun:

> He syngeth in his voys gentil and smal,
> "Now, deere lady, if thy wille be,
> I praye yow that ye wole rewe on me,"
> Ful wel acordaunt to his gyternynge.
>
> (3360–63)

The Song of the Lord that Absolon should be singing appears later in
the tale, in juxtaposition to the music of Nicholas in bed:

Ther was the revel and the melodye;
. . . .
Til that the belle of laudes gan to rynge,
And freres in the chauncel gonne synge.

(3652–56)

Given the character of friars elsewhere in *The Canterbury Tales,* however, there is not much likelihood that these "freres" actually practice the love that they sing. Chaucer's most original and ironic use of the Song of the Lord is a subtle sign of the religion of the flesh in *Troilus.* When Pandarus seems to hear "belles" sounding at the miracle ("merveille") of Cupid, by which Criseyde has agreed to give "blisse" to Troilus, and when at the same time he urges Venus to "maken melodye" (3.187–89), Chaucer has created an absurd inversion of the consecration and the music of the Mass, as was first pointed out by Robertson.[56] More conventional is the punning sign of the name "Alisoun" for Chaucer's tender-hearted woman. By imitating the song "kyrie eleyson" ("Lord, have mercy") of the Mass, the name becomes a subtle sign for false erotic mercy, as one Middle English lyric suggests.[57] Altogether, Chaucer's Songs of the Lord are a highly varied and original body of simple signs.

Chaucer's wholly figurative musical sign for cupidity, the "olde daunce," the explanation of whose meaning we also owe to Robertson, is a conventional sign in poetry that grows out of the scriptural New and Old Song and may hardly need to be mentioned. The Wife of Bath implicitly knows "the olde daunce" of love (A 476) in the same sense as the "olde vekke" in the *Romaunt* knows it, and she is a "devel" who "hadde lerned of love's art" and "knew all the olde daunce" (4286–300). The Wife also knows it implicitly in the same sense as the governesses who "han falle in freletee, / And knowen wel ynough the olde daunce" in the Physician's Tale (78–79). Pandarus also "koude ech a deel / The olde daunce, and every point therinne" (3.694–95) as he brings Troilus to Criseyde's bed. It is implicitly this "olde daunce" of cupidity that Pandarus earlier twice asks Criseyde to begin (2. 111–12, 221–22), and that she also consciously intends when she asks Pandarus, "How ferforth be ye put in love's dance?" (3.1105). These are all foreshadowing signs for her "amoureuse daunce" in bed with Troilus (4.1431). As a sign, although the "olde daunce" has the scriptural meaning of Christian *cupiditas* (preferring created things to their Creator), in poetry it has the same general meaning as the "daunce" of the "elfe queene, with her joly compaignye" in the Wife of Bath's Tale, and the "carole" of Myrthe in the *Romaunt.*[58] It contrasts in meaning with the "carole" of the seven virtues in Dante's *Purgatorio* (cantos 29–31), the "balade . . . in carole-wyse" in *The Legend of Good Women* (G 200–23), the healthy "daunce" of the widow in the Nun's Priest's Tale (4030), and the ironic "newe daunce" that Troilus only seems to have led (2.553).

The third strand of musical tradition, the mythological, offers a relatively small number of musical images that were used frequently, especially after A.D. 1150, as signs or exempla of virtues and vices. The main sources were the Roman poets, especially Ovid, but also Virgil, Statius, Claudian, Martianus Capella, and to a lesser extent, Horace. Their musical material was interpreted as signs, mainly moral but also at times as theological and naturalistic signs, by a goodly number of medieval mythographers from Fulgentius in the sixth century to Boccaccio, Ridewall, Bersuire, and Walsingham in the fourteenth.[59] Medieval poets assimilated these signs, through rhetorical training and reading, from both the Romans themselves and the mythographers. In Roman poetry as in philosophic tradition, poetry itself, of course, is a kind of song. Chaucer gives us a glimpse of this tradition in *Troilus*, which is a "song" (3.1814) that the poet "sings" (2.56). Like scriptural signs, mythological signs of music can vary in meaning. Venus can represent *mundana musica* or erotic delight; Orpheus's music can signify eloquent wisdom or effeminizing pleasure, as in John of Salisbury and Alan of Lille among others.[60] Even Apollo played a seven-reed pipe ("fistula") on earth for the seven years he was a human, although in heaven, where he is the god of music as well as prophecy, archery, medicine, and wisdom, he plays his lyre.[61] Whereas the nightingale in scriptural tradition represents the soul praising God, in mythological tradition Philomela generally signifies lost chastity or eroticism. Likewise, but less frequently, the Muses also, as we have seen, can signify foolish inspiration as well as virtuous inspiration. Other musical figures signify only vices, such as the Pierides, who challenged the Muses; Marsyas, who challenged Apollo; and Misenus, who challenged Triton to musical contests, all of whom signify pride.[62] Almost always, the music of the Sirens is sensual, of Bacchus riotous, and of Hymen virtuous.[63]

Among Chaucer's musical signs from mythology, the music of Venus is most abundant and the music of Apollo is most oblique. Chaucer vividly associates Venus with music for the same reason that mythography as a whole does, because music is alluring and "voice instead of face has been a bawd for many," as Ovid says, or because song is one of the "hooks" of Venus to Boccaccio and Claudian.[64] The music of Cupid, or Love, is identical with that of his mother for most literary purposes. As with most of his musical signs, Chaucer's music of Venus enriches the meaning of his settings and characters but usually does not control that meaning. From the *Romaunt*, Chaucer knew that Love "is discordaunce that can accorde, / And accordaunce to discord" (4715–16), where the emphasis is on "discord." In *The Complaint of Mars*, Venus is the "verrey sours and

welle / . . . Of soun of instrumentes of al swetnesse" (174–79), phrasing
which suggests a contrast to the spheres as the "welle of musik and
melodye" in the *Parliament* and to the *summum bonum* as the "welle of alle
goodes" in the *Consolation*. [65]

Chaucer shows increasing sophistication in his signs of Venus. In *The
House of Fame* no musical signs appear in the temple of Venus (119–39).
In the Knight's Tale, among all the "circumstances of love" are "festes,
instrumentz, caroles, daunces" (A 1930–32), and Venus has a "citole" in
her right hand (1959), which differs slightly from the more conventional
conch shell of Bersuire and other mythographers, but coheres clearly
with the tradition of the sensual Venus. [66] In *The Parliament*, however, the
frenetic endless dancing of "women inowe . . . al dishevele . . . yer by
yeere" around Venus's temple (232–35) is a more subtle and original
sign for the punishment of sinners, who "Shal whirle aboute th'erthe
alwey in peyne" (80), as Scipio says earlier.

Other signs of Venus's music are more conventional than that in the
Parliament, but they are developed with more vividness. In the Merchant's Tale she "daunceth" with her erotic firebrand before the bride of
January "hir knight" (E 1727–28, 1778); and in the Squire's Tale "who
koude telle you the forme of daunces / . . . Swich subtil lookyng and
dissimulynges" (F 283–85) that "daucen lusty Venus children deere"
(F 937) unless it were Lancelot? Her other dancers include her "servant"
the squire Aurelius (937), who "syngeth, daunceth, passynge any man"
(F 929); and implicitly the Squire of *The Canterbury Tales*, who "koude
songes make and wel endite, / Juste and eek daunce, and . . . sleep
namoore than dooth a nyghtyngale" (A 95–98). With more originality, at
the top of Fortune's wheel (3.1714), Love's servant, Troilus (3.1794),
revels in Venus's music implicitly, "In suffisaunce, in blisse, and in syng-
ynges" (3.1716); and in his singing (3.1743) he likens ironically an illicit
human music ("accord" of lovers' "lawe of compaignie") with the great
world of music of "stowndes concordynge" and "elementz that ben so
discordable" (3.1744–57). It is the music of Venus again when Troilus
"began for joie th' amorouse daunce" and delighted "as the briddes,
whanne the sonne is sheene, / Deliten in hire song in leves grene"
(4.1431–32). When related to Boethius's *Consolation*, the music of Venus,
or physical "delit," is one aspect of the music of the Goddess Fortune
who "kan to fooles [Troilus in this instance] so hire song entune, / That
she hem hent and blent, traitour comune" (4.4–5).

The music of Apollo in Chaucer is much less abundant than that of
Venus and wholly indirect except in the Manciple's Tale, even though
Phoebus himself is mentioned often. As in the invocation to *The House of
Fame*, book 3, imitated from Dante's *Paradiso* (canto 1), Apollo in
Chaucer is generally the "god of science and of light" (1091), but apart
from the Manciple's Tale his music appears only in allusions to the story

of Midas's donkey ears, and here without any mention of the god him-self. The point of Midas's donkey ears, of course, is that Midas was too deaf to music and wisdom to realize that Apollo played more sweetly on his heavenly lyre than the satyr Pan did on his seven-reed pipe. Chaucer uses these donkey ears as a fairly subtle, though not original, sign that his characters Troilus and "Alisoun" of Bath are deaf to the music of wisdom or heaven. Pandarus is most vivid with this sign and amusingly echoes Lady Philosophy's similar speech to Boethius, another thrall of Fortune:

> What! slombrestow as in a litargie?
> Or artow like an asse tó the harpe,
> That hereth sown whan men the strynges plye,
> But in his mynde of that no melodie
> May sinken hym to gladen, for that he
> So dul ys of his bestialite?

(1.730–35)

Implicitly, Troilus is like an ass to the harp, or deaf to the melody of true wisdom (which is not Pandarus's worldly wisdom), just as Boethius is in book 1 of the *Consolation*. The Wife of Bath ironically reminds us of her own deafness to wisdom when she introduces into her Tale a digression on Midas' "asses eres" and urges us to read Ovid for the rest of the story (D 952–82). The cupidinous wisdom she does know is implied in her Prologue by her vinous dancing and nightingale song, and in her Tale by the vanishing "daunce" of the "elf-queene" (or succubus) from which Arthur's knight foolishly hopes to learn "som wysdom" (D 989–96). Later, I shall return to Apollo in the Manciple's Tale.

The fourth tradition of medieval musical signs, poetic tradition, is enormous, of course, larger than any other written tradition except the scriptural, but it actually does not introduce many signs relevant to Chaucer that we have not already encountered in the previous three traditions. Although poetic tradition may actually have provided the immediate sources for many of Chaucer's signs, if not most of them, the ultimate medieval sources for most musical signs in all poets are the philosophic, scriptural, mythological, and social traditions. The works of several poets that Chaucer knew well abound in musical signs. Alan of Lille mingles abundant music from philosophy, scripture, and mythology in the *Complaint of Nature* and *Anticlaudianus:* the concord of nature, the melody of spheres, the liberal art music, the music of body and soul, the concord of the virtues, the "frenzied lyre" of Orpheus and the sacred orchestra of Hymen, God of marriage.[67] Dante makes abundant use of discordant noise in *Inferno,* psalms in *Purgatorio,* and dancing/singing spheres and angels in *Paradiso* as signs, respectively, of sin, penitence, and eternal joy. Musical signs are especially original and abundant in his Earthly Paradise.[68] *The Romance of the Rose* was perhaps more germinal for Chaucer than any other poem, with its vivid use of erotic birdsong, like that of the Sirens, its elaborate daunce or carole of Myrthe (described over several hundred lines and condemned by Resoun), its melody of the spheres, its songs of the Shepherd's Park, and its extravagant orchestrations by Pygmalion.[69] There is no need at present to detail the abundant music or songs of lovers, gods, virtues, and birds that Chaucer could have found in plenty in French poets, especially Machaut and Froissart, and in Boccaccio.[70]

Since many signs found in poetic tradition have been discussed already in relation to other traditions, only one of the musical signs that Chaucer derives mainly from poetic tradition will be mentioned now, and that is the song of many birds. We have seen earlier that multiple birdsong is twofold in meaning. As a sign of charity and praise, singing birds derive from scriptural tradition, for instance the apocryphal *Testament of Adam*, Ambrose's *Hexaemeron*, Rabanus Maurus, and many other sources.[71] In poetry, the sign appears vividly in Dante's Earthly Paradise (*Purgatorio*, 27.7–18). We have seen already Chaucer's use of this sign of virtuous love in *The Book of the Duchess* and *Parliament of Fowls*. It also appears in this sense in *The Legend of Good Women:*

> And thus thise foweles, voide of al malice,
> Accordeden to love, and laften vice
> Of hate, and songen alle of oon acord,
> "Welcome, somer, oure governour and lord!"
>
> (F 167–70)

With more originality, and slightly differently because only one bird sings, Chaucer uses birdsong as a controlling sign of charity at the start of the *Complaint of Mars*, on Saint Valentine's Day, "with seint John to borowe":

> Yet sang this foul—I rede you al awake,
> And ye that han not chosen in humble wyse,
> Without repentynge cheseth yow your make;
> And ye that han ful chosen as I devise,
> Yet at the leste renoveleth your servyse;
> Confermeth hyt perpetuely to dure,
> And paciently taketh your aventure.
>
> (15–21)

Birdsong as a sign of erotic delight, on the other hand, develops mainly in poetic tradition, with support from the bestiaries. One of its earliest uses available to Chaucer appears in Claudian's elaborate Epithalamium for the Emperor Honorius, where only the birds that Venus approves may sing in her paradisaic retreat on Cyprus. Perhaps its most influential use occurs at the opening of the *Roman de la Rose,* where it strongly inclines the dreamer to concupiscence. From here it becomes a topos in Middle French allegories that were known to Chaucer, such as Machaut's *Fonteinne amoureuse* and Froissart's *Paradys d'Amours.*[72] As mentioned already, Chaucer's own use of general birdsong as a sign of lubricity in the General Prologue and Sir Thopas is important thematically. More incidental uses of this erotic sign appear in *Troilus* (4.1429–35), in the Nun's Priest's Tale (4391), and in the Squire's Tale on Cambuskan's birthday:

> In Aries, the colerik hoote signe.
> Ful lusty was the weder and benigne,
> For which the foweles, agayn the sonne sheene,
> What for the sesoun and the yonge grene,
> Ful loude songen hire affecciouns.
>
> (51–55)

After briefly sketching the last tradition of music, we shall return to Chaucer's own most original poetic use of musical signs.

The social tradition of music is also enormous in extent and perhaps more difficult to control in meaning than the other four traditions. Some of the meaning of music in social tradition has to be inferred from the other four traditions we have sketched. We know from scriptural tradition, for instance, that the idea of a music of the Lord and of the Devil would have been widespread in society. It would have been learned in the school of the Prioress' Tale where "children lerned hir antiphoner / ... Fro word to word, acordynge to the note" (1709, 1737). We can infer from poetry such as *The Canterbury Tales* and the *Decameron* some of the uses and meaning of music among the nobility, and also among commoners, as in Chaucer's amusing descriptions of noble feasts and squires' musical skills, and in Boccaccio's pictures of virtuous polite recreation.[73] There is surely some distortion of historical reality in such pictures as the feasts in the Knight's Tale and the Squire's Tale, however, and there is obvious hyperbole in the musical contortions of the squire Aurelius and the clerk Absolon, who are most likely based on literary sources, such as Pygmalion in *The Romance of the Rose,* as much as on known social behavior. Chaucer probably illustrates for us most of the actual social situations in which music was practiced. He shows music associated with the liturgy, the education of clerks and squires, the entertainments of the nobility and merchants, the social pastimes of the commons, including pilgrimages, and the pursuit of love. He mentions many of the musical instruments and kinds of songs common in his day, as studies have shown.[74] Nevertheless, his abundant irony and exaggeration should be enough to keep us from viewing many of his musical descriptions too confidently as an actual historical record.

Other sources for the social tradition of music are more strictly historical than poetry is, and therefore more reliable, but they also require tactful interpretation. These sources include penitential manuals, histories, and the records of noble houses and guilds, but there is not space at present to do more than suggest these materials. The Parson's Tale illustrates the general tendency of penitential manuals. It warns tersely against "curiositee of *mynstralcie,* by which a man is stired the moore to delices of luxurie" (445). This view is confirmed by more personal penitential works such as Henry of Lancaster's well-known confession in *Le Livre de seyntz medicines* that dancing and song are not necessarily sinful, but are a dangerous occasion of sin.[75] Historical narratives generally deemphasize the danger of song and dance in noble houses, as in Froissart's description of the great Smithfield Tourney of 1390 where on Sunday night there was "elegant dancing in the queen's apartments, in the presence of the king and his uncles, and other barons of England, with ladies and damsels, continuing till it was day" and on Tuesday night in the bishop's palace where "the repast was elegant and costly, and the dancing continued all night."[76] Undoubtedly, there was more occasion of sin at such affairs than Froissart suggests. From public records, we can acquire some evidence of the social ideal of music. The "Pui" was a social fraternity of prosperous merchants in several European cities, and its "Festival of the Pui" is described in the London *Liber custumarum.* The festival was established "in honor of Our Lord Jesus Christ . . . for the nurturing of good love, courteous solace, joy and gladness; and for the annihilating of wrath, rancor, and all vices," and it included contests "to honor, cherish, and commend all ladies" by means of songs on the theme of "the becoming pleasance of virtuous ladies," even though no ladies were allowed to be present.[77] This social record confirms from another direction the constructive role for music that exists in all four other traditions. On the other hand, penitential works confirm that a good deal of unvirtuous music existed. As a whole, therefore, social tradition confirms the dual role of musical signs in poetry, to signify both virtue and vice.

Since most of Chaucer's signs discussed thus far are what I have called single signs or vivid contrasts, it now remains to discuss a little more fully three of his most original and subtle uses of musical signs: (1) an elaborate combination of signs, (2) the symbol "melodye" in *The Canterbury Tales,* and (3) the musical frame of *The Canterbury Tales.* The most original and elaborate combination of musical signs in Chaucer is found in the description of Chauntecleer just before he is seized by the fox, although the wedding of old January offers a close second in elaborateness.[78] As the scene of Chauntecleer's fall opens, his self-destructive erotic nature is revealed amusingly by the sign of the singing mermaid:

> and Chauntecleer so free
> Soong murier than the mermayde in the see;
> For Phisiologus seith sikerly
> How that they syngen wel and myrily.
>
> (B² 4459–62)

The bestiaries leave no doubt about the evil singing of mermaids.[79] Next, as Daun Russell begins to flatter Chauntecleer, he uses ironically a musical sign that ought to remind human Chauntecleers of the higher nature they should try to imitate:

> "For trewely, ye have as myrie a stevene,
> As any aungel hath that is in hevene."
>
> (4481–82)

Russell goes right on with a second sign, "Boece," that is also intended to allay Chauntecleer's fear through flattery, but which is actually a more subtle reminder than angel song of the foolish nature of Chauntecleer's music:

> "Therwith ye han in musyk moore feelynge
> Than hadde Boece, or any that kan synge."
>
> (4483–84)

If the learned Chauntecleer were not being blinded by flattery, he would recall, as mentioned earlier, that Boethius advocated the primacy of reason in music, not feeling.

The next sign, that of Chauntecleer's "fader," is perhaps even more subtle. Literally, it is an effective appeal to Chauntecleer's pride; allegorically it is an ironic reminder of the "fader" of all humans, Adam, who sang with "heart" rather than reason while closing his eyes to truth, and it is also another ironic reminder in the tale of the wrong use of the hour of dawn, a time for praise:

> "Save yow, I herde nevere man so synge
> As dide youre fader in the morwenynge.
> Certes, it was of herte, al that he song.
> And for to make his voys the moore strong,
> He wolde so peyne hym that with bothe his yen
> He moste wynke, so loude he wolde cryen.
> . . . .
> That ther nas no man in no regioun
> That hym in song or wisedom myghte passe."
>
> (4491–501)

Immediately afterwards, the musical sign in "Daun Burnel the Asse" is only implicit:

> "I have wel rad in 'Daun Burnel the Asse,'
> Among his vers, how that ther was a cok,
> For that a preestes sone yaf hym a knok
> Upon his leg whil he was yong and nyce,
> He made hym for to lese his benefice."
>
>   (4502–06)

Daun Russell uses the allusion only to praise Chauntecleer's father for
wisdom and to flatter Chauntecleer, but as with the sign "Boece," Daun
Russell himself misses the main point. The rooster in "Daun Burnel" *did
not sing* when he should have sung, and Chauntecleer ought to follow his
example by *not singing*.[80] Chauntecleer would then show true wisdom
instead of his usual folly. (Actually, the rooster in "Daun Burnel" did not
show true wisdom in his situation because he was motivated by revenge.)

Another detail in "Daun Burnel" is a subtler sign on Chaucer's part.
The rooster in "Daun Burnel" also plays the role of a cantor of the Mass,
thus suggesting the clergy. This implication coheres with several musical
details in Chaucer's own tale which suggest that the tale is an allegory
about the clergy (both secular and monastic perhaps).[81] That allegory is
especially encouraged by the first description of Chauntecleer's singing:

> His voys was murier than the murie orgon
> On messe-dayes that in the chirche gon.
> Wel sikerer was his crowyng in his logge
> Than is a clokke or an abbey orlogge.
> By nature he knew ech ascencioun
> Of the equynoxial in thilke toun;
> For whan degrees fiftene weren ascended,
> Thanne crew he, that it myghte nat been amended.
>
>   (4041–48)

The choices of detail, "murie orgon," "messe-dayes," "abbey orlogge"
are obvious reminders of the priesthood, and "ascencioun" and "degrees
fiftene" are perhaps subtle reminders of it. Given the Nun's Priest's
subtlety, they are not likely to be just decorative, and their implications
tend to be confirmed by a later passage in which Chauntecleer "knew by
kynde, and by noon oother loore, / That it was pryme, and crew with
blisful stevene" (4386–87). The "loore" suggested here is the rational
knowledge of when to sing the Divine Office, of which "pryme" is one
conspicuous part. The earlier "degrees fiftene" (4047), moreover, is not
literally accurate since, in the thirteenth and fourteenth centuries, roos-
ters were not believed to crow every hour.[82] The detail therefore
suggests a figurative meaning or sign, and there is a relevant sign in the
psalter that priests sang each week. The "degrees fiftene" suggests
Psalms 119 to 133, which were universally regarded as the "canticum

graduum," the Song of Ascent or, as Rolle says, the "sange of degres." It consists of fifteen steps, or degrees, and signifies "spiritual stages in the ascent to charity."[83] It reinforces subtly Chauntecleer's preference for descending. This early sign of spiritual love in the tale coheres well with the later scene of Chauntecleer's fall. As Daun Russell ends his elaborate combination of musical signs, he amusingly begs Chauntecleer to sing by "seinte charitee," that is, implicitly, to sing as he would the "degrees fiftene," or the Song of Degrees, that supposedly he knows so well by "kynde" (4386):

> "Now syngeth, sire, for seinte charitee,
> Lat se, konne ye youre fader countrefete?"
>
> (4510–11)

Like many priests of his day, however, by singing in lechery and pride, Chauntecleer "countrefetes" his father Adam instead of his father *caritas*.

This ends Chaucer's elaborate combination of signs at the fall of Chauntecleer, but one more sign remains in the tale. The noise and cacophony of wind instruments brought on by Chauntecleer's fall is a fitting and vivid musical sign for the folly of his previous singing at Lauds (a love duet—4069) and at Prime (a love revel—4388–94), and of his ignoring the true song of "degrees fiftene":

> So hydous was the noyse, a, *benedicitee!*
> Certes, he Jakke Straw and his meynee
> Ne made nevere shoutes half so shrille
> . . . .
> Of bras they broghten bemes, and of box,
> Of horn, of boon, in whiche they blewe and powped,
> And therwithal they skriked and they howped.
> It seemed as that hevene sholde falle.
>
> (4583–91)

With just a suggestion of Judgment in the last line, the trumpets of brass, wood, horn, and bone mainly signify moral discord, and perhaps also worldly pride, as the horn players do in *The House of Fame*. Altogether, by suggesting strongly an allegory of clerical negligence, Chaucer's musical signs in the Nun's Priest's Tale are not just figurative enrichment, but major determinants of his meaning, as they are in the *Duchess* and the *Parliament*.

The complex sign or symbol "melodye" in *The Canterbury Tales*, first proposed by Robertson, is not a major determinant of meaning, but a device that gives symbolic enrichment and thematic continuity to the work. Although this symbol in Chaucer generally carries rather conventional meaning each time it appears, its placement, its vividness, and its variety of meanings make Chaucer's use of the symbol highly original. Moreover, in the last poetic tale, the Manciple's Tale, when it is combined with other musical signs, this symbol does become a major determinant of meaning, and it also serves to "frame" *The Canterbury Tales* in the same general way that Chaucer has framed other poems and individual tales with musical signs.

The Canterbury Tales open with a memorable "melodye" of nature, or the flesh. This song of nightingales is a sign of purely physical desire that helps to orient the careful reader to the idea of two loves and that also prepares for the entirely disparaging use of musical signs in the rest of the General Prologue. A vivid contrast to this concupiscent music appears at the start of the Knight's Tale, where the "melodye" of Theseus, clearly associated with his wisdom and chivalry, is a sign of harmony in the soul and society:

> What with his wysdom and his chivalrie,
> He conquered al the regne of Femenye,
> . . . .
> And thus with victorie and with melodye
> Lete I this noble duc to Atthenes ryde.
>
> (865–73)

This melody echoes the philosophic tradition of music in Chalcidius and others, where the best "symphonia" is justice, in which reason rules, emotions execute, and appetites obey.[84] At the end of the Knight's Tale, the "bliss and melodye" (3097) of reasonable marriage appear. Within this frame of two virtuous melodies there exists a moderate amount of antithetical concupiscent music in the songs of Palamon and Arcite, the temple of Venus, and in mildly extravagant feasting.

The Miller, out to "quite," in part, the Knight's unrealistic view of the harmony of marriage, begins with the seemingly virtuous "melody" of Nicholas's *Angelus ad virginem*, but soon shows it deteriorating to the "melody" of adultery, and finally to the dissonance of Nicholas's practical joke and the ensuing noise. The Reeve's Tale continues the thematic symbol vividly by applying it to the gross snoring and flatulence of Symkyn's family:

> This millere hath so wisely bibbed ale
> That as an hors he fnorteth in his sleep,
> Ne of his tayl bihynde he took no keep.
> His wyf bar him a burdon, a ful strong;
> Men myghte hir rowtyng heere two furlong;
> The wenche rowteth eek, *par compaignye.*
>   Aleyn the clerk, that herde this melodye,
> He poked John, and seyde, "Slepestow?

Herdestow evere slyk a sang er now?
Lo, swilk a complyn is ymel hem alle,
A wilde fyr upon thair bodyes falle!"

(4162–72)

This "melodye" can be viewed as a further deterioration of the rational melody of Theseus, in one sense even inferior to the perverted rationality and deceiving sweetness of Nicholas and Alisoun's melody, since it exists in the elemental unthinking noise of drunken sleep. Here again the sign enriches description but hardly controls its meaning. Some amusing control is offered, however, by the night "song" of "complyn" (4171), which was associated particularly with quiet nights, sobriety, and repentance.[85]

The contrast between the harmony of reason and the allurement of the flesh continues in the use of this sign in the Clerk's and the Merchant's Tales. Walter goes to select his virtuous bride with "many a soun of sondry melodye" (271), but January is cuckolded in a sensual garden where

. . . Pluto and his queene,
Proserpina, and al hire fayerye,
Disporten hem and maken melodye
Aboute that welle, and daunced, as men tolde.

(2038–41)

This seemingly attractive "melodye" is actually infernal, a variety of the Old Song and dance. It is only one instance of numerous signs of *musica lasciuia* in the Merchant's Tale, including erotic abuse of the divine Song of Songs.[86] The infernal "melodye" of Fayerye is picked up again in Sir Thopas, as we have seen, and there it is implicitly contrasted to the spiritual music of the little clerk found in the Prioress' Tale, although the symbol "melodye" does not itself appear in that tale.

A similar implicit contrast, without the symbol itself, also occurs between the Wife of Bath's and the Friar's Tales. The "elf queene," who "Daunced ful ofte in many a grene mede" (D 861, 991–96), again embodies infernal power. She is contrasted implicitly to the virtuous old woman in the Friar's Tale, who is "an old wydwe," a "ribibe" (1377) and an "old rebekke" (1573). Although the second of these unusual terms suggests a pun on "Rebbecca," who was a commonplace moral sign of ideal faith or an allegorical sign of the church, both of the terms literally mean a kind of stringed musical instrument or fiddle, the rebec.[87] Since stringed instruments were so abundantly interpreted in scriptural tradition as signs for service of God, especially for mortifying concupiscence or observing the decalogue, Chaucer seems to imply subtly such a religious meaning here in the terms "ribibe" and "rebekke." These musical signs cohere well with the pious character of the poor widow. By contrasting infernal "daunce" with supernal "ribibe," they add lightly to the general contrast of the foul "olde wyf" to the pious "old wydwe."

Other musical signs in the Tales are implicitly related to the theme of "melodye" even if the symbol itself is not mentioned, as we have just seen that it is not in the Wife's and the Friar's Tales. The erotic "musik" and "accord" of Chauntecleer implicitly continue the sensual melody of the elf-queen and of Nicholas. So too does the elaborate music of Aurelius, who is just possibly contrasted to David, the greatest singer of scriptural tradition:

> He syngeth, daunceth, passynge any man
> That is, or was, sith that the world bigan.
>
> (F 929–30)

The misguided nature of Aurelius's passion, however, is suggested by the extravagance of his music and his resemblance to a fury:

> Of swich matere made he manye layes,
> Songes, compleintes, roundels, virelayes,
> How that he dorste nat his sorwe telle,
> But langwissheth as a furye dooth in helle.
>
> (F 947–50)

In contrast to this individual passion of the Franklin's Tale, the preceding Squire's Tale presents a picture of social eroticism at the birthday of Cambuskan partly with musical signs: "loude mynstralcye," the dance of "lusty Venus children deere," and "eek the wyn, in al this melodye" (F 268–97). The license of this scene may also reflect the highly discordant narrative techniques of the tale. It is difficult to say of the Squire, as he does of Gawain, that "accordant to his wordes was his cheere, / As techeth art of speche hem that it leere" (F 103–4).

The theme and symbol of virtuous "melodye" appears next in the Second Nun's Tale at the marriage of St. Cecilia. Here it is an obvious sign of the genuine Song of the Lord, in contrast to the earlier corrupt "belles" of the Monk, the "offertorie" of the Pardoner, the "trentals" of the Summoner's "frere," the "pryme" of Chauntecleer, and other abuses of the sonorous Song of the Lord.[88] As noted earlier, it also helps to make more vivid the Pauline spiritual music of Cecilia:

> And whil the organs maden melodie,
> To God allone in herte thus sang she.
>
> (G 134–35)

Although Chaucer ties his Life of Saint Cecilia closely to the Canon's Yeoman's Tale in various thematic ways, he does not contrast these tales with musical signs, as he does several earlier pairs. As a whole, however, Chaucer's virtuous "melodye" shows a surprising completeness, though most likely it is accidental. Whereas the "melodye" of Theseus suggests philosophic tradition ("wysdom") and that of Walter social tradition (a Marquis going for his bride), Cecilia's "melodye" is vividly scriptural. When we add the last instance of virtuous "melodye," that of mythologi-cal Phoebus in the Manciple's Tale, Chaucer has managed to use in his poetry all the traditions of virtuous musical signs.[89] Conversely, his cor-rupt "melodye" is equally complete: the libidinous scriptural songs of Nicholas, the gross unreason of Symkyn's family sleeping, the erotic social feasting of Tartarye, and the mythological evil of elf-queens.[90]

In the Manciple's Tale, Chaucer's major symbol unexpectedly takes on a new meaning and gives an unusual musical frame to the Tales as a whole. That a meaningful frame may be deliberate is suggested by his careful use of musical structures elsewhere. The dream in *The Book of the Duchess* is framed by the songs of Lauds and the twelve bells of Vespers, in *The Parliament of Fowls* by the "melodye" of the spheres and the "roundel" of birds in "evene accord," and the Knight's Tale is framed by the melodies of wisdom and marriage. In these three works both sides of the frame are virtuous. In the Miller's and the Nun's Priest's Tales, musical signs move from deceiving piety to obvious discord. At the end of *Troilus* the melody of the spheres is a norm for previous uses of music, including the "voice of wrath" of Thesiphone at the start (1.6–11); and earlier the mythological songs of lost chastity sung by the swallow ("pro-igne") and the nightingale provide a frame for Criseyde's assent to love.[91] Finally, there are obvious contrasts of pious and erotic music in the Prioress-Thopas and Clerk-Merchant pairs of tales. A meaningful frame in *The Canterbury Tales,* therefore, would not be surprising, and might be a new piece of evidence that Chaucer intended the Manciple's and the Parson's Tales to be contiguous.[92]

Other external evidence also helps to create a presumption that Chaucer may be doing something unusual with the "melodye" and abundant music of this tale. Neither his likely source in Ovid nor Gow-er's analogue in *Confessio amantis* uses any musical material.[93] Moreover, the Manciple's lack of control over his narrative, his admission that he is not "textueel" (H 235, 316), the suggestion that his "word" does not "accorde with the dede" (208), and his fear of the Cook's jangling all suggest that his own tendentious and repetitive "sentence" in the tale may be undercut by Chaucer with more significant implications, as the poet undercuts other cupidinous pilgrims. Finally, the Parson's Tale shows surprising relevance, in general and in details, to the deeper meaning that is suggested in part by the musical signs of the Manciple's Tale.

The tale begins with a vivid picture of Phoebus that suggests the tradi-tional god of music:

> Pleyen he koude on every mynstralcie,
> And syngen, that it was a melodie
> To heeren of his cleere voys the soun.
> Certes the kyng of Thebes, Amphioun,
> That with his syngyng walled that citee,
> Koude nevere syngen half so wel as hee.

(H 113–18)

Although the Manciple calls Phoebus "the mooste lusty bachiler" and "the semelieste man" and errs in exalting Phoebus's singing equally with his playing, this picture amusingly evokes the *god* who was associated with wisdom, prophecy, and healing, as well as with the Muses and music.[94] The contrast to Amphioun, builder of Thebes, suggests Phoebus's superiority to passion and injustice, which Thebes connotes in the Knight's Tale, the *Inferno, Thebaid,* and mythography.[95] The divine implications cohere with the usual ideal of Apollo or Phoebus in Chaucer as the "God of science and of light" and the god that asses cannot hear.[96] The divine implications of Phoebus are also encouraged at the start by two allusions to the serpent "Phitoun" killed by this best of archers (109, 128). As in the Parson's Tale (325, 330), the serpent inevitably suggests infernal evil.

Chaucer also cleverly makes the Manciple significantly wrong in another musical detail about Phoebus. The Manciple sets his tale "When Phebus dwelled heere in this erthe adoun" (105), but he speaks of him as playing "every mynstralcie" and as bearing "in his hand a bowe" (129). Ovid and the mythographers explicitly tell us, however, that when Phoebus was banished from Olympus by Jove to Elis and Messenia, he dressed as a shepherd, carried a staff rather than a bow, and played a seven-reed pipe rather than his usual lyre.[97] With this contradiction of details, Chaucer implies two points: first, that the Manciple (like the Wife of Bath) is not "textueel" or to be trusted in his story-telling, and, second, that Phoebus signifies a genuinely divine, not human, power. While the mythological Phoebus was dwelling on earth, he did not carry the implicitly divine "harpe, and lute, and gyterne, and sautrie" (268) that he possesses in this tale. These are the stringed instruments of "David in his psalmes," which have been abused so frequently earlier in *The Canterbury Tales* by the Friar, Nicholas, Absolon, and others. Here at the end, however, these stringed instruments provide a meaningful contrast to the Miller's bagpipe that led the pilgrims out of town (A 565–66).

The Manciple would have us think of Phoebus as a human, one who commits the sin of "rakel ire" (289), or "hastif ire" in terms of the Parson's Tale (541), yet Chaucer deliberately emphasizes his truly divine nature with musical and other signs. The Manciple urges us to read "David in his psalmes" (345) about the sin of jangling, but much more vivid in those pious songs is the image of God's anger and his arrows of vengeance.[98] The same image appears in Chaucer's *ABC*, "the bowe bent in swich maneere / As it was first, of justice and of ire" (29–30). In *The Complaint of Mars,* Phoebus implies divine ire and justice, "the torche . . . that al this world will wrie" (91), and his epithet there, "the candel of jelousy," (7) helps to interpret the "jalous" Phoebus of the Manciple (144). In the Parson's Tale, God is "the stierne and wrothe judge" at the day of doom who sits over the "horrible pit of helle" (168), and in The Manciple's Tale Phoebus slings the crow "out at dore . . ./Unto the devel," that is, to hell (307). In Ovid's tale, Coronis, the unfaithful *lover* of Phoebus, acknowledges that he is right to kill her, but grieves the loss of their child, whereas in the Manciple's Tale, as in the *Ovide moralisé,* Coronis is an unfaithful *wife,* a traditional metaphor for the human relation to God, and no mention is made of Aesculapius, who does not fit well with the Manciple's own special pleading. All of the details cited so far cohere with one interpretation known in the fourteenth century. In the *Ovide moralisé,* after a literal interpretation of Ovid's tale (not to betray one's master's wife), there is an "autre sentence" in which Apollo signifies "divine sapience," Coronis "nostre humanite," the adultery "mortel vice" with "terriennes delices," the crow "le dyable," and Aesculapius the "soul in grace" (which is Chaucer's subject in the next tale).[99] This deeper sentence in Chaucer's tale has been argued before, but not with emphasis on the musical details.[100]

Besides the superb stringed "mynstralcie" of Phoebus, other musical signs support the idea that Chaucer's intention is to bring out an allegorical meaning of divine punishment of sins. The exquisite singing of the crow, as well as its speech, is clearly the gift of Phoebus, not of nature, since he can take it away:

"Thou songe whilom lyk a nyghtyngale;
Now shaltow, false theef, thy song forgon,
And eek thy white fetheres everichon,
Ne nevere in al thy lif ne shaltou speke."

(H 294–97)

Such power implies that Phoebus is divine and not simply human, as the obtuse Manciple would have him. Moreover, here the nightingale song of the crow suggests the long tradition of virtuous nightingales which Chaucer does not draw upon in any other work.[101] Earlier, the song of the crow is described so as to suggest the song of angels in contrast to worldly nightingales:

Therwith in al this world no nyghtyngale
Ne koude, by an hondred thousand deel,
Syngen so wonder myrily and weel.

(136–38)

"In al this world" and "an hondred thousand" suggest another world,
where "le dyable" rejoiced with angel song before his fall. Although
"myry" singing in Chaucer is nearly always concupiscent, as in the Friar's
"murye note" (A 235) and Sir Thopas (B² 2024), it can also be spiritual, as
in the "murie organ / On messe dayes" (B² 4041).

The crow's song of betrayal, moreover, suggests the motivation of
envy, which is especially characteristic of "le dyable":

> This crowe sang "Cokkow! cokkow! cokkow!"
> "What, byrd!" quod Phebus, "what song syngestow?
> Ne were thow wont so myrily to synge
> That to myn herte it was a rejoysynge
> To heere thy voys? Allas! what song is this?"
>
> (243–47)

Implicitly this is the Old Song of envy and malice. The "cokkow" is
associated with the bitter goddess "Jalousy" in the Knight's Tale (1930)
and *The Parliament* (252), and also with self-gratification in *The Parliament*
(605). In the Parson's Tale, "accusynge . . . is lyk the craft of the devel,
that waiteth bothe nyghte and day to accusen us alle" (511). The pleasure
of the crow over Phoebus's misfortune is more vivid in its answer to his
question:

> "By God!" quod he, "I synge nat amys.
> Phoebus," quod he, "for al thy worthynesse,
> For al thy beautee and thy gentilesse,
> For al thy song and al thy mynstralcye,
> For al thy waityng, blered is thyn ye
> With oon of litel reputacioun,
> Noght worth to thee, as in comparisoun,
> The montance of a gnat, so moote I thryve!
> For on thy bed thy wyf I saugh hym swyve."
>
> (248–56)

To strengthen this interpretation, we find abundant evidence in the
Parson's Tale for associating the crow with the envy of the devil: "The
seconde spece of Envye is joye of oother mannes harm; and that is
proprely lyk to the devel, that evere rejoyseth hym of mannes harm"
(492). The Parson also uses a metaphor that resembles the crow's "Cokkow": "hem that sowen and maken discord amonges folk . . . been they
likned to the devel, that evere is aboute to maken discord" (641–42). He
also connects the betrayal of the devil to the soul's death: "Certes, synful
mannes soule is bitraysed of the devel by coveitise of temporeel prosperitee, and scorned by deceite whan he cheseth flesshly delices . . . and
atte laste it is slayn fynally" (275). All this is what happens in the Manci-

ple's Tale: the crow is envious and devilish, it sows discord, and it betrays the wife so she is slain.

Phoebus's "sorweful herte" (263) and great "sorwe" (267, 291) suggest the virtuous anger of the Parson: "The goode Ire is by jalousie of goodnesse, thurgh which a man is wrooth with wikkednesse and agayns wikkednesse . . . nat wrooth agayns the man, but wrooth with the mysdede of the man, as seith the prophete David" (539–40). Even more suggestive of divine sorrow for sin is Phoebus's destruction of his instruments, signs of spiritual joy:

> For sorwe of which he brak his mynstralcie,
> Both harpe, and lute, and gyterne, and sautrie.
>
> (267–68)

This end of music suggests the famous passage of "David in his psalmes" (345)—to whom we are referred by Chaucer—in which the musicians of Israel hang up their instruments in Babylon because, as Rolle says, they wish to "withdraw God's words from hounds and swine as long as they despise holy love." Also in Rolle, as elsewhere, white crows signify men of virtue and black crows men in sin whom the devil receives as his birds.[102] So Phoebus flings the "traitour" (271) crow "to the devel" (307), and the Manciple reiterates that "a wikked tong is worse than a feend" (320).

The evidence thus creates a strong likelihood that at the end of *The Canterbury Tales* we have some of Chaucer's most original musical signs. For the first time in the Tales, the symbol "melodye" connotes divine nature and virtue itself. We also find the joyous spiritual song that God gives to his creatures, and the sorrowful end of spiritual song or joy that sin produces. Even though these signs are obscured by the Manciple's ineptitude, their implications are significant evidence that Chaucer had other intentions. Like other Chaucer poems, therefore, *The Canterbury Tales* also has a significant musical frame, creating a contrast between the "melodye" of physical desire at the beginning and the "melodye" of spiritual joy at the end of the work. The sober Parson's Tale would not have been an appropriate place to close this poetic, symbolic frame. The Manciple's Tale is the right place, however, because it is poetry. Its implications of divine judgment can then serve to prepare obliquely for the explicit treatment of divine judgment in the Parson's Tale. Whatever Chaucer may have intended earlier, his last intention was to place the Manciple's Tale just before the Parson's.

Chaucer's poetry, then, is rich with musical signs from several medieval traditions, and these signs cannot be understood adequately without some knowledge of these traditions. Many of the signs are conventional, but still fetching; others are original and often subtle. On balance, compared to other late medieval poets, Chaucer is a creator of unusual and subtle musical signs, not only in elaborate combinations, in the symbol "melodye," and in overall musical frames for works, but also in single signs and in striking contrasts.

CHAUCER'S
USE OF SIGNS
IN HIS PORTRAIT
OF THE PRIORESS

CHAUNCEY WOOD

Because Chaucer does not use the word *symbol,* and because the English form of the word in its literary, representational sense did not become widespread until the Renaissance, I do not like to use it in discussions of Chaucer's poetry. We can, however, be very comfortable talking about signs in Chaucer, for his understanding of the term is clear and simple. The Parson, for example, observes that tears are one of the signs of true contrition, while the Friar in the General Prologue claims rather differently that to give to a poor order of Friars is "signe that a man is wel yshryve."[1] We see, then, that Chaucer uses the word *sign* much as Saint Augustine did when he said that a sign is "a thing which causes us to think of something beyond the impression the thing itself makes upon the senses."[2] Thus, Augustine goes on, smoke is a sign of fire, and a trumpet call is the soldier's signal to advance or retreat, depending upon which call or sign is employed.

Most literary discussions of signs begin and end with their identification. We can, for example, identify the garlic, onions, and leeks of the Summoner's diet as signs of the Old Man of the senses, an identification based upon the appearance of these foods in the book of Numbers in the Old Testament, coupled with a study of medieval interpretations of the biblical signs. Similarly, as Rodney Delasanta has observed, we can identify the horses of the Canterbury pilgrims as signs of their moral integrity, and make the rough axiom that the moral worth of the character is inversely proportional to the equine quality of the horse, and conversely.[3] With many signs in Chaucer's poetry, however, identification is only a first step in the process of literary analysis, because he is fond of using signs playfully. A sign can be given an amusing and significantly false definition, for example, as with the Friar's self-serving claim that giving to a poor order is a sign that a man is contrite. Chaucer also refers signs to unexpected things upon occasion, so that our tentative, hypothetical identification turns out to have been wide of the mark. Tears, for example, were cited by the Parson in the passage mentioned previously as a sign of contrition. We might reasonably expect, therefore, that tears in the Prioress would be a sign of contrition, but instead her weeping turns out to be a sign of grief for dead mice and chastised dogs.

When we consider the medieval habit of defining meanings of things both *in bono* and *in malo* it follows that the identification of signs in Chaucer will frequently be a dodgy business, for medieval signs typically have more than one meaning. This means that identification, which I said earlier is sometimes only a first step, turns out to be a very difficult step. However, an approach in which more than one possible meaning is kept in mind will permit us to consider Chaucer's use of signs, in a way that will involve identification as both a first and a last step in a process that treats the possible identifications and actual manipulation of a sign as a continuum rather than as two temporally separate events.

An example will help here. It is relatively easy to adduce historical and literary evidence for many signs in Chaucer that give different, often diametrically opposed, yet equally well-supported meanings or identifications. This is the sort of thing that has led Florence Ridley to observe that most of the arguments about Chaucer's Prioress end in a draw.[4] Consider the Prioress' name, Madame Eglentyne. The name is certainly a sign, but the eglantine or sweet briar rose can signify many things. As a person's name it has long been known to be a name for heroines of medieval romances. As a flower its thorniness might be contrasted *in malo* with the rose without thorns, the sign of the Virgin Mary, but there are also several instances in which the eglantine is said *in bono* to be the plant used for the crown of thorns on Christ's head, and indeed one can find the word used for the Virgin's rose as well.[5] We are thrown back, then, upon the poem itself. We shall have to decide whether the Prioress is named for a heroine of romance or for the Blessed Virgin in terms of the rest of her portrait rather than by an appeal to primary sources. Moreover, because her name is given to us in the fourth line of a forty-five line description, I think it quite likely that Chaucer intended the name to be equivocal—at that juncture—in our experience of the portrait. As Stanley Fish has pointed out, all readers make numerous "anticipatory adjustments" or "partial closures" in their experiences of a text, and it is my contention that Chaucer plays upon our tendency to do this in his portrait of the Prioress.[6] This is not to suggest that Chaucer's works are hopelessly ambiguous or that he intended all value judgments to be left up to the reader. Rather, the choices (sometimes difficult choices) of possible identifications of signs do not merely lead to meaning but in a sense embody it. Because the reader is continuously having to reassess his tentative choices of meaning, meaning becomes, to borrow from Fish again, an event. One of Chaucer's portraits in the General Prologue is like a work of medieval art in that the correct identification of separate, subordinate signs is required for the correct interpretation of the portrait as a whole, but is unlike a painting in that the audience's approach to the signs can be strictly controlled by the poet. That is, while the artist who paints a picture can only emphasize or deemphasize significant features through size, color, and placement, and the artist who illuminates a book can determine response only to the extent that he employs openings and registers, the artist who draws a word picture reveals his signs in a sequence he determines absolutely, and which an auditor must follow and a reader probably will follow. This becomes, therefore, an important element in literary strategy; there is a very real sense in which the portraits in the General Prologue can only be reread.

Because nuns were such familiar figures in both fourteenth-century life and literature, Chaucer could depend upon his readers to anticipate his statements to a degree and could then manipulate signs and the things signified accordingly. Indeed, it is important to note that Chaucer's portrait of the Prioress is *not* like conventional satires on nuns, which regularly accused them of concupiscence. Both in subject matter and in form Chaucer is working out a satiric approach new to his age. In the portrait of the Prioress there are signs that are apparently misunderstood, that are given in an unexpected order, unexpectedly qualified, inaccurately or inadequately defined, or left out altogether in spite of high expectations. It is this process of manipulation of the signs and of the reader's responses that I want to examine. It is a process that depends upon identification of signs for its beginnings, but that ultimately has as its goal the description of the art of Chaucer's art rather than an identification of its subject. Although the word is currently unfashionable, this essay is really an appreciation. To be sure, though, the examination of *how* Chaucer creates his effects will at times lead us to an understanding of *what* he is saying that would otherwise not have been available, and that kind of result is a welcome bonus in this kind of study. If we are agreed that Lowes was on the right track when he said that the portrait of the Prioress showed the "engagingly imperfect submergence of the feminine in the ecclesiastical," we may inquire more precisely as to the manner of presentation of this, which will result in a nicer estimate of the degree of imperfection, the level of submergence, and the warmth of our engagement. Similarly, Malone's comment that "religion hardly enters into Chaucer's description" and that where it does Chaucer gives it a "worldly twist" will be seen to constitute the very essence of Chaucer's satiric technique, despite Malone's protestations that Chaucer would not do anything "so gross as poking open fun at [the Prioress]." [7]

The most basic kind of sign I wish to examine may be introduced by an appropriate passage, again from Chaucer's Parson's Tale. The Parson distinguishes between inner and outer Pride, and further notes that the outer is a sign of the inner:

> Now been ther two maneres of Pride: that oon of hem is withinne the herte of man, and that oother is withoute. . . . But natheles that oon of thise speces of Pride is signe of that oother, right as the gaye leefsel atte taverne is signe of the wyn that is in the celer.
>
> (409–11)

Outer pride, then, is the sign of inner, spiritual pride, and the Parson goes on to explain that one typical manifestation of outer pride is in "outrageous array of clothyng" (412). Just as the bush that was used as a tavern sign signified the wine in the cellar not visible to the eye, so the fine fur trimming of the Monk's robe, as Edmund Reiss has observed, indicates inner, spiritual pride, also a condition only visible through exterior signs. For the Prioress, though, Chaucer's use of clothing as a sign is somewhat more oblique. We may note to start that one of his techniques in presenting clothing as a sign in the portrait of the Prioress is what I have called "unexpected qualification." Her wimple, for example, is a garment that could be worn by lay folk as well as clerics. Indeed, the Wife of Bath is "ywympled wel" (A 470) which in her case probably means that she wore a bright, expensive, ample covering for her neck and around her face—something that would coordinate nicely with her new shoes, her enormous hat, her ten pounds worth of coverchiefs, and her red stockings. A wimple on a nun, however, one imagines somewhat differently, for its function is not to be showy, not to indicate by its lavishness the owner's wealth, not by its color or novelty to call attention to itself or its owner, but to do the opposite: to cover up the potentially attractive neck and to minimize the face of the woman who has discarded earthly for heavenly concerns. Since it is clear that the Prioress' wimple should be a sign of inner purity or otherworldliness, corresponding to her having taken the veil spiritually, it comes as no small surprise that Chaucer qualifies it thus: "Ful semyly hir wympul pynched was" (151). The wimple's incidental aesthetic quality, the seemliness or nicety of its pleating, is what is stressed, and this quality in fact runs counter to its anticipated function as a sign. Indeed, two techniques have been employed here: the inappropriate sign, a pleated as opposed to a plain wimple, and the unexpected qualification. Since the word "semyly" has a certain ambiguity the effect of the whole is to play upon our tendency to make partial closures. Reading as far as "Ful semyly hir wympul" we could understand either "her wimple was quite seemingly, appropriately . . ." or we could understand "her wimple was quite becomingly, pleasingly. . . ." And indeed, the word "pinched" itself *could* mean no more than pinched in at the sides—something appropriate for a nun or any outdoor traveler. What Chaucer has done is to create a line of poetry that is potentially or momentarily equivocal, although not so when seen as part of the whole description.

Jill Mann, one of the most perceptive critics of the General Prologue, has noted even more specifically regarding the Prioress' wimple that the Middle English *Ancrene Wisse* specifically disapproves of the pleating of a nun's wimple.[8] This kind of historical information is especially valuable, for it permits the modern critic to examine both Chaucer's intentions and his methods more exactly. If a nun should not wear a pleated wimple at all, then one that is pleated "ful semyly" tells us that not only has the Prioress done something she should not have done, but has done it with some care!

Mann's further points regarding the Prioress concentrate on conventional satires of nuns from estates literature, and as she herself notes, while there are many resemblances between the nuns satirized there and the Prioress satirized by Chaucer, the resemblances are to some extent misleading.[9] In most of the conventional satires of nuns, the ultimate charge against them is unchastity or indeed lubricity, whereas the description of the Prioress suggests a woman who is more sentimental than sensual; more a victim of pride than of lust. To be sure, Chaucer uses some elements of conventional satire on nuns in his portrait and it would be possible to suppose that he would go so far as to depend on his audience's anticipation of a conventional attack. However, the evidence—incomplete as it is—suggests otherwise. Most of the strategies Chaucer uses make the best sense if we assume that he hoped his audience would anticipate the description of a praiseworthy nun. If we wish to examine Chaucer's methods of satire we shall profit more from an examination of the literature describing proper nuns and their behavior than from the satires of them, for Chaucer's particular satire is, as noted earlier, atypical.

Having already studied Chaucer's use of the wimple, let us consider the larger issue of the Prioress' clothing generally. Certainly this is of primary importance not only for her portrait but for any of the portraits in the Prologue. Indeed, Chaucer has promised that he will tell us three main things about each character once he has defined "whiche they weren": his or her "condicioun," which seems to suggest both physical and spiritual condition equally (or variously); his or her "degree," that is, social standing, and his or her "array" (38–41). Clothing, then, because featured so prominently as an external "condicioun," will undoubtedly function as a series of signs of inner "condicioun," precisely in the manner suggested in the passage cited earlier from the Parson's Tale. And, to be sure, from the very beginning we see the "parfit" Knyght's modest fustian, the less perfect Squire's elaborate embroidery, and the Yeoman's forest green. The first three portraits prepare us to expect a description of the nun's garb, and also to anticipate a sign in that clothing, just as in the earlier portraits. Moreover, not only does the text prepare us to anticipate an outer sign of inner qualities in the Prioress' array, but the literature of medieval England has other descriptions of what a nun's array was and what it meant. We may cite a typical and helpful example from the writings of Chaucer's literary friend John Gower:

> When a girl is to be a nun, first she is clothed in black garments and her hair cut off. She disfigures her body on the outside in order that her spirit within may be beautiful and grow pure white, being filled with love of God.[10]

First she is clothed in black. Of course, there is nothing more basic to the condition of a nun than her dark habit indicating her rejection of the world. And, in a kind of mirror form of the Parson's two species of inner and outer pride, here exterior humility (the disfigured body) indicates inner humility—a virtue making the soul beautiful. If we look at the illumination in the Ellesmere manuscript the most significant, striking aspect of the Prioress is her black habit—a far cry from the clothes of the Wife of Bath. To satirize the Prioress, then, one of the more delicate of Chaucer's devices is omission. The word "black" is not in fact used in her portrait, although the reader would have every expectation that it would be. We find "graye," "coral," "grene," and "gold," but no black, brown, or white, the colors we would most expect on a nun. As for her habit itself, we get very little description of this at all, and what we have comes late. We have noted the attractively pleated wimple; to this Chaucer adds a "ful fetys" (157) or handsome cloak, which again puts the emphasis on an incidental aesthetic quality actually opposed to the cloak's anticipated function as a sign of rejection of the world. Thus, in the first pilgrim we meet where array might be expected in real life to be a sign of the "condicioun" of its wearer, Chaucer hardly touches upon the character's array at all, other than to describe it as inappropriately fancied up or titivated. Where one would expect blackness to be a sign of unworldliness we find stylishness as a sign of worldliness.

In addition to postponing, deemphasizing, and unexpectedly qualifying the most expectable sign in the portrait of the Prioress, her habit, Chaucer uses other large strategies in his portrait. If we remember the Parson's remarks about outer pride as a sign of inner pride, it would be easy enough to assert that for all of Chaucer's pilgrims the information Chaucer gives us about their external qualities—what they wear, what they say, what they do—will be a system of signs of internal "condicioun." In the specific instance of the Prioress, this can be borne out by reference to medieval writings about nuns such as the *Ancrene Riwle.* While there is no specific evidence that Chaucer knew this particular work or expected members of his audience to know it, nevertheless manuscripts have come down to us in French, Latin, and Middle English, suggesting a great popularity. One can safely argue that its ideas are conventional and would have been widely understood.

The *Riwle* begins by drawing a distinction between the outer and inner life:

> There are many kinds of rules, but I shall speak here of two out of all of them. . . . The one governs the heart and keeps it untroubled. . . . This rule is always interior, guiding the heart. . . . The other is completely external, and governs the body and its actions. It gives directions about all outward behaviour, about eating and drinking, dress, singing, sleep, and vigil. This is "bodily exercise" which according to the Apostle, "is profitable to little." It is much like a rule of the science of mechanics, which serves the science of geometry. So this [external] rule exists merely to serve the other. The other is the lady, this her handmaid, for all those actions which belong to the outer rule serve only to govern the heart within.[11]

The rule governing the outer life, then, that which sets the standards of dress we have been concerned with, is ultimately not important, for the essence of a nun is the inner life, and the rule that is important is the inner rule, the rule of the heart. While for all the pilgrims the outer description (rhetorically the *effictio*) is the sign for inner *notatio*, this will be even more the case for the nun, whose black, simple garment is the sign that she has rejected the outer for the inner life. We await, then, Chaucer's move from the outer characteristic to the inner; from the less important outer rule to the more important inner one. We await this for some time, and when it finally appears it is not what we really anticipated at all.

Some of the fun in all of this, of course, depends upon the somewhat neutral nature of the tone of the description of the Prioress. As the portrait opens we are really not sure whether this is to be an encomiastic portrait, like that of the Knight, or whether it is to be a broad satire like the portrait of the Monk that will follow. Chaucer tells us "which" she is, and then tells us what she does. No single detail is necessarily satirical; yet each one seems not to be what we expect in the description of a nun. We have noted that we might have expected Chaucer to begin with a description of her habit, but instead he tells us how she smiles (not very much) and how she swears (not very much)! Chaucer's strategy of description in this portrait is almost exactly the opposite of that used in the portrait of the Knight. There he began by noting the Knight's knightly qualities: he is a worthy man, he has always loved chivalry, truth, honor, freedom, and courtesy. With the Prioress, however, we begin by noting a

host of qualities that are tangential to the contemplative life, subsidiary
to the "inner rule," or not contributive to the proper behavior of a
Prioress. We shall eventually arrive at a consideration of the Prioress'
conscience—something essential to consider in a nun—but before we get
to that Chaucer tells us how she smiles, how she swears, what name she is
called, how she sings the divine service, how she speaks French, how she
eats, how she deports herself, and, finally, why she does these things: in
order to imitate courtly demeanor!

> Ther was also a Nonne, a Prioresse,
> That of hir smylyng was ful symple and coy;
> Hire gretteste ooth was but by Seinte Loy;
> And she was cleped madame Eglentyne.
> Ful weel she soong the service dyvyne,
> Entuned in hir nose ful semely,
> And Frenssh she spak ful faire and fetisly,
> After the scole of Stratford atte Bowe,
> For Frenssh of Parys was to hire unknowe.
> At mete wel ytaught was she with alle:
> She leet no morsel from hir lippes falle,
> Ne wette hir fyngres in hir sauce depe;
> Wel koude she carie a morsel and wel kepe
> That no drope ne fille upon hire brest.
> In curteisie was set ful muchel hir lest.
> Hir over-lippe wyped she so clene
> That in hir coppe ther was no ferthyng sene
> Of grece, whan she dronken hadde hir draughte.
> Ful semely after hir mete she raughte.
> And sikerly she was of greet desport,
> And ful plesaunt, and amyable of port,
> And peyned hire to countrefete cheere
> Of court, and to been estatlich of manere,
> And to ben holden digne of reverence.

It is only after this twenty-four-line section that we finally turn away
from outer qualities to inner in order to examine the Prioress' conscience. Moreover, in order to signal the importance of this shift,
Chaucer marks it with a very pivotal "but." "But, for to speken of hir
conscience" he tells us, and we think, ah, at last we get to something we
expect in a description of a nun—something that will tell us directly
about her inner, spiritual "condicioun," something that will test the quality of the "wine in the cellar" that has been our governing analogy. And,
Chaucer, laying it on thickly, builds us up even more:

> *But,* for to speken of hire *conscience,*
> She was so *charitable* and so *pitous*
> She wolde *wepe,* if that she saugh . . .

If she saw what? Again, I think, Chaucer teases us into a partial, and in this case a very premature closure. Responding to the key words "conscience," "charity," "mercifulness," and "weeping," we cannot help but think that Chaucer is headed in a serious direction. We expect him to conjure up an image of human or divine suffering that stirs the Prioress' cultivated instincts of mercy and charitableness and causes her to weep: the weeping then being a *sign* (of course) of her conscience as promised. But what she sees is a mouse, caught in a trap. A more bathetic substitution would be hard to imagine. As Robertson has pointed out, it is the most anticlimactic of a series of anticlimaxes in the portrait.[12] R. E. Kaske has objected to this interpretation on the grounds that the word "conscience" *can* have a meaning approximating "sensibility of feelings," which he would connect with the suggestions in the text that the Prioress corresponds to a heroine of a medieval romance.[13] While Kaske's evidence is scanty and depends in turn upon a vexatious passage, nevertheless it is attractive to imagine "conscience" as having both a primary and a secondary meaning, for it would be another instance of Chaucer's playing upon our anticipatory adjustments. To some degree we expect a nun's conscience to be a conscience; to some degree we suspect that this nun's conscience may be very different. However, the addition of charity to the word-picture strongly points towards a moral interpretation of the word conscience, and as both Robertson and Steadman have observed, the Prioress' charity turns out to be as misplaced as her conscience is ill-defined—glaringly so, since the proper objects of charity will be defined in Chaucer's portrait of the Plowman.[14] By manipulating the outer signs in the ways described, Chaucer makes it more difficult than it would otherwise be to determine the direction he will take when he arrives at inner meanings, and it is precisely this suspense that makes the anticlimax comic.

To work well an anticlimax needs to be hinted at a bit or its effect will be to astonish us unexpectedly rather than amusingly to confirm a growing suspicion. Chaucer does prepare us, and he does so in two ways. First, the choice of things described is, as I have remarked, either beside the point or actually contraindicated for a nun. This is fairly simple, and for some time scholars have noted that certain seemingly irrelevant elements in the portrait, such as her table manners, are in fact, because borrowed from the carnal advice of La Vieille in the *Romance of the Rose* and ultimately from Ovid, positively undesirable in a nun.[15] Similarly, the Prioress' smiling in a simple and coy (that is quiet) way and her elaborate name of Eglentyne have been shown by Lowes to be inappropriately borrowed from the vocabulary of the medieval romance. Secondly, Chaucer not only adduces questionable details of behavior, but he is given to qualifications. The most insistent of these, in the portrait as a whole, is the use of the emphatic "ful," which functions like modern English "very." Chaucer repeats this word so often that one is led, however indirectly, to feel that he is in fact protesting too much. Consider, if you will, the following: the Prioress is "ful symple and coy" in her smiling, she sings the divine service "ful weel," and, as if that were not admiration enough, she sings it in her nose "ful semely." She speaks French "ful faire and fetisly," and her table manners are the result of her concern "ful muchel" for courtesy. The manners are stressed again when we are told that she reaches for meat or food "ful semely"—surely one of the few encomiastic descriptions of meat-reaching in the poetry of any language. The effect of the whole, the narrator goes on, is that she is "ful pleasaunt," a description that is presumably reinforced by the subsequent modification of her wimple, which we remember is "ful semely" pinched, her cloak, which is "ful fetys," and her mouth, which is "ful smal."

There simply is nothing like this in any of the other portraits, although Chaucer does repeat variants of the word "worthy" to reinforce the claim that the Knight is indeed a worthy man. Here, though, the effect is different because the repeated word is different. The net result of all this "ful"-ness is, if you will pardon the pun, fulsome. By qualifying virtually every action, characteristic, feature, or garment with "ful" Chaucer overpraises the Prioress and creates a subtle and very entertaining irony. Irony is the art of condemning while seeming to praise, and Chaucer here brings it about by praising everything—even meat-reaching. We might accept "ful simple" smiling, or singing of the divine service "ful weel," but we are less willing to hear it sung in the nose "ful semely," while her provincial French is curiously described as "ful faire." It is perhaps wrong to say that this series culminates in her reaching for her meat or food in a "ful semely" manner, for although that is perhaps the most jarring use of the phrase in the portrait—especially if "raughte" means "belched" rather than "reached"—the technique is cumulative more than climactic and in a sense we only appreciate the separate uses of the word when we have read or heard all of them.[16] As Phyllis Hodgson has pointed out in her admirable edition of the Prologue, the details seem progressively less "seemly" for a Prioress, to which one can add that the repetition of the word "semely" also forces us to question its meaning, for it can mean no more than "appropriately" or it can, by its insistence on the decorum of outer behavior, on seemliness as a quality to be observed, call our attention to a mistaken concern by the Prioress for external rather than internal qualities; for the world rather than the spirit.[17]

Words, as Saint Augustine pointed out, are the commonest types of signs, and just as Chaucer manipulates things that are signs (like the Prioress' habit) and actions that are signs (like the Prioress' weeping), he also plays games with words, using the technique of inadequate or inaccurate definition to signal something quite different. Let us return to the

Prioress' conscience for an illustration. Insofar as our governing image of the bush and the wine is concerned, the Prioress' outer characteristics should be the signs and her conscience the referent, but, because words can be signs of different things, the pattern is a bit more complicated. Signs refer to other signs. Because of the ambivalence of the outer signs in the portrait of the Prioress, we are uncertain in our reading as to whether her inner conscience will be good, bad, or nonexistent. Will there be wine, vinegar, or an empty cellar? Or will there be a sign in the cellar saying "temporarily out of stock?" Instead of moving from an outer sign to an inner characteristic, Chaucer moves from outer signs to a *word*, which, we have seen, turned out not to be the sign of the inner characteristic we anticipated.

Thus, we thought that the word *conscience* would be a sign for what it normally is a sign for in Chaucer: conscience—inward knowledge; awareness of right and wrong, as when Prudence tells Melibee that "the substance of a man is ful good, whan synne is nat in mannes conscience" (1635). Yet Chaucer gives us a wholly inappropriate illustration of this sort of conscience, the weeping over dead mice, which either denies the moral meaning or, perhaps, changes it into a worldly, sentimental meaning. In the end, though, sentiment hardly constitutes a conscience for a Prioress at all, and the effect is to have a sign with no referent. Chaucer calls our attention to the bush outside the tavern, then displays wine barrels within. Empty wine barrels.

Other words are also ambivalent signs, and one closely linked with "conscience" is "reverence." We remember that the Prioress is eager to "ben holden digne of reverence." The context is important:

> [She] peyned hire to contrefete cheere
> Of court, and to been estatlich of manere
> And to ben holden digne of reverence.
> But, for to speken of hire conscience . . .

The three important words here are "conscience," "reverence," and "countrefete." Note to start that the Prioress actively seeks worldly reverence in contrast to the Parson, who is disinterested in pomp and reverence, and does not trouble to "spice" his conscience, which I understand to mean he does not try to cover up what he finds in his conscience that is distasteful. Robinson's suggestion that his conscience is not overly refined or overly scrupulous strikes me as unlikely in that very encomiastic portrait:

> He waited after no pompe and reverence,
> Ne maked him a spiced conscience,
> But Cristes loore and his apostles twelve
> He taughte, but first he folwed it hymselve.[18]

If the Prioress' desire to be held worthy of reverence in the world is dubious, and if her conscience is ultimately nonexistent, we may inquire further into Chaucer's use of the deliciously equivocal word *counterfeit,* which is crucial in any discussion of signs, for it declares the presence of a false sign. The Prioress is at pains to "countrefete cheere / Of court, and to been estatlich of manere," which raises several questions: should she do this, and is she able to do this? That a nun should not seek to be like a noble lady, should not seek worldly reverence, has been fairly widely agreed upon, and we need not pursue the issue. To what extent a nun can imitate a courtly appearance is more to the purpose. The word itself is glossed by Robinson along with a defense of the Prioress: while granting that her manners are "gently satirized," he nevertheless thinks that "countrefete means simply 'imitate' without the implication of dishonesty." Here again Robinson seems to put the cart before the horse, offering a definition based upon his interpretation of the text rather than interpreting the text as possible definitions suggest.

Of course Chaucer can use "counterfeit" to mean simply "imitate," as he does when Criseyde asks Troilus if he proposes to counterfeit a jealous child (3.1168). At the same time, though, it can certainly mean to imitate in order to deceive, as it does in *The Legend of Good Women* when Jason is said to feign truth and counterfeit pain in order to advance his suit with different women (1368–76). In the context in which the word occurs in the portrait of the Prioress it is hard to imagine that some element of deception would not attach itself to the meaning of the word, since no matter how she smiles, speaks French, and watches her table manners, her station in life is that of a nun, a Prioress, and if her habits are of the court her habit is of the cloister. A nun cannot be a courtly lady, although she might have been born into a courtier's family, because she has made vows to reject the world. Indeed, the more she imitates the "cheere / Of court," the more she falsifies her role as a nun. A Prioress who counterfeits courtly behavior becomes a counterfeit nun. This is not a gray area. The *Ancrene Riwle* says plainly enough that "courtly manners in an anchoress . . . have often resulted in the end in sin and shame."[19] Robinson's protestation that there is no implication of dishonesty in Chaucer's use of the word "counterfeit" misses the point. Insofar as the Prioress is a nun counterfeiting a lady she is dishonest with the world and with herself. If courtly manners are the sign of a lady, they are as surely not the sign of a nun. Insofar as the word *counterfeit* is itself a sign, it is a sign that tells us not to believe other signs! The word *counterfeit* is at the center of Chaucer's chiastic play with words, ideas, and signs.

The word *reverence* operates in close connection with the Prioress' desire to counterfeit the "cheere of court," for the goal of her affected behavior is "to ben holden digne of reverence." Because the word "reverence" has at the same time a secular and a religious sense, its function

here is to cut both ways. The worldly, secular reverence the Prioress
seeks is the same quality the Parson rejects, waiting after no pomp or
reverence, and which seems to characterize the Sergeant who is so well-
versed in the letter of the law:

> Discreet he was and of greet reverence—
> He semed swich, his wordes weren so wise.

(A 312–13)

The Man of Law is, like the Prioress, someone who wants to seem something other than what he is. He "semed bisier than he was," and seemed
to be a man of reverence because of his wise words—or at least the
narrator says they were wise. Some doubt is cast on the Man of Law's
speech when it is put in context, for immediately preceding his description the Clerk is set forth as the paradigm of good speech, learning and
teaching with speech that was "seyd in forme and reverence." The
Prioress ignores the spiritual dimension of reverence for its worldly
counterpart; she ignores the reverence due to God for the reverence she
hopes to receive as a counterfeit lady. But even here the irony is complex, for in her striving after a worldly esteem unsuitable to one of her
vows, the Prioress lets go by the board the rather high estimation of
society she could command by virtue of being a Prioress.[20] The word
reverence is a sign for two things, and the play of one against the other
constitutes the real meaning of the meanings.

We may close our examination of the Prioress' inner life as Chaucer
does: by a return to her conscience, this time coupled with a tender
heart. If we remember that the description as a whole is forty-five lines
long, the brevity of Chaucer's attention to the inner life is all the more
remarkable:

> But, for to speken of hire conscience,
> She was so charitable and so pitous
> She wolde wepe, if that she saugh a mous
> Kaught in a trappe, if it were deed or bledde.
> Of smale houndes hadde she that she fedde
> With rosted flessh, or milk and wastel-breed.
> But soore wepte she if oon of hem were deed,
> Or if men smoot it with a yerde smerte;
> And al was conscience and tendre herte.

We might be a little surprised by the switch from a description of conscience to a description of pets to a reiteration that we have been talking
about conscience all along, but we should be surprised only if we had
taken Chaucer's definition of conscience at face value in the first place.
Scholars have noted that the Prioress should not have dogs at all and that

she would better exemplify charity by feeding the poor than by feeding her illegal pets.[21]

We may, however, look a little more carefully at the close of the passage on conscience, where Chaucer links it with a "tendre herte." The Prioress' tender heart has been seen by some to be a correct definition of the function of conscience, and by others to be merely a factual statement of real if misplaced sympathy. However, the coupling of conscience and tender-heartedness is more arresting when we remember that in the passage we examined from the *Ancrene Riwle* on the outer and inner rules, the word *heart* was used three different times as a synecdoche for the inner or spiritual life. In other words, since the outer rule is to serve the inner, the whole focus of a nun's life is to perfect her heart. And there is very little in the *Riwle* to suggest that sensitivity to the plight of dogs and mice constitutes such perfection. The *Riwle* does say that the heart is properly involved with a good conscience, with true charity, and correctly directed mercy. All the words Chaucer uses in his description of the Prioress (her conscience, charity, being "pitous" and her heart) are to be found in the *Riwle,* but the actions Chaucer describes as nominal proofs of these things—the weeping over dogs and mice—are of course inappropriate definitions. Just how inappropriate may be seen by a closer look at the definitions in the *Riwle.* The nuns are advised that the inner rule "governs the *heart* and keeps it untroubled and free from the wounds and tumours of an unhealthy *conscience.*" This rule, furthermore, while it "is always interior, guiding the *heart,*" also constitutes the "*charity* of which the Apostle speaks, which comes from a *pure heart,* [not, we note, from a tender one] and a good *conscience.*"

The good conscience and the pure heart in this text may be amusingly contrasted with the Prioress' outer-directed preoccupations. Finally, the quality of mercy, the tenderness and capacity for being "pitous" that has tempered much otherwise adverse criticism of the Prioress, is spelled out in the *Riwle.* Mercy is important to the author of the *Riwle,* not as something to be shown to dogs or even to people, but to be hoped for from God: " 'Extend thy mercy,' says the psalmist, 'to them that know thee' by true faith, 'and thy justice,' that is righteousness of life, 'to them that are right in heart.' . . . The psalmist says: 'Do good, O Lord, to those that are good, and to the upright of *heart* ' " (p. 1). These are hardly sentimental injunctions. The nuns are told to direct their hearts properly so that a particular kind of charity, one dependent upon a good conscience, a pure heart, and true faith, will make them like those towards whom the Psalmist hopes God's mercy will be directed. It is necessary to note again that there is no evidence to suggest that Chaucer actually knew the *Ancrene Riwle,* but certainly it is arresting to consider that in his portrait of the Prioress, in the little subsection on conscience, all of the most important words used in the *Riwle* are employed, with none of their carefully defined meanings. It is almost as though Chaucer, working with conventional materials about nuns, was trying to create one who was exactly the opposite of what a nun should be.

Following the short discussion of the Prioress' supposed conscience, Chaucer again turns to externals, describing the Prioress' wimple, cloak, and beads, and also describing her face in some detail, commenting on her eyes, nose, mouth, and forehead. Almost sixty years ago Lowes noted that the description of the Prioress' face was dependent upon conventions of medieval love poetry and was transferred, as Lowes amusingly puts it, "with all its blushing associations thick upon it, to the nun." More recently Kevin Kiernan has observed that because the "descending catalogue" of the rhetoricians—the standard prescription for describing a beautiful woman—continued in its full version to a description of the entire woman from head to toe, with a tacitly provocative, non-Aristotelean excluded middle, there is a certain suspense in this description of a woman who is also a nun.[22] What, we wonder, is Chaucer going to do? What will he say? But, as with so much in this portrait, Chaucer's joke is to raise expectations only to retreat into a calculatedly equivocal "conclusion" in which not very much is concluded. The descending catalogue does not descend. For our present purpose it is worth remembering that any convention, including a rhetorical convention, is a sign. Saint Augustine makes it clear that some signs are literal and some figurative (p. 43), and among figurative signs meanings can differ rather arbitrarily, not because of the nature of the thing, but because of "agreement and consent to its significance" (p. 60). The descending catalogue is such a sign, and rather typically Chaucer does not simply use it; rather he manipulates it. Again our job has been first to identify and then to explicate.

One of the more intriguing parts of the catalogue of the Prioress' person is the amusingly evasive description of her as surely "nat undergrowe." As with so many of the details, our interpretation here will depend upon our judgment of the portrait as a whole. Muriel Bowden, for example, thinks Chaucer means only that the Prioress was "well-proportioned" (p. 95), while Phyllis Hodgson more cautiously asks if she is not "unexpectedly large, and so somewhat comic and a bit pathetic?" (p. 85). In a more neutral vein, G. J. Engelhardt has taken it to mean "physically mature."[23] Part of the difficulty in discerning Chaucer's meaning here is that the Prioress' overall size is related to the size of her forehead:

> But sikerly she hadde a fair foreheed;
> It was almoost a spanne brood, I trowe;
> For, hardily, she was nat undergrowe.

As Robinson's notes tell us, the forehead has occasioned considerable controversy. To begin with, there is some question whether the forehead should have been visible in a properly wimpled nun, and further whether the large forehead was a sign of beauty or of stupidity. At any rate, whatever the significance of the large forehead, Chaucer is at pains to connect it with her large size, and I find it difficult to imagine that by connecting the large forehead with large size he means only to say that she was well-proportioned. I think rather that he wanted to imply that she was larger than most people, and, if he was using litotes, that indeed she was very much not undergrown.

Now there are two ways to arrive at that state: through inheritance of a large frame or through an appetite for large meals, which leads to obesity. Few critics have read the passage this way, but in a portrait that tells us how the Prioress handles morsels, how she wets her fingers, how she wipes her lips, how she reaches for meat, and how she drinks, we may be excused for concluding that Chaucer meant us to think of the Prioress as corpulent.[24] This in turn would be another departure from the advice to nuns given in the *Riwle*, wherein they are told to lead a "hard life" (p. 57). Indeed, a nun's thin body should be a sign of spirituality, as the author of the *Riwle* makes clear in an extended metaphor of the anchoress as bird. Here are signs that explain other signs:

> True anchoresses are called birds because they leave the earth, that is, the love of all worldly things, and because of the longing of their hearts towards heavenly things, fly upward towards heaven. . . . Those birds fly well that have not much flesh, like the pelican, and many feathers. The ostrich and other such birds, because of their great weight of flesh, make only a pretence of flying, beating their wings while their feet remain always near the ground. So with the sensual anchoress who lives for the pleasures of the body and cultivates her own comfort; the weight of her flesh and bodily vices prevent her from flying, and though she makes a pretence and great commotion with wings . . . and though she has some appearance of flying and looks like a holy anchoress, whoever looks closely will laugh her to scorn, for her feet, that is her desires, keep her always near the earth. (pp. 58–59)

This illuminating passage not only tells us something about corpulence in nuns, but about the claims of the body versus the claims of the spirit generally. Even more to the point, it is an excellent example of the medieval attitude toward those who fall short of their calling. It does not say that people will smile sympathetically at them, or show amused tolerance, or exhibit gentle raillery, or any of the kinds of things modern critics are accustomed to saying about Chaucer's attitude toward the Prioress. Rather it says that nuns who live for the pleasures of the body and for comfort will be laughed to scorn. The extent to which the Prioress may be said to live for the body is debatable, but it is abundantly clear that she does not live for the spirit. If we pass from the analogy between the nun and the pelican to that between the nun and the night-raven, the significance of the Prioress' actions are clearer, for the author of the rule says that a nun should fly in the night, that is in private, "seeking heavenly food for [the] soul" (p. 67). Whether or not the Prioress eats too much earthly food, she does not partake of enough heavenly food. There are signs here and we should be alert to them. Chaucer's audience would, as Chaucer undoubtedly did, judge her performance as a nun more negatively than we are accustomed to do.

It remains to examine the Prioress' beads and brooch.

> Of smal coral aboute hire arm she bar
> A peire of bedes, gauded al with grene,
> And theron heng a brooch of gold ful sheene,
> On which ther was first write a crowned A,
> And after *Amor vincit omnia.*

While coral and green rosary beads might strike us as so self-contradictory as to be invented by Chaucer for the occasion, there were in fact such things in the fourteenth century, and John B. Friedman has shown that they were particularly favored by aristocratic ladies.[25] We can, then, associate the Prioress' fashionable beads with her general concern to imitate courtly ways. Insofar as the beads are a sign, however, they are significant in a slightly different way. When the artist of the Hoccleve portrait drew his picture of Chaucer, he portrayed him holding a rosary—presumably as an outer sign of inner devotion, since the pilgrim is not so described in the text. That rosary is dark brown or black.[26] The word-portrait of the Prioress is totally different. Her rosary is not, as we should particularly expect in a nun, an outer sign of inner devotion, but an outer sign of inner worldliness. While the *Ancrene Riwle* urges nuns "never to be idle," but "work or read, or be at beads, and in prayer," the Prioress' beads are displayed rather than used.[27] And, as with the wimple and the cloak, Chaucer calls our attention to an incidental aesthetic quality which, because it occurs in a sign that in other contexts would possess a very modest aesthetic value but great spiritual value, has the remarkable effect of transforming the meaning of the sign into the opposite of what it might have meant if somewhat differently described.

While a Prioress might properly carry rosary beads, the appended brooch seems surely to be worn in violation of precept. The *Ancrene Riwle* advises nuns not to wear either a ring or a brooch (p. 187), and, as with her showy rosary, even if she were not violating an external rule she is certainly not operating in the inner spirit fostered by St. Benedict when she attaches a gold brooch to a green and coral rosary. The whole effect is to transform the normally spiritual into something that makes a primarily aesthetic appeal.

The motto on the brooch, *Amor vincit omnia,* long ago attracted the critical judgment of John Livingston Lowes, whose remarks have been so influential that he seems to have had the first and last words on the subject.

> The motto on the Prioress's brooch was a convention with a history. The line . . . is, as everybody knows, from one of Virgil's eclogues. There it refers, of course, to the way of a man with a maid. But by a pious transfer, which took place long before Chaucer . . . the line was converted to the use of love celestial. . . . And it is precisely that happy ambiguity of the convention . . . that makes Chaucer's use of it here . . . a master stroke. Which of the two loves does "amor" mean to the Prioress? I do not know; but I think she thought she meant love celestial.[28]

For the passage to work the way Lowes claims it does, it is necessary that the two possible meanings of *amor vincit omnia* be essentially equal in frequency, so that the Prioress' presumed translation is as valid as an earthier meaning. However, Lowes does not make a very good case for this. In the only place where he adduces evidence for his claim he actually cites only one text, which in fact reads "sed quia scriptum est: caritas omnia vincit." The same vagueness is found in Sister Madeleva's claim that it is "one of the commonest of epigrams among religious," which she asserts without evidence.[29]

Now one would not want to state that *amor vincit omnia* could not have a significance *in bono* in the Middle Ages; it could and did, and John Gower, for example, uses it in a good sense in the Prologue to his *Tripartite Chronicle* and in *Vox clamantis,* book 6, chapter 14. However, its original, Virgilian sense was almost certainly stronger, since it was undoubtedly a school text. Gower uses it that way in *Vox clamantis,* book 5, chap. 3; it is used with an overt reference to Virgil in the climactic passages closing the *Romance of the Rose,* and employed much the same way in Benevenuto da Imola's commentary on the carnal lovers in Dante's *Inferno.* While it would not be possible to resolve the matter definitively, it seems likely that the Virgilian sense would be so strong that the real joke is in the Prioress' inability to fathom the commonplace erotic sense of the text. Instead of stressing her innocence or pure-mindedness, as Lowes does, we might better stress her ignorance of Virgil, or perhaps her inability to distinguish between *amor* and *caritas,* or her lack of good sense. If there is anything a nun should not be it is ambiguous regarding the world around her. The joke about not knowing or understanding Virgil is precisely the same joke Chaucer used earlier in her portrait when he ascribed to her table manners that arose from a misreading or misunderstanding of the *Romance of the Rose,* and it is of a piece with her knowing French, but only provincial French. In-

deed, a certain ineptitude with classical or foreign languages is a common satiric touch in medieval English literature. We remember, for
example, the amusing scene in which Avarice in *Piers Plowman* thinks
that "restitution" is French for robbery, and Chaucer himself has the
Summoner spout Latin phrases without any real knowledge of the language, while Chauntecleer confidently and disastrously translates *"mulier
est hominis confusio"* as "Womman is mannes joye and al his blis."
   If indeed Chaucer is setting the Prioress up as one who reads im-
properly, he may well have received the inspiration from his friend John
Gower, who described nuns as having biblical rather than classical reading deficiencies: "[Some nuns] think the Scriptures permit them to do as
they do, because frequently they simply read the text and are not concerned about the gloss" (*Vox clamantis*, book 4, chap. 13). Of course,
Chaucer's great triumph in creating a character who does exactly this
with biblical texts is in his portrayal of the Wife of Bath, who does her
own glossing, but he may have picked up a hint for the Prioress as well.
Insofar as the Prioress' brooch would be perceived by her to be a sign, we
would probably assume (with Lowes) that she construed its legend in a
good sense, and wore it as a sign of her spirituality. Of course, since it is
jewelry, and prettily carved, its supposed spiritual significance is undercut. Insofar as the legend is Virgilian and carnal, the brooch is a sign
without a referent, for there is nothing to indicate that the Prioress is
carnal herself. She is not, after all, much like the Wife of Bath in her
behavior. The brooch, then, may be a sign of the Prioress' shallow understanding of commonplace Latin tags, as her table manners are a sign
of an imperfect understanding of French. And this shallowness is significant, for as St. Augustine says of biblical reading, "many and varied
obscurities and ambiguities deceive those who read casually, understanding one thing instead of another. . . . I do not doubt that this situation
was provided by God to conquer pride by work" (*On Christian Doctrine*, p.
37). There is a culpable ignorance in the Prioress.
   The portrait of the Prioress ends much as it began: with reference to
something unexpected or inappropriate. The portrait opened with a
description of the Prioress' smiling as full simple and coy, and although
Lowes long ago noted that these are typical words to describe a heroine
of romance, and editors of the text have been at pains to point out that
"coy" meant only "quiet," Chaucer's common use of the phrase "coy as a
maid" suggests that the Prioress displayed more a girlish than a medita-
tional smile. So with the brooch. Whatever the possible meanings of its
legend, no one in Chaucer's audience could ignore its well-known sensual origin, so its effect (if not the Prioress' intention for it) is womanly
rather than godly.
   I promised at the outset to try to assess a little more exactly Lowes's
contention that the Prioress' "amiable foibles" show her to be "charm-

ingly human," and therefore constitute a "delightfully imperfect submergence of the woman in the nun."[30] I think it is fair to say that the
submergence is so imperfect as to constitute only a little dampening, for
where, after all, is the nun? Nuns normally lived under a version of the
Benedictine rule which enjoined above all else obedience, poverty, and
celibacy. The Prioress' dogs and jewels show her disobedience of the rule
and at the same time compromise her poverty, while her celibacy can
only be surmised. The further supporting pillars of discipline, lack of
property, labor, claustration, and diet, are similarly inapplicable. The
Prioress owns property (her gold brooch), is out of her cloister, dines
well on fine food, and does no labor that we hear of.[31] In a similar vein, if
we remember our examination of the *Ancrene Riwle*, we found that the
inner, more important rule emphasized purity of heart, which in turn
depended upon an "unblemished conscience, free from the awareness of
sin that has not been forgiven through Confession" (p. 2). There is
nothing in the portrait to suggest that the Prioress takes much care for
her sins, for her conscience, or for the inner rule at all. She is too busy
with her external appearance. In forty-five lines of description, the only
references to anything that might be construed to have to do with what a
nun might properly be occupied with are the four lines describing her
singing of the divine service and her wearing rosary beads, and in both
cases outer form rather than spiritual function is stressed.

In conclusion, the judgments of most scholars about the Prioress seem
strangely affectionate. Every sign in the portrait of the Prioress points to
her worldliness—the very antithesis of the essence of monasticism. And,
as a nun who wants to be a fashionable lady she ends up being neither.
She is nothing. Indeed, as Robert P. Miller has pointed out to me, this
portrait of an unspiritual Prioress, packed with equivocal signs, is followed directly by reference to the very spiritual Second Nun, who in the
General Prologue is not described at all.

Chaucer does not hate the Prioress, and he does not condemn her as
vigorously as he does, say, the wayward Monk, but he has been at some
pains to portray a completely failed ecclesiast. I cannot agree with Lowes
that there is something delightful, amiable, or charming in her failure as
a nun, although the satire itself is a literary delight. Moreover, I cannot
agree with F. N. Robinson that "if it can be called satire at all [it] is of the
gentlest and most sympathetic sort," nor can I concur with Florence
Ridley's conclusion that the treatment is "only mildly satirical." Peter S.
Taitt's assertion that she is characterized "in terms which imply that she is
an appropriate figure for her situation in life" is diametrically opposed
to the assessment made here.[32]

What we have in the portrait of the Prioress is a careful description of
a nun who is not a nun, much like the Monk's portrait that follows.
Robert B. White, Jr., has demonstrated in superb fashion that the Monk

is methodically portrayed as differing point by point from the monastic norm.[33] If Chaucer "looked upon [the Prioress] with affection" as Donaldson contends,[34] it would be the affection of an artist for a well-executed piece of work, not the affection of a man of the world for a nun of the world. The reason for so much critical mercy and tenderhearted-ness may well arise from Chaucer's deft manipulation of signs. In this particular portrait, much more than in any of the others, Chaucer plays games. The larger strategies of delay in getting to the inner life, in devoting so much of the portrait to her table manners, and of reassuring us nevertheless that all is well, have for some critics perhaps worked too effectively. The signs, too, are subtle. We have no Miller's wart, no Wife's red stockings, no Monk's fat swan. We have instead a series of signs that are inappropriate, that are calculatedly equivocal, or that refer to inner qualities that are themselves ambivalent or suggest ambivalent defini-tions. While the portrait depends upon the author's inviting more than one anticipatory response at a time, our ultimate responses are by no means left up in the air. The use of literary strategy, the manipulation of signs, and the subordinate word games, which are, as we have seen, kinds of uses of signs too, have as their goal the portrayal of an imperfect nun. And if we find an imperfect nun with nice manners, well-fed dogs, and showy jewelry to be attractive in any sense other than as an artistic creation, I think we must do so on our own initiative, not from Chaucer's words. The signs do not warrant affection. If the bush outside a tavern is the sign of the wine within, then the signs here lead us to the equivalent of an empty cellar. An inspection of Chaucer's use of signs shows that his goal was not to arouse our affection but rather to inspire us in medieval fashion to "laugh her to scorn."

RESURRECTION AS DRAMATIC ICON IN THE SHIPMAN'S TALE

GAIL McMURRAY GIBSON

In recent years criticism of Middle English texts has been punctuated by the catch-word "irony," a word which actually describes a complicated variety of responses to the demands of a text. Modern commentators often use the word generically to signify the commonest kind of audience manipulation, what the fifth-century encyclopedist Saint Isidore of Seville called *allegoria*—simply "saying one thing and meaning another."[1] For the modern reader who must labor to retrieve the meaning of the surface fiction as well as that significance left unsaid, "irony" often means saying one thing which to an audience in a distant past meant another. It is thus only slowly that we have come to understand that while medieval literature is sometimes explicit and didactic in open and direct ways, it is just as often peopled by unreliable narrators, set with deliberately shaped enigmas, and undergirded with allegorical subtexts which may be of sustained or of local kinds, which may be used both humorously and as moral counterpoint to a main text. In the Miller's Tale, for example, the medieval audience's knowledge of the theologically motivated comedy of the Noah's Flood plays[2] moved beneath the surface to inform their understanding of Chaucer's fictions concerning poor John the Carpenter, his wife, and his tubs. Chaucer asked his audience both to delight in the fabliau humor of a ribald tale well told and to recognize with considerable ruefulness the serious perversion of God's order which the domestic turmoil of the tale pictures in microcosm. That Chaucer's eagle in *The House of Fame* should swear by Saint John (whose saintly attribute *is* the eagle), or that in *Gawain and the Green Knight* the porter at the castle set upon a hill should swear by the St. Peter of the heavenly gates are smaller but no less instructive manipulations. We may call them ironies if we choose, moments in which a reader or listener is asked to understand a pattern of congruence and noncongruence that is stated by wit rather than by words.

Whatever skepticism[3] arises in response to such "close readings" of texts whose presentation was usually oral (and thus temporal) rather than spatial may be answered in part by the observations of Jean LeClercq about the "muscular" reading and active reminiscence of texts in the Middle Ages,[4] or by Frances Yates's study of the formidable memory systems of classical and medieval culture.[5] And as H. J. Chaytor has written, nothing is "more alien to modernity than the capacious medieval memory which, untrammelled by the associations of print, could learn a strange language with ease and by the methods of a child, and could retain in memory and reproduce lengthy epic and elaborate lyric poems."[6] Ultimately, the vexing question of just how much could be seized and retained from medieval texts can best be answered by those texts themselves. Although we know nothing about the *Pearl* poet or even about the audience for which he wrote, the incandescent perfection of *The Pearl* survives as mute testimony to the enormous expectations that poet possessed about his audience's powers of recognition. Even if some of the numerical and linguistic patterning of *The Pearl* lies so inapparent that it, like the highest sculpted boss of an immense cathedral, seems designed for divine rather than human eyes, there is no doubt that the poem presupposed a wide variety of mental actions—recognitions, corrections of the dream-narrator's inadequate responses, and an understanding both lyrical and reverent at the close of the poem and its circle. *The Pearl* is as perfect a vernacular example as can be found of a medieval text aspiring to the Augustinian aesthetic of difficulty, celebrating the sheer, heady beauty of that which must be hard-sought to be found.[7]

That Chaucer intended his poetic fictions to afford the listener or reader that same pleasure of discovery seems abundantly clear. In a thought-provoking essay entitled "Chaucer and the Visual Arts" V. A. Kolve has outlined the kinds of "memorial images" which Chaucer concealed in his *Canterbury Tales* somewhat as the *Pearl* poet concealed symbolic numerology and the emerging circle emblem in *The Pearl.* Such symbolic images, Kolve argues, "create a certain residue in the mind," exert a kind of pressure upon the hearer's mind and memory which gives the whole tale a "powerful intellectual, artistic and imaginative coherence."[8] Thus, the runaway mare in the Reeve's Tale, Kolve suggests, while meaningful as a literal detail of fabliau plot, is more fully a kind of iconic—and laconic—image of man's unbridled lust run away from his reason.[9] The Reeve's Tale is an intensely visual tale—the runaway horse exists there as concretely as the bedroom window or the tubs of the Miller's Tale—but there are other stories told by Canterbury pilgrims whose nodal meanings lie in larger patterns of symbolic actions and resonant dialogue rather than in single images, which contain ironic manipulations of a dramatic rather than of a strictly visual kind. It is clear that there is much surface "drama" in *The Canterbury Tales*—intrusions, interruptions, protests, the interludes of prologues and endlinks—but perhaps not as apparent are the dramatic icons, compressed symbolic and allusive playings, which lie beneath the literal surface of the narrative. One such dramatic icon appears in the neglected Shipman's Tale, in the guise, so I will argue, of a parodic enactment of Christ's Resurrection appearance to Mary Magdalen.

One recent book on *The Canterbury Tales* calls the Shipman's Tale a "funny but unsavory tale" which some think "the most immoral of the tales."[10] It is curious to me that it is never remarked by those readers who would dismiss the Shipman's Tale as a bawdy product of Chaucer's good humor or his cynicism just how strangely incongruous to its fabliau plot is the note of urgency on which the tale begins. After only four lines of narrative, the teller of the tale, presumably originally intended by Chaucer to be the Wife of Bath[11] (who has her own interests in scarlet gowns), abruptly abandons the beginning of a speech about "sely hous-bonde" and the expensive clothes and parties of beautiful, willful wives to interject an intrusive and strangely ominous note. "Swiche salutaciouns and contenaunces / Passen as dooth a shadwe upon the wal" says a voice which sounds more like Chaucer's Parson than the irrepressible Alys. "But wo is hym that payen moot for al!" (8–10). Although it is possible to understand this woe and these words as literal comment on the debts of husbands hard-pressed by the Dame Alyses of the world, the sermon-like warning that all these revels—these "salutaciouns and contenaunces"—will pass away, and the haunting allusion to the shadow on the wall point as ominously as did the writing on Belshazzar's wall to a serious subtext of implication. With deft strokes Chaucer frames in our minds the questions, "How must such things be paid for? Why is the paying woeful?" These questions on a literal level prepare for the coming tale's preoccupation with "pay" and with the fabliau's final comic reckoning. But these strange words of warning and of woe also serve to frame the tale with the inevitability of that much larger and nontemporal reckoning; like the morality drama *Everyman,* the tale begins by reminding us of the final necessity of reckoning our lives and our talents before God. This doubleness of implication continues: The husband must clothe his spouse in expensive gowns, says the narrator, since those clothes are worn "al for his owene worshipe" (13). I doubt that many in Chaucer's audience would have missed this curiously ironic inversion of the famous gospel sermon which taught men and women to take no heed for their raiment but, like the lilies of the field, to worship the Lord who lovingly cares for and clothes them (Matthew 6:28–30).

The words *pay* and *array* ironically yoked in the opening lines of the Shipman's Tale are also repeatedly joined in rhyme throughout the narrative and dialogue.

The sely housbonde, algate he moote *paye,*
He moot us clothe, and he moot us *arraye,*

Al for his owene worshipe richely,
In which *array* we daunce jolily.

(11–14)

For his honour, myself for to *arraye*,
A Sonday next I moste nedes *paye*
An hundred frankes, or ellis I am lorn.

(179–81)

And I shal *paye* as soone as ever I may.
For by my trouthe, I have on myn *array*,
And nat on wast, bistowed every deel.

(417–19)

The plot of the Shipman's Tale, of course, concerns a wife's unscrupulous efforts to pay for expensive new clothes; the mere repetition of these two words need not require explication. But if we pause to consider the significance of *array* within the context of the whole *Canterbury Tales*, our response to the conspicuously echoed *pay* and *array* is somewhat altered. The *Chaucer Concordance* reveals that the only other tale by Chaucer in which the word *array* appears with greater frequency is the Clerk's Tale, Chaucer's version of the Petrarchan parable about the soul's testing by God.[12] Both the simple white shift which patient Griselda wears in her humility and the glorious golden robes bestowed upon her by the husband who, like the God he figures, loves and tries and restores her, emblematize Griselda's spiritual perfections. It is clear that Chaucer's two wives and their array—the chaste, spiritual garments of Griselda and the merchant's wife's adulterous and worldly clothing—may be seen as foils for each other; Griselda is as worshipful in her patient endurance of Walter's trials as the merchant's wife is unscrupulous in her dealings with the hapless husband she so ironically professes to "worship."

If we allow ourselves to look at these two kinds of array with the hindsight afforded by the Parson's Tale, we can see clearly explicated in sermon what we see by inference in the fictions themselves: "I woot wel," says the Parson "that [wives] sholde setten hire entente to plesen hir housbondes, but nat by hire queyntise of array."

St. Jerome seith [the Parson continues] that "wyves that been apparailled in silk and in precious purpre ne mowe nat clothen hem in Jhesu Christ." . . . / Seint Gregorie eek seith that "no wight seketh precious array but oonly for veyne glorie, to been honoured the moore biforn the peple." / It is a greet folye, a womman to have a fair array outward and in hirself be foul inward.

(933–35)

To the Parson's authorities (Jerome and Gregory) might be added the words of Saint Paul from 1 Timothy 2:9–10 and especially from Romans 13:13–14—words indelibly inscribed in the medieval imagination by the moving account of Saint Augustine's conversion in his *Confessions:* "And in silence I read the first passage on which my eyes fell: 'not in rioting and drunkenness, not in chambering and impurities, not in contention and envy: But put ye on the Lord Jesus Christ [sed induimini Dominum Iesum Christum], and make not provision for the flesh in its concupiscences.' " [13] Saint Paul's counsel that every Christian clothe himself in Jesus Christ was heeded by Augustine at that epiphanal moment; when he renounced his old life, he put on symbolic garments of belief and was made a new man.

Array in the context of a medieval pilgrimage is thus a serious theme. Clothing is not only the sociological clue to mankind's "condicioun" and "degree" as Chaucer demonstrates so brilliantly in the General Prologue, but is an image for the acceptance of the Christian life or its rejection. Men may, as the Parson says, be clothed in worldly silk and purple—or be clothed in Christ. When the once-doubtful Thomas of the Middle English *Towneley Plays* finally places his hands in the bloody sides of the risen Lord and believes, he makes a long joyful speech in which he declares that he will give away all his worldly garments—hat, mantle, girdle, coat, purse of silk. Thomas needs these things no longer, he declares, for "Ihesu, that soke the madyns mylk / ware noght bot clothes of pall." [14] Thomas's speech and actions are gestures of humility and of charity, but they are even more fundamentally dramatic images of his new life. He puts on Christ, abandoning his own earthly garments as Christ abandoned the useless grave-clothes in the tomb. Just so the symbolic white garments worn by the newly baptized and by the clergy at the Easter season represented in concrete visual terms the renewed life and faith celebrated with the mystery of Christ's Resurrection. As a twelfth-century English homily instructs, so must men's souls be clad in the white garments of purity, if we too would "come to our arising." [15] For Christ's Resurrection from the dead prefigures the universal Resurrection and Judgment; we may rise clad in the white raiment of the blessed and be saved. But to reject God's array is to be damned, as an Easter sermon from John Mirk's *Festial* warns in no uncertain terms:

> þen as wele as hym schall be þat comyþe to þys fest wele arayde in Godys lyuere, cloþyd in loue and scharyte, als euell schall hym be þat comyþe yn fendys lyuere, cloþyd in envy and dedly wraþe; for þes, as the gospell tellyþe, schall be taken and cast into the prison of hell. [16]

To paraphrase the Shipman's Tale, we must pay for our array.

But though Chaucer's Parson and his real-life counterparts offer useful lessons for understanding the expectations of Chaucer's audience as they listened to the Shipman's Tale, far more important are clues beneath the surface of the text itself, clues which to an attentive audience would have united the echoing words *pay* and *array* of the fabliau plot into a cohesive theme. For Chaucer has actually placed within the central episode of the Shipman's Tale a Resurrection of his own—a parodic drama of Christ's appearance to Mary Magdalen—which performs the same kind of ironic undercutting of text which the Noah's Flood play achieves in the Miller's Tale. And much like the sacral parody of Noah's flood in the Miller's Tale, Chaucer's parodic Resurrection play creates a witty pattern of simultaneous congruence and opposition to the sacred event it invokes; it is both Resurrection and anti-Resurrection.

Chaucer's staging of his "Resurrection" drama begins with the visit of Daun John to the merchant's house in line fifty-one of the tale: The servants, Chaucer says, were as glad to see the monk as a fowl is glad when "the sonne up riseth." Although the sun/Son pun was a frequent verbal play in Middle English poetry,[17] and although Chaucer's enthusiasm for puns was certainly no less legendary to his own audience than it is to modern students, this simple remark in its context seems straightforward, unremarkable. There is nothing yet in the tale, beyond the nagging memory of the curious opening lines, to suggest that Chaucer intended anything more here than a casual simile about birds and sunrises. But then, only twenty-five lines later, we are offered another arising, not only a rising-up, but a rising up on the third day. "The thridde day, this marchant up ariseth," Chaucer tells us. This merchant then makes his way to his counting house to survey his ledgers and his finances. And still again, a few lines later, we are told that Daun John "was rysen in the morwe also." Daun John, arisen on this third day goes to a garden where he "walketh softe" (93) and where he meets the merchant's comely wife. By the time this third reference to an "arising" appears—all three of these within the space of forty lines of text—any good listener among Chaucer's audience must have been alerted to the possibility that Chaucer was up to something more than pulling his characters from their beds. And so must we, for the word *arise*, of course, just like the Vulgate *surgere*, means both the leaving of a bed and the Lord's leaving of His tomb.[18]

Why a garden might be an appropriate setting for a lover's tryst—even so business-like a tryst—hardly requires explanation, but neither would it have needed explanation to Chaucer's audience why this garden might appropriately be linked with the "arising" of the monk. For it was in a garden, said the Gospel of John, that Jesus first made his appearance after his Resurrection from the dead, and it was there in the garden that the weeping Magdalen found him. So preoccupied was Mary Magdalen with the empty tomb, says the Gospel, that she at first mistook her risen

Lord for the gardener (John 20:15). This scene of mistaken identity giving way to joyful affirmation of Christ's miracle is a dramatic moment in the Gospel; by the late twelfth century it had literally been made drama in the dozens of liturgical plays which reenacted Christ's appearance to Mary Magdalen as part of the yearly ritual observance of the Easter miracle.[19] In fact, we know that one such Latin *Hortulanus* play was performed by nuns at Barking Abbey near London, the same abbey where the Elizabeth Chausir who scholars have often argued was Chaucer's own daughter or sister took her vows in 1381.[20] And by Chaucer's day, every vernacular Corpus Christi cycle would have contained a play of this garden meeting of Resurrected Christ and Mary Magdalen. All four of the extant English cycles contain lengthy *Hortulanus* scenes; indeed Catherine Dunn has suggested that

> the encounter between Mary and the risen Christ is the most crucial dramatic moment in the entire cycle, for it is the *peripeteia* (in the Aristotelian sense), the recognition and reversal that suddenly transform the Passion catastrophe into a glorious fulfillment.[21]

That this meeting between Christ and Mary Magdalen occurs in a garden was of great interest to medieval exegetes, who interpreted the garden as the typological perfection of Adam's fallen garden or as a moral emblem of mankind's own soul.[22] In the *Digby Play of Mary Magdalen* when Mary confesses that she had at first mistaken her risen Lord for "Simond, the gardener," Jesus delivers a sermon about this moral significance of the garden, explaining that he is in truth the gardener, for

> Mannys hartt is my gardin here.
> Therin I sow sedys of vertu all the yere;
> The fowle wedes and vicys, I reynd up by the rote.
> Whan that gardin is watteryd with teris clere,
> Than spring vertuus, and smelle full sote.[23]

Despite the fact that the monk Daun John is, by vocation at least, a man of God, and despite the fact that Chaucer carefully observes that the monk is thirty years old (26)—the number of spiritual perfection and the age, said Saint Augustine, of all the inhabitants of heaven when they will be resurrected from the dead at the Last Judgment[24]—he is obviously miscast for the role of resurrected Saviour. The garden of the Shipman's Tale encloses not those virtuous seeds of the Digby play, but the rank corruption of a man and a woman ruthlessly preoccupied with the business of finances and of sex. The single gratuitous reference to the "mayde child" who has accompanied the merchant's wife to that garden—a child who conveniently disappears for the rest of the narrative—emphasizes the defiled innocence of the meeting and of its garden setting.

It is possible that the "mayde childe" is part of the Resurrection pattern as well, an allusion to "the other Mary," who in the Gospel and in the liturgical Easter dramas accompanied Mary Magdalen to Christ's sepulchre.[25] For it is clear that Chaucer makes of the merchant's wife a Magdalen playing a perverse version of a *Hortulanus* play, a play in which the prostitute-made-saint is replaced by a contemporary Magdalen who will contract to prostitute herself both within and without her marriage. Chaucer's Magdalen weeps not at the sight of the empty grave clothes in the tomb as did the Magdalen of the Easter dramas, but at the thought of her unpaid clothing bills. Lamenting in "sorwe" and "drede," the merchant's wife bemoans by that "ilke Lord that for us bledde" (178) that she must find a hundred franks to pay for the new clothes she has bought (so she says) for her husband's honor, "myself for to arraye" (179). The conniving and adulterous wife sounds more than a little like the Mary Magdalen before conversion, like, for example, the Magdalen of the *Benediktbeuern Passion Play* who sings thus of the world's fleshly pleasures:

The world's pleasure is sweet and agreeable,
Its society is delightful and elegant.
There are allurements of the world for which I long . . .
I'll pamper my body, caring for nothing else;
I'll deck it out in an array of brilliant finery.[26]

The Magdalen of the *Benediktbeuern* play will later, like the doubting Thomas of the *Towneley* cycle, put aside all worldly garments at the moment when the sinner becomes saint. And at this point, so a rubric from the play text instructs, Mary Magdalen was "to put aside her worldly attire and put on a black mantle; and let the lover withdraw."[27] Chaucer's Magdalen, of course, will never withdraw from the world in black mantle and tears of repentance, but remains resolutely throughout the tale an adulteress who shamelessly sells her favors and delights in her finery. For the Shipman's Tale's audience, this ironic identification of the merchant's wife with Mary Magdalen is aided by a mental association which Chaucer established in his introductory portrait of the teller he finally decided to assign to the tale: The Shipman's barge, Chaucer has told us in the General Prologue, "ycleped was the Maudelayne" (410).

It is not only a remembered name but a remembered image which Chaucer asks his audience to call to mind as they hear of that perverse Resurrection appearance in a garden. In nearly any English parish church in the fourteenth century, a worshipper could see before him the familiar icon of Christ's appearance to the Magdalen, that traditional image of entreaty and stern rejection called the *Noli me tangere*.²⁸ The Magdalen reaches out joyfully to touch the risen Lord as Jesus recoils from her, raising his right hand in a gesture both distancing and blessing. *"Noli me tangere,"* Christ says to Mary Magdalen in the Gospel and in the Resurrection plays,²⁹ as he urges Mary not to rely on the tangible proof of the sensory world, but to believe in the spiritual mystery. Much as the lamb ludicrously placed in a child's bed inverts Nativity images in *The Second Shepherd's Play*,³⁰ Chaucer's meeting between monk and merchant's wife is a precisely inverted image of the *Noli me tangere*, the most outrageous moment in Chaucer's comic perversion of the Easter drama. For instead of cautioning "touch me not" the monk responds to the wife's offers of services in bed with quick and forthright action:

> And with that word he caughte hire by the flankes,
> And hire embraceth harde, and kiste hire ofte.
>
> (202–03)

This perverse recognition scene, in which Christ is played by a lecherous monk and Mary Magdalen by an adulterous wife with a shrewd business sense, creates a comic inversion of a *Hortulanus* play, but it is a parody that comments ruefully on its own imperfections even as it entertains. With a single early-morning embrace in a garden, Chaucer juxtaposes the amoral world of the fabliau for an instant with the moral universe— and the implications are serious. As Chaucer has told us from the beginning, such "salutaciouns" may pass like the shadow on a wall, but must finally be paid for.

The parodic sub-drama continues in the Shipman's Tale narrative as Chaucer shifts the dramatic icon from garden to counting house. The merchant's wife hurries from the monk's embrace to the door of the room where her husband sits occupied with his record books and his tallies. *"Quy la?"* inquires the husband. And the wife replies, "Peter! it am I." The significance of the name of Peter for the Reverend Skeat lay in its proof that "even women used to swear."³¹ But it is not altogether clear whether the name is an oath by Saint Peter, appropriately invoked here before a locked door, or whether it is the actual name of Chaucer's merchant. Chaucer and his audience knew from Easter sermons and from Resurrection plays both liturgical and vernacular, that it was to Peter that Mary Magdalen ran with the news of Christ's Resurrection. Although Christ in the Gospels merely instructed Mary to bear the news *"ad fratres meos"* (to my brethren), medieval texts almost always specify that Mary went directly to Peter, the tormented disciple who had thrice betrayed his Lord. The angel at the abandoned tomb told Mary to go to Peter, explains the Middle English *Southern Passion*, in order to save him from wanhope ("and that he ne come in wanhope; / the aungel nempnede his name").[32] Thus it is that Peter is nearly as inevitable a character in the *Hortulanus* drama as the Marys and Christ. Rubrics in the *Chester* and the *N-Town* Resurrection plays indicate that Mary Magdalen goes directly from the garden to Peter; in the *Towneley* mystery play cycle, it is Christ Himself who instructs Mary Magdalen,

> By name peter thou call and say that I shall be
> Before hym and them all myself in galyle.[33]

The only other disciple, by the way, who regularly appears in the Latin and vernacular *Hortulanus* plays is John, Christ's beloved disciple, who races Peter to the tomb,[34] and who may well explain Chaucer's choice of name for the monk, Daun John. The merchant's wife, who is otherwise nameless in the tale, once swears an oath by Mary which, by creating the same ambiguity of syntax as the Peter oath, suggests her own appropriate name in the Resurrection paradigm: "Marie, I deffie the false monk . . ." (402) she tells Daun John after she discovers the monk's double dealings. The merchant's wife is, as we have seen, not a type of Mary Virgin, but of the Mary who was a sinner, an unrepentant Magdalen. The comic mix-up of roles signaled by these names—Mary embracing the beloved disciple in a garden, then plotting to betray Peter the betrayer—all these things were, I suspect, part of the humor of Chaucer's witty appropriation of the Resurrection drama.

Thus the fabliau plot that Chaucer has created at once evokes and is opposed by the Resurrection drama unknowingly and burlesquely enacted by monk, wife, and merchant in the Shipman's Tale. There is no miracle but that of an unscrupulous ruse; there is no good news brought back breathlessly from the tomb. The characters in the tale may hear Mass and swear to adultery on their breviaries, but the comic human creatures of the tale are, of course, oblivious to what Chaucer knew, and to what the hearers of the tale knew only too well: The Resurrection dramas do end in the counting house, for the plays of Christ's Resurrection and Pentecostal charge to his apostles are followed in the mystery play cycles by the play of Doomsday, by that play in which each man and each woman is resurrected from the dead, and in which, as the *Towneley* "Last Judgment" says, "ilk man for his self / shall answere for his dede."[35]

When the merchant's wife in annoyance with husband and ledger books blurts out, "The devel have part on alle swiche rekenynges" (218), she has unwittingly pronounced God's own judgment on them all. She invokes, in fact, precisely that justice which is so conspicuously absent from the resolution of Chaucer's fabliau plot. The puzzling lack of temporal justice which many critics have interpreted as evidence of

Chaucer's light intentions in the Shipman's Tale actually serves, I believe, to emphasize the violation of order in the tale and even to suggest to Chaucer's audience the seriousness of that other cosmic justice beyond the false world of fabliau. The triumphant answer of the wife who cheerfully promises to pay "abedde" for all debits satisfies the husband of Chaucer's tale, as indeed all clever wives seem to satisfy cuckolded husbands in the fabliaux. But Chaucer's bawdry is undercut by a drama and a resonance of implication which renders that disordered resolution as morally reprehensible as it is ludicrous. For if Chaucer's characters have no fates beyond the pages of the tale, his audience did. In God's own counting-house the final awe-full tally would be made, and those who had not clothed themselves in Christ's array would not live again, but would be, as Chaucer's Parson relentlessly reminded them, cast miserably into hell, "naked in body as of clothyng, save the fyr in which they brenne." And where then will be, asks the Parson, "the gaye robes, and the softe shetes, and the smale shertes?" (195–96).

The art of the Shipman's Tale lies not in the sinners-in-the-hands-of-an-angry-God rhetoric of the Parson who, approaching the very gates of the symbolic city of his pilgrimage, speaks with the bluntness of his urgency, but rather lies in Chaucer's devastating, comic vision. Chaucer's first brief warning of judgment to come, the echoing rhymes of "pay" and "array" with their homiletic associations, the repetitions of "arising" on a third day which set the stage for a comic Resurrection drama complete with Magdalen, beloved disciple (who has usurped his host's wife as well as his Lord's place), and a betrayed Peter—all these things create the brilliantly ironic moral of Chaucer's fabliau: "We must pay for our array." The Shipman's Tale is a ribald story told with relish and with skill, but it bears compressed within it a drama which yokes that ribaldry to a serious context of meaning. Chaucer invites us to laugh at these scheming characters and at ourselves—but also to remember that other garden and that final counting-house.

THE BOOK OF THE DUCHESS:
SECULAR ELEGY OR
RELIGIOUS VISION?

JAMES I. WIMSATT

This paper represents an attempt to rationalize an apparent incompatibility in what I have written on *The Book of the Duchess*. On the one hand, I have looked to its French background, which has led me to emphasize its close ties to fourteenth-century French secular love poetry. On the other, I have dealt with the religious significance that shows up when one studies its text in the light of Christian tradition.[1] Although the treatments seem to me separately sound, when brought together they appear to postulate quite different readings of the poem. This is a paradox. In literature, of course, paradox is often good, and in literary study it is not necessarily bad. In this case, exploration of it is at least interesting.

My approach to the problem is through consideration of poetic kind, genre. One's interpretation of a work is, as E. D. Hirsch, Jr., asserts, "genre-bound." "An individual trait," he states, "will be rootless and meaningless unless it is perceived as a component in a whole meaning." The reader will make implicit assumptions about the "kind of utterance" he confronts—its "intrinsic genre"—and he will understand its parts in accordance with them.[2] On the basis of these he will make decisions about potentially ambiguous statements. Let me offer a simple example from *The Book of the Duchess*. At the beginning of the poem the narrator says that he has suffered a sickness for eight years; but, he continues, let us pass over that, "For there is phisicien but oon / That may me hele."[3] Now I suppose that we have only to be familiar with basic conventions of English poetry to understand that *sickness* and *physician* in this context are meant in a figurative sense. The narrator does not have leprosy or angina, and he is not looking to some notable leech of unmatched medical knowledge for a physical cure. However, recognizing the figurative nature of the expression does not wholly solve the interpreter's problems. For there are at least two figurative meanings, both widely attested in medieval literature, which may be applied to one's understanding of these words. In the one case, the sickness may be seen as moral and the physician as Christ. In the other, we may think of it as a love sickness, and the lady-love as the only potential healer.[4] The reader's interpretation will depend on the kind of poem he conceives he is confronting: if it is a love poem the metaphorical sickness will be of the heart; if a religious poem, it will be of the soul. Respectable modern interpretations of the work offer both readings, the one chosen depending not on the immediate context, which offers no definitive indication, but rather on the kind of poem the critic believes himself to be reading.

Similar elements throughout Chaucer's poem, it seems, invite on the one hand a secular reading, and on the other a religious interpretation. It is this ambiguity that my previous studies reflect, and that I look to determination of the poem's genre to resolve. I will cite a further, more complex, example. In *The Book of the Duchess,* after the dreamer speaks of his sickness and his sleeplessness, he tells of reading the tale of Seys and Alcyone, which leads to his sleep and dream. In his dream he awakens in a springtime setting and soon finds himself riding out with the Emperor Octavian on a hunt for a hart, which is chased and lost. The dreamlikeness of the action invites, almost demands, that we look for figurative significance. But again there is more than one possibility. Who is the Emperor Octavian here? Is he to be understood in the context of the hunt-of-love tradition as Octavian the medieval romance hero leading a hunt of love for a lost "heart"?[5] Or is he the historical Emperor Octavian of Rome, seen as he sometimes was as a figure for Christ, here hunting the human soul? One may also see the hart as Christ, another common figure, and the hunters of Octavian as representative of his Roman crucifiers.[6] Again, the reader's perception of the genre will guide the interpretation.

The center of the poem, the Black Knight's complaint and tale of his love, is no less equivocal. When the Knight describes his first sight of White and exclaims, "By God, and by his halwes twelve, / Hyt was my swete" (831–32), how are we to understand the elaborate expletive here? Or how about his words a few lines later which echo a statement of Christ's describing heaven?

To gete her love no ner nas he
That woned at hom, than he in Ynde;
The formest was alway behynde.[7]

In both cases the assertions about White carry potential ecclesiological reference, whereby she can be seen as in some manner as a figure for the Church. Depending on the literary type he thinks he is confronting, the reader will take such reference seriously and see it as a part of the characterization of White, or he will dismiss it as playful or simply accidental.

Were these passages that I have cited isolated examples of secular/spiritual ambiguity, with one or the other type of meaning clearly predominant in the poem, then we could dismiss the one and embrace the other, or at least find the less prominent dependent on the more prominent. However, it can be shown, I think, that there are similar examples throughout, involving words, lines, and passages. As a consequence, the whole of *The Book of the Duchess* seems susceptible to interpretation either as a poem that centers on human love, or as one that is concerned primarily with spiritual matters. This is the problem on which I bring to bear a consideration of genre. This supplies no quick solution, however. There exists a secular/spiritual ambiguity in medieval type to match the ambiguity found in the individual parts of Chaucer's poem. There is an established medieval classification of secular love vision that the *Duchess* seems to fit into, and there is also a family of religious visions that use conventional love imagery to which the elegy also seems to conform. We thus seem to be involved in a hermeneutic circle, to use Hirsch's characterization.[8] We move from the parts to the whole, then back to the parts, with no resolution. The ambiguous elements of the poem match the equivocal generic expectations that we develop from the text.

Fortunately, there are extrinsic materials that, used judiciously, may properly be called upon in determining more specifically the typal affiliations of the *Duchess*. The abundance of sources that Chaucer used, which have been quite thoroughly identified, provide one kind of these. Relevant historical material and Christian tradition supply another. It happens that these involve the poem more deeply in ambiguity. But if we follow them through we find the ambiguity more interesting and revealing, and finally less confusing. We will look to the sources first.

The sizeable list of writers whom Chaucer drew on for his elegy indicates his early wide reading; it includes Ovid, Statius, Virgil, the two poets of the *Roman de la Rose*, Machaut, and Froissart.[9] By far the most important of these in quantitative terms is Chaucer's older contemporary, Guillaume de Machaut. A dozen of his lyrics and long *dits amoureux* provide situation and language to such an extent that the *Duchess* has been called a servile imitation of the Frenchman's work.[10] Chaucer's poem has been defended successfully against this charge. Nevertheless, as I have tried to show elsewhere, Machaut's *dits,* which represent a distinct development with a numerous progeny, are very nearly allied to Chaucer's elegy; the données of the English work are remarkably similar to those of Machaut's poems. In both cases, experiences of an individualized narrator who interacts with other individuals, generally his superiors, are central. Personifications are few and are subservient to the semirealistic narrative—they are not, as they are in the *Roman de la Rose,* vital elements of philosophical analysis. The idealized nature settings are suitable to remarkable happenings, but marvels do not dominate. The narrative tends to be static, with courtly conversation the main mode of exposition, and there is a great emphasis on courteous behavior. The vicissitudes of the love experience, described in a standard jargon, is the great subject. Such matters show clearly that Chaucer's elegy is associated in kind with the family of love narratives originated by Machaut.

We can be even more specific about the generic relationships here. There is a developed sub-genre of Machauvian *dit* to which the *Duchess* more particularly belongs. The poems of this group I have called narratives of complaint-and-comfort.[11] These works turn on the complaint of a lover over separation from his beloved, the lament being followed by a proffer of comfort from a counsellor or the loved one. In the *Duchess* Chaucer uses three Machaut *dits* of this kind, the most important for his overall plan being the *Dit de la Fonteinne amoureuse*. Machaut wrote the *Fonteinne amoureuse* to comfort the Duke of Berry in his imprisonment in England, where he was separated from his young wife. Like the English elegy, it involves a somewhat awkward narrator, representing the poet, who comforts a young lover, the ducal patron thinly disguised. Chaucer's work was recognized by his contemporaries as a complaint poem in the Machaut tradition; this is definitively proven by a later French work, Froissart's *Dit dou Bleu Chevalier,* which unmistakably imitates both the *Duchess* and Machaut's poems in its offering solace to another ducal patron.[12] There are several additional highly regarded members of this sub-genre in still later literary generations. All of the poems evidently are addressed to troubled patrons. The last of the line is Spenser's *Daphnaïda*, called by Tucker Brooke, "Spenser's most consummate tribute to medieval art and to his great predecessor."[13]

The Book of the Duchess, then, is a *dit amoureux* of the complaint-and-comfort type, and we will expect to find the kinds of meanings in the poem that are characteristic of the type. The genre identification should help decide whether "physician" is a metaphor for Christ or for the lady, and whether the hart signifies the lost beloved or the soul. For the poems in the Machaut tradition it seems that the secular reading is indicated. In these works a physician is a figure for the beloved lady,[14] and it is lovers who are presented as hunters and prey. In them the lover invokes God to emphasize his strong feelings rather than to spiritualize the subject matter,[15] and the very occasional biblical echoes carry little evident religious suggestion. References which appear equivocal in the *Duchess* thus do not usually seem equivocal in the French *dits.* The *Fonteinne amoureuse* and Chaucer's other models in the type, on the face of it at least, do not seem susceptible to a religious reading, nor is there much which suggests that Froissart and the others who later wrote complaint-and-comfort poems picked up spiritual meanings from Chaucer or Machaut.

Seen as a *dit amoureux,* therefore, *The Book of the Duchess* will have a secular interpretation. As such a poem, it submits to the reading that the major line of criticism has given it. In the main, critics have emphasized its character as an elegy for an impressive and beautiful lady, Blanche of Lancaster, offering human comfort to her bereft knight, John of Gaunt, and thence to all her admirers. In his influential essay on the work, Bertrand Bronson expresses this point of view very well. In his conclusion he avers that the "lesson" of the elegy "is the age-old one of resignation and human acceptance of life and death, of thankfulness for past felicity, of the comfort of precious memories, of the dignity of self-mastery in spite of Fortune's 'false draughtes dyvers.'"[16] The other works of the type submit to a similar interpretation. In a medieval way, they deal with the handling of human problems—with "coping." As one would expect from Chaucer, he contrives a pattern of consolation with more finesse and imagination than did either his model, Machaut, or his successors in the complaint-and-comfort group, but the intent of all is much the same, to offer human consolation for an earthly separation.

Where does this take us with the *Duchess?* Establishing its place among *dits amoureux* does confirm its standard interpretation as a poem concerned with human love and consolation. Does this rule out a religious interpretation? Within the framework adopted for the investigation here, it may seem that it does. We have assumed that meanings will be understood as they are components of a generic whole, and we have found that the potential spiritual readings are not realized in the genre to which we have assigned Chaucer's poem. *Dits amoureux* do not exhibit a notable secular/spiritual ambiguity. There is, however, at least one way in which the spiritual meanings could still be realized; this is if the *Duchess* belongs also to a second genre which will accommodate them. Such a second independent genre seems improbable; it is not a common literary phenomenon. Nevertheless, I believe there are good arguments for finding a second genre in *The Book of the Duchess.* In making a case for it I will call especially on the second class of extrinsic material I mentioned above, the relevant historical material and the Christian tradition.

To begin with, I would note that there are obvious good reasons for not dismissing a potential religious interpretation out of hand. As has been indicated, the apparent secular/spiritual ambiguities are not common in the French *dits amoureux.* But they are pervasive in Chaucer's poem. It is therefore much more difficult to attribute them to chance or to incidental word-play. Furthermore, there is the impressive insistence of Chaucer's narrator that his dream has transcendent significance. Granting that the prayer for sleep that precedes his dreaming seems frivolous, one may still find his statement about the dream quite seriously intended:

Such a lust anoon me took
To slepe, that ryght upon my book

Y fil aslepe, and therwith even
Me mette so ynly swete a sweven,
So wonderful, that never yit
Y trowe no man had the wyt
To konne wel my sweven rede;
No, not Joseph, withoute drede,
Of Egipte, he that redde so
The kynges metynge Pharao,
No more than koude the lest of us;
Ne nat skarsly Macrobeus,
(He that wrot al th'avysyoun
That he mette, kyng Scipioun).

                                                        (273–86)

Though claims of important meaning occur in other *dits amoureux,* in no
other of these poems and in no other of Chaucer's dream poems is the
claim of meaning so emphatic. Nor is it expressed in terms so suggestive
of supernatural content. To describe the dream as "ynly swete" is to
associate it by way of conventional terminology with medieval narrative
of edifying spiritual content. Beneath the husk of the grain and the shell
of the nut is the sweet kernel within.[17] The narrator elaborates accordingly: it was more than a revelation of things to come such as Joseph
might interpret; it was more than a cosmic fable such as Macrobius could
gloss; it was quite beyond the wit—the rational powers—of any man. The
manifest suggestion is that the dream embodied ineffable spiritual truth.

The narrator awakens in his dream to the song of birds. The description of their singing and of the ideal atmospheric conditions evokes a
paradisal locale, thus continuing to suggest that the dream has spiritual
content. Chaucer's sources for these lines contain hints of such matters,
but they remain hints, and they are not carried through. His description
of the birds' song is of critical importance to my case:

Me thoghte thus: that hyt was May,
And in the dawenynge I lay
(Me mette thus) in my bed al naked,
And loked forth, for I was waked
With smale foules a gret hep
That had affrayed me out of my slep,
Thorgh noyse and swetnesse of her song.
And, as me mette, they sate among
Upon my chambre roof wythoute,
Upon the tyles, overal aboute,
And songen, everych in hys wyse,
The moste solempne servise
By noote, that ever man, y trowe,
Had herd; for som of hem song lowe,

Som high, and al of oon acord.
To telle shortly, att oo word.
Was never herd so swete a steven,—
But hyt had be a thyng of heven,—
So mery a soun, so swete entewnes,
That certes, for the toun of Tewnes,
I nolde but I had herd hem synge;
For al my chambre gan to rynge
Thurgh syngynge of her armonye.
For instrument nor melodye
Was nowhere herd yet half so swete,
Nor of acord half so mete.

                                                    (291–316)

In the series of superlatives here, particularly significant is the description of the birds' "servise"—a religious term—as the most solemn that
man had ever heard. Also striking is the statement that there was never
such a sweet song except of a heavenly thing. In the source in the *Roman
de la Rose* the term *service* is used,[18] but Chaucer adds "moste solempne";
and whereas in the *Roman* the birds are said to sing like heavenly
angels—a simile—Chaucer states directly that only the heavenly equalled
the birds' song. More important, indeed quite central, to my argument is
the pun in the next lines in the narrator's statement that he would not
have given up hearing the birds "for the toun of Tewnes." The double
meaning that may be found here directly mirrors the secular/spiritual
ambiguity that seems to be present throughout the poem. As I see it, the
religious meanings in the pun supply a key clue to the second genre of
the elegy. The pun therefore provides the setting-off point for the re-
mainder of this paper.

The most obvious meaning for "toun of Tewnes," particularly as modern editors have capitalized it, is "city of Tunis," referring to the African
city, the successor of Carthage, that was a wealthy center of medieval
Islam. By this reading Chaucer's dreamer states that he would not trade
his dream for the riches of Tunis, this being an appropriately grandiose
material price to put on an experience that has human value.[19] But there
are even more suggestive possibilities. Bernard F. Huppé and D. W.
Robertson, Jr., note that "toun of Tewnes" in Middle English also can
signify "tune of tunes" and "town of towns." The former is equivalent to
Song of Songs or Canticle of Canticles, the name of the biblical love
poem, and the latter evokes New Jerusalem as presented in the Book of
Revelations, the Apocalypse.[20] These suggestions may well strike a
reader of the poem as overingenious, particularly if he sees it as confined
to the *dit amoureux* type and therefore offering no context for the punning meanings. Nevertheless, the more closely one inspects the poem
and its relevant materials, the more probable it seems that these mean-

ings point to another genre to which the *Duchess* belongs. They connect Chaucer's vision poem with biblical visions and other works that are highly appropriate to the occasion of the poem, the death of Blanche of Lancaster. Furthermore, their potential validity and effect are enhanced by other uses in the *Duchess* of the two books of the Bible in question. Before developing these points, though, I want to discuss an intriguing piece of secondary evidence supporting the puns that has emerged from my study of the manuscripts of Guillaume de Machaut's *dit, Le Jugement dou Roy de Behaingne,* which is line-for-line the most important source of the *Duchess.*

The *Roman de la Rose* is Chaucer's primary source for the birds' song at the beginning of the dream. In this section he also draws importantly on a similar nature passage in Machaut's *Roy de Behaingne.*[21] For the problem here one word in the Machaut passage that describes the birds' song is crucial. In all manuscripts of the poem but one it is said that the birds sing "pour la douceur dou joli *temps* nouvel" (21) [because of the sweetness of the lovely new *time*]. In manuscript J alone, the manuscript that seems by all odds the closest to the one Chaucer used, the birds sing not because of the "new time," but rather for the "joli chant nouvel" [the lovely new *song*].[22] "New song," I suspect, helped to inspire Chaucer's puns and perhaps even suggested material for the elegy, for it evokes both Canticles and the Apocalypse.

"Canticum novum," "new song," has strong biblical resonance; the phrase appears in three books of the Bible: Psalms, six times; Isaiah, once; and the Apocalypse, twice.[23] Its most vivid and celebrated use is in the Apocalypse where the 144,000 virgins sing the "new song" before the throne of the Lamb (14:3). The medieval currency of this scriptural scene is indicated, for instance, in the Middle English *Pearl* where the Maiden speaks of the virgins' "note full nwe," and of their "nwe songe" before the Lamb.[24] Of what exactly do the virgins sing? The usual gloss has it that the new song concerns "the Incarnation, for which the world exults and the angels sang."[25] In medieval tradition the Incarnation also is usually seen as the primary subject of the *Canticum canticorum.* Inevitably *Canticum canticorum* and *Canticum novum*—no doubt the two most famous *cantica* of the Bible—were associated. Thus Hugh of St. Cher says, "What else is this New Song but the desire of the Incarnation. . . . Whence the book that begins, 'Let him kiss me with the kiss of his mouth,' in which the desire of the Incarnation is expressed, is called the Canticle of Canticles."[26]

In his source in the *Roman de la Rose,* then, Chaucer read of birds who sang a "beautiful service" like "heavenly angels"; in the passage of Machaut that he uses he found birds singing a "new song," the song preeminent among songs celebrating the Incarnation, appropriate to angels and the virgins before the throne of the Lamb. Canticles and the

Apocalypse simultaneously are evoked, leading the English poet, we may think, to suggest in a pun that the solemn service of his angelic birds was beyond even the heavenly songs of those inspired books. His dreamer would not have foregone listening to the birds for the "toun of tewnes."

This evidence from Machaut is arresting; in the manuscript that by all evidence is closest to Chaucer's source manuscript, the birds' song has anagogic implications directly pertinent to both spiritual meanings in the double pun, and this is the only manuscript in which these implications are present. The support this reading offers, though indirect, is of a rare and valuable kind, involving as it does external evidence applicable to a major poetic crux. But of course it does not entail certitude about the puns; it only contributes to the case for them. More compelling support comes from an assessment of Chaucer's certain and probable uses of Canticles and the Apocalypse in the elegy proper.

Direct allusions to the Canticles, some of which Friedrich Klaeber noted eighty years ago,[27] appear especially in the description of Fair White. Her neck, like that of the bride of Canticles, seems a tower of ivory (*BD* 946; Cant. 7:4). Her complexion, like the bridegroom's, is white and red (*BD* 905; Cant. 5:10). She is said to be unique like the phoenix (981–84) in words that recall the uniqueness of the bride: "One is my dove, my perfect one is but one, she is the only one of her mother" (6:8). And just as White would be the chief mirror among ten thousand (971–74), so the bridegroom is declared to be "chosen out of thousands" (10:10), and the bride "most blessed among sixty queens, eighty concubines, and maidens without number" (6:7–8).[28]

There also seems to be echoes of Canticles in the hunt section, as one perceptive critic has noticed.[29] The major elements of Chaucer's hunt sequence appear in one brief passage of Canticles (2:8–13). At the beginning of this passage the bridegroom is said to be like a hart which leaps over the hills, evoking for commentators the bridegroom of Psalm 18 (6–7), who in the manner of the sun traverses the sky.[30] The Canticles bridegroom next pauses to stand outside the windows of the bride. In familiar words he calls her to come out, "for winter now is past, the rain is over and gone. The flowers have appeared in our land, the time of pruning is come. The voice of the turtle is heard in our land. The fig tree hath put forth her green figs." After this summons he seems to leave, for she shortly calls him to "return," to be like a "young hart" (2:17). The *Duchess* offers an impressive parallel to this part of Canticles in the section which follows the description of the birds' song. The dreamer sees the sun shining through his chamber windows in an inviting paradisal atmosphere. He goes out to join in a hunt of the hart, but the hart disappears into the wood. Then he wanders into a land where the "poverty" (410) of winter is forgotten, myriad flowers bloom, and "al the woode was waxen grene: Swetnesse of dew had mad hyt waxe" (414–15).

The Apocalypse is also directly echoed in Chaucer's poem. This book's subject matter, of course, is the last days: Antichrist, the Second Coming, and the Millennium. In the Black Knight's lament he at one point describes himself in terms of those who according to the Apocalypse are tormented by scorpion-like locusts in the last days. He cries,

> The pure deth ys so ful my foo
> That I wolde deye, hyt wolde not soo;
> For whan I folwe hyt, hit wol flee;
> I wolde have hym, hyt nyl nat me.
>
> (583–86)

This is simply a versification of Apocalypse 9:6, which Chaucer translates in the Parson's Tale: "They shullen folwe deeth, and they shul nat fynde hym; and they shul desiren to dye, and deeth shall flee fro hem" (216). There are related apocalyptic suggestions in the figurative chess game in which the scorpion-like Fortune triumphs over the Black Knight's queen.[31]

The elegy's most striking echo of the Apocalypse is one which Huppé and Robertson have perceived.[32] Late in his book Saint John reports that he saw "New Jerusalem, coming down out of heaven from God, made ready as a bride adorned for her husband" (Apoc. 12:2). He goes to a high mountain to see descending the bright-walled city with its pearly gates (21:10). In *The Book of the Duchess,* similarly, after the Black Knight reveals to the dreamer that Fair White is dead, the dream comes to a conclusion with a vision of a castle:

> With that me thoghte that this kyng
> Gan homwardes for to ryde
> Unto a place, was there besyde,
> Which was from us but a lyte.
> A long castel with walles white,
> Be seynt Johan! on a ryche hil.
>
> (1314–19)

Here is another outstanding example of the pervasive secular/spiritual ambiguity in the poem. Chaucer hides in these lines an enigma with not one but two solutions. The first solution parallels an acrostic in Machaut's *Fonteinne amoureuse,* in which the poet hides his own name and that of the Duke of Berry, whose troubles are the subject of his poem. So in lines 1318–19 Chaucer ingeniously inserts the Christian names of the couple who provide his subject, John and Blanche ("white"), together with their major titles, Richmond ("ryche hil") and Lancaster ("long castel"). But this is only half. In the same lines and words, Chaucer also invokes the author of the Apocalypse ("seynt Johan") and points to his shining heavenly city on its height.

Among all the ambiguities of the poem the most significant phraseological ones are those which open and close the dream, the "toun of Tewnes" at one end and the white-walled castle at the other. The former indicates the value of the vision and the latter designates its end, its goal. Both point, on the one hand, to the human vision concerned with comforting John on the death of Blanche, the dream which the narrator finds worth the wealth of Tunis, and, on the other hand, to the Christian vision that looks heavenward, the vision which the narrator thinks of a value comparable to the Canticle of Canticles and New Jerusalem. The ambiguities in these two passages epitomize the whole of Chaucer's poem, which may be seen as one great serious pun with distinct secular and spiritual referents, or as one large enigma, with secular and spiritual solutions, both valid. The genre which provides the frame of reference for the spiritual interpretation has its prototypes in the biblical books these passages evoke, the Apocalypse and the Canticle of Canticles. Other important medieval works in the genre are the Eden cantos of Dante's *Purgatorio* and the Middle English *Pearl*.

The meaning found in this kind of work is definitely spiritual. It is unlike, however, the meaning which Christian commentators found in secular epic and romance narrative, in which they saw valuable allegorical lessons hidden beneath attractive fictions. It is also unlike the historical books of the Bible, in which exegetes found allegorical significance embodied in the literal events described. The genre I am proposing is, as in the latter case, biblical; but it is characterized by texts that on their face are figurative, as Canticles and the Apocalypse were seen as figurative. Canticles was thought of as a poem on the Incarnation in the guise of a wholly metaphorical marriage song, and the Apocalypse as a revelatory vision presented figuratively.

The works of this genre present a kind of visionary experience that is definable in the terms of medieval theology; the kind of perception that exegetes postulated for Saint John's narrative in the Apocalypse seems also applicable to Canticles and the medieval works in the genre. The definition of it used by commentators originates in Saint Augustine's characterization of the three types of human perception in his commentary on Genesis. Francis X. Newman, in applying Augustine's classifications to *The Divine Comedy*, explains the three types succinctly:

The first . . . is the *visio corporalis*, the literal sight of the eye or, more generally, knowledge by means of the external senses. The second is the *visio spiritualis* or *imaginativa*, knowledge by means of the imagination. In "spiritual" vision we do not see bodies themselves, but images that have corporeal shape without corporeal substance. Dreams, for example, are a sub-class of *visio spiritualis*. The third and highest of the classes of vision is *intellectualis*, the direct cognition of realities such as God, the angels, *caritas*, etc., which have neither corporeal substance nor corporeal shape.[33]

Augustine cites the Apocalypse as the specific example of the second mode, the spiritual vision, and exegetes after him were given to explaining the Apocalypse in such terms.[34]

In view of the contents of Canticles it would seem appropriate to classify it with Saint John's vision as "spiritual." In discussions of Augustine's three modes of perception commentators do not refer to Canticles, perhaps because of the problems of interpretation that its erotic images and historical references present,[35] but in other contexts medieval writers associate its mode with that of the Apocalypse. Ambrose Autpert, for instance, finds that both books have the same kind of "mystical sacraments" hidden under a veil of figurative expression.[36] Other linkings of the two biblical texts that bear on the interpretation of the *Duchess* appear in three vernacular works: *Pearl, Purgatorio,* and a gloss on the French *dit,* the *Échecs amoureux.* The prose commentator on the *Échecs,* a love allegory, claims that the poem uses the same manner of speaking "in parables and indistinct figures" as Canticles and the Apocalypse employ.[37] The claim is of interest in the present discussion for its description of the mode of the two biblical books and for its association of them according to mode. It is also significant in its positing that a nonbiblical poem has spiritual meaning like that of divine works. The French poem itself and the specific interpretation assigned are not particularly relevant here. The *Échecs* does not, like *The Book of the Duchess,* betray on the surface potential spiritual meaning, nor does it make notable use of Canticles and the Apocalypse. More pertinent in these matters are *Pearl* and *Purgatorio,* which do use these books and have patent spiritual meaning.

The procession of the Church in cantos 29 to 31 of *Purgatorio* is based largely on the Apocalypse, with details at its very center coming from Canticles. Such salient features as the candlesticks that lead the procession, the elders who represent the books of the Bible, and the emblems of the evangelists are from the Apocalypse. The griffin who draws the cart of the Church is identified with the bridegroom of Canticles, and Beatrice appears on the cart in response to the reiterated summons of the bridegroom, "Veni, sponsa" [come, my spouse].[38] *Pearl,* too, uses the two books prominently. The extensive depiction of New Jersualem is wholly drawn from the Apocalypse. And from the beginning of the poem the Maiden is closely associated with the spotless bride of Canticles.[39] She reports having been called to heaven in words of the bridegroom:

Cum hyder to me, my lemman swete,
For mote ne spot is non in þe.

(763–64)

The two poets readily assimilate material from the two biblical books to their poetic visions.

Newman argues persuasively that Dante's three canticles present in turn Saint Augustine's three modes of perception, with *Purgatorio*, like the Apocalypse that it uses, representing *visio spiritualis*. The vision in *Pearl*, probably inspired by Dante's scene in Eden and heavily dependent on the Apocalypse, seems of much the same order. Since Augustine saw dreams as included among spiritual visions, *Pearl*'s use of the dream reinforces this supposition. Though Chaucer's elegy for Blanche differs more obviously in content from both of these works than they do from each other, and though its use of the Apocalypse is not so integral, *Pearl* and Dante's pageant still are near relatives of the *Duchess* in its religious aspect. All three have common biblical sources and substantial similarity in the manner of presentation. Each of the three is dominated by an impressive female personage, who while alive was very important to the central male figure. Furthermore, as I have shown in articles on Blanche and Beatrice, all three females are analogically related to the Virgin Mary by means of Christian reference that includes Apocalypse and Canticles.[40] Since the Virgin is the archetype of the perfected soul, the analogy imputes to Blanche a heavenly status to match that established directly for Beatrice and the Pearl Maiden in their poems.

What I posit, then, for *The Book of the Duchess* is membership in a genre of religious vision which provides a frame-of-reference for its potential spiritual meanings, just as the complaint-and-comfort genre provides a frame for its secular significance. The two highly figurative books of the Bible are the archetypes of this religious genre. For several reasons, I posit for the *Duchess* in addition an especially close link with Canticles. In the first place, in Church tradition Canticles provided prime *topoi* for consolatory writings on the order of Chaucer's elegy. Moreover, the historical circumstances of Blanche's life and death made reference to it especially suitable. And finally the biblical song supplies the one likely precedent for Chaucer's composing in two genres.

I will elaborate a bit on these points. In using Canticles in the elegy for Blanche Chaucer aligns the poem with a long Church tradition. From early time Canticles was employed by the Fathers and prominent churchmen in memorial literature to impute heavenly status to the departed. In a sermon in 392 after the death of Valentinian II, Saint Ambrose uses much of the phraseology of Canticles in dramatizing the ascent of the young emperor's soul. At the culmination of his description—to cite only a short passage—the *Logos* greets the soul with the exclamation of the *sponsus:* "How beautiful art thou, and how comely, my dearest, in delights" (Cant. 7:6); thereupon Valentinian's brother Gratian, already in heaven, runs forward to lead the newly arrived soul, while admiring angels praise Valentinian in the language of Canticles.[41]

Saint Jerome makes similar use of Canticles in a situation that is like Chaucer's. Chaucer writes to comfort his patron on the death of his wife, the devout Blanche. Jerome writes to comfort the son of his devout disciple Paula on her death. He suggests in the words of Canticles Paula's happiness at being called to heaven: "Immediately when she heard the bridegroom calling, 'Arise, come, my dearest, my beautiful one, my dove, for behold the winter is now past, the rain has gone,' joyfully she responded, 'Flowers have appeared in the land, the time of pruning is come.'" Subsequently, under the influence of such powerful models, similar uses became common.[42] The tradition lies behind the narration of the soul's ascent after death in the twelfth century *Liber meditationum,* known from its traditional ascription as "Augustine's Meditations," which remained popular in England through the Renaissance. Its effusive depiction of the happiness of the soul departing the world is a collection of allusions to Canticles. I quote a limited part from a sixteenth-century English translation:

> Happie is the soule, which departing from the earthlie body goeth directlie into heaven; secure it is and quiet, and feareth neither enimie, nor death. . . . How cheerefullie goeth she out, hasteneth, runneth, when al amazed she heareth her beloved saieng unto her on this wise: "Arise my love, my faire one, and come awaie. The flowers appeere in our earth; the time of the singing of the birds is come, and the voice of the turtle is heard in our land. . . . Come awaie my chosen, my faire one, my dove, mine unspotted one, my spouse, come awaie, and I will put thee into my bed chamber because I have longed after thy beautie.[43]

For the whole Middle Ages Canticles provided ready material for presenting the sanctified soul's entry into heaven.

Canticles thus was eminently suitable for the elegy for Blanche. The analogy between the Virgin and Fair White which Chaucer develops in the poem increases this suitability, for the bride of Canticles often was seen specifically as Mary, as well as the generic perfected soul. There is evidence, moreover, that the historical Blanche had a special devotion to Mary. She was born into an especially pious family on March 25,[44] the Feast of the Annunciation, and she and John of Gaunt were particular patrons of the Carmelite Order, which proudly identified itself as the Order of the Blessed Virgin Mary.[45] According to Thomas Speght, Chaucer's Elizabethan editor, it was on Blanche's request that Chaucer wrote his "A B C," a poetic prayer to the Virgin.[46] Appropriately, Blanche died on September 12, within the Octave of the Nativity of the Virgin. Her death occurred thereby in the one season of the year when Canticles figured in the Sarum liturgy.[47] Interpreted widely as concerned with the Assumption, the time of Mary's death and entry into

heaven, Canticles became prominent in the liturgy of that feast, celebrated August 15. By natural attraction, it entered into the Masses and
Offices of the Nativity of the Virgin, which followed closely on September 8. Thus the biblical poem, expressive of the Virgin's Assumption,
was prominent in the religious services the day Blanche died and its
anniversaries thereafter. The special historical appropriateness of the
Marian analogy and of Canticles to Chaucer's commemoration, then, is
also manifest.

Substantial evidence therefore suggests that Canticles is the work most
relevant to the spiritual meaning of the English elegy. The biblical poem
also supplies, I think, Chaucer's model for a composition with separate
and simultaneous secular and religious interpretations. Throughout the
history of Christian exegesis, the author of Canticles was said to be
Solomon, master of a thousand wives, and his poem a marriage song.
The book at the same time was seen as a love song of Christ, inspired like
all of the Bible by God. As a secular epithalamium it submits to a human
reading which includes topical reference; and as a poem of mystical
vision, it has spiritual interpretation. Just so, I propose, *The Book of the
Duchess* carries meaning as a topical love poem of the complaint-and-
comfort type, and also as a spiritual vision like *Pearl* and Dante's Eden
cantos.

The main obstacle to seeing such influence on Chaucer's handling of
genre is that commentators insisted that the images of Canticles have no
carnal reference. Isidore of Seville in an influential preface, for instance,
finds that in this book Solomon bypasses visible things and contemplates
the celestial under the semblance of the bride and bridegroom.[48] He
thus denies that Solomon was referring to his marital experiences. Such
a view as applied to *The Book of the Duchess* apparently would deny that
Blanche of Lancaster is a subject, even though her name is used in the
poem just as Solomon's is used in Canticles. In both cases this seems
extreme, and for Canticles it proved exegetically awkward. Interpreters
had a hard time getting past the physical referents of the kisses, breasts,
lips, cheeks, and thighs, as well as Solomon's name. I will adduce just one
example of their failure to exorcise the worldly; the example is a forceful
one, Saint William of St. Thierry, close friend of Saint Bernard of Clairvaux, and of course thoroughly orthodox. In glossing Canticles William
makes the usual comment that the spiritual sense carries the meaning
and that the images of carnal love are without significance. At the same
time, in apparent contradiction, he states that the book may be said to
concern Solomon's marriage to the daughter of Pharoah, and he subsequently supplies historical glosses for the two parts of his commentary,
finding, for instance, that the text speaks of Solomon's taking his wife
into his cellars and into his chamber.[49] Other exegetes likewise regularly
betray a sense that carnal referents are in some manner present,[50] and

my supposition is that Chaucer—less constrained by theoretical scruple—thought of Canticles as having a secular significance. He saw it, I think, as a poem somehow concerned with Solomon's marital experience, as well as a vision with meaning independent of such experience having to do with the Incarnation, Assumption, and other meetings of heaven with earth. I strongly suspect that it was Chaucer's model for composing in two genres at once, producing independent secular and spiritual interpretations.

While the Apocalypse is not as close in mode to the vision of the *Duchess* as is Canticles, on the spiritual plane at least it is of the same family. As a presentation of the final days, furthermore, it also has general relevance to the occasion of Chaucer's work, since all deaths are foreshadowings of the final end. Potentially, moreover, in Chaucer's mind it may have had specific relevance to the time. Viewing the end of the world as imminent was not unusual in the Middle Ages, nor in fourteenth-century England, and Blanche's death may have seemed to Chaucer a culminating sign. The 1360s had begun well for Europe and England. King John of France was a captive of war in England, and Pierre of Cyprus toured the Continent promoting a new crusade. But by the later years of the decade the great advantages England had gained from the Black Prince's victories evaporated in the diplomacy of delay practiced by Charles V of France, John's son. And Pierre's Crusade, together with most of the European crusading spirit, fizzled out after the capture and abandonment of Alexandria in 1365. Froissart says that Blanche died "young and pretty." She was also the mother of five Lancastrian children, very wealthy and powerful, and much beloved. Her death may have held powerful eschatological significance for the young Chaucer.[51]

Factors of history and scriptural tradition thus combine with the sense of the text to fix the *Duchess* in the genre of religious works that I have posited. There remains, of course, the problem of specifying its interpretation—what exactly it means spiritually. Certain aspects of this interpretation seem clear. As with Beatrice and the Pearl Maiden in their poems, the work celebrates the heavenly status of Blanche's soul, and in the celebration of her the Blessed Virgin and the Church also participate. The Knight, left behind, is a figure for desperate souls, not only of those deprived of Blanche's edifying influence, but of all souls in a world that seems cut off from the normal channels of grace flowing to the earth through the Virgin and the heavenly Church. For the narrator, as for Dante and the dreamer in *Pearl,* the experience described instructs him in the nature of the paradisal and heavenly. Of less certain significance are features like the hunt of the hart and the chess game with Fortune. The difficulty is not that one cannot find meanings, but that it is difficult to settle on a single meaning. Indeed, it seems characteristic of works in this religious genre which I have proposed that they submit to multiple interpretation. One wonders just how open-ended the *Pearl* poet meant the interpretation of his vision to be; modern readings of it certainly exhibit substantial diversity. The Canticle of Canticles had three well-established lines of exegesis with any number of possible variations. There is a lesser range of potential readings for Chaucer's elegy than for Canticles, no doubt, but it is quite conceivable that Chaucer did not intend that the spiritual interpretation be fixed for all of the poem. Without devoting much more attention to the individual parts of the work, in any event, I would be overbold to suggest a more precise reading.

What I have proposed already is bold enough. To imagine an author writing a poem in two genres at once, each demanding a distinct interpretation, taxes credulity. It suggests a tour de force like that involved in devising a complex jig-saw puzzle that can be put together in two ways to make two different and coherent pictures. Yet I am proposing more than a tour de force. For it seems that *The Book of the Duchess* not only is coherent in both types that it embodies, but also that it is an artistically impressive example of both. Undoubtedly, it is the best of the very respectable group of French and English complaint-and-comfort poems, offering human comfort for human separation. And as a figurative presentation with spiritual significance, it seems no unworthy companion for its impressive biblical and vernacular fellows. Were the claim made for any less a poet than Chaucer, the achievement might appear impossible.

We know, though, that mastery of genre is one great mark of Chaucer's genius. Each of his dream poems represents a separate literary type, and next to the Bible *The Canterbury Tales* presents probably the most interesting study that literature offers of diversity in kinds. In conveying meaning Chaucer with great virtuosity employs the devices and conventions of each type to appropriate effect. Moreover, he achieves irony and humor by importing into his narrative materials that are foreign to the genre he is working in. I have recently attempted to demonstrate how he does this in *Troilus and Criseyde*.[52] A great body of material in the work suggests alternatively that it is an epic, a romance, or a theodicy; but Chaucer undercuts each of these types ironically, leaving only a poignant realism. In the Miller's fabliau he plays with romance conventions to wonderful effect. In the Nun's Priest's beastfable he humorously employs devices of both the epic and the philosophical narrative. The list of his uses of one genre to achieve effects in another may be extended. In no work of his outside the *Duchess*, however, are meanings from two genres realized separately and simultaneously. Though the *Duchess* is the earliest of Chaucer's long original poems, it is without doubt the composition of a sophisticated literary man. Despite the puzzle it presents, even because of the puzzle it presents, we would hardly trade it for the "toun of tewnes."

FROM CLEOPATRA TO ALCESTE:
AN ICONOGRAPHIC STUDY OF
THE LEGEND OF GOOD WOMEN

V. A. KOLVE

I t is a truth universally acknowledged that Cleopatra is an odd candidate for inclusion in a *Legend of Good Women*—as is Medea, whose larger fame includes the slaughter of her own children, and as would have been (if the poem were finished) such other virtuous ladies as Helen of Troy, Tristan's Iseult, and Canace, who "loved hir owene brother synfully" (*CT* B¹ 79). Chaucer promises us the stories of them all. But before we rush to conclude that his choices are ironic and the *Legend* a simple parody, we must note among this company other ladies whose fame is of a different kind. Thisbe, Dido, Lucretia, Philomela are there as well—love's victims, not love's criminals—to say nothing of Alceste, the Prologue's queen, whose legend was meant to conclude the whole. No irony attends these latter choices, and Chaucer reserves no parodic modes specifically for the former—whose a priori claim to place must seem to anyone problematic indeed.¹ The moral heterogeneity of this company of Love's saints constitutes the greatest of the many puzzles intrinsic to the poem, and in this paper I wish to think about it in some new ways, by attending closely, first of all, to the Legend of Cleopatra. Though her credentials are as dubious as any, her story is given structural as well as thematic importance by a strict command from the God of Love: "At Cleopatre," he says to Chaucer, "I wol that thou begynne" (F 566). If that is a directive few critics have followed, perhaps it is because in our age the Prologue has effectively become the poem. Cut free from the legends it was meant to introduce, it is read as though it were likely to contain within itself the completion of all its meanings.² A closer look at the *Legend of Cleopatra* can serve not only as a case study in the iconographic mode of Chaucer's literary imagination, but can also lead us—after a survey of the materials available to Chaucer for his projected legend of Alceste—to some more appropriate ways of regarding *The Legend of Good Women* as a whole.

We do not know precisely from what source or sources Chaucer derived his knowledge of Cleopatra's history. His version of her life is so brief (124 lines) and so much occupied with inventions entirely his own (including a vivid description of the sea-battle at Actium) that there are insufficient grounds on which to judge. A few textual details, none substantive in importance, suggest that the *Epitome rerum Romanorum* of Florus, written in the second century A.D., or its thirteenth-century redaction in the *Speculum historiale* of Vincent of Beauvais, may have been at hand. Boccaccio's *De claris mulieribus* remains a possibility as well, not for any influence that can be demonstrated upon Chaucer's opening Legend, but because, as a collection of lives of famous women, it offers the closest formal antecedent in medieval literature to *The Legend of Good Women* as a whole, and because it too includes Cleopatra. But the search for sources is unlikely ever to approach the vital center of the poem, for it is clear that Chaucer deliberately suppressed most of Cleopatra's history, what we may call in sum "the Cleopatra tradition," and significantly altered almost every part that he retained.[3] The passionate, fickle, and ambitious queen familiar to us from the historians, Boccaccio, and Shakespeare is missing from Chaucer's verse, as is any detailed notice of her life prior to her love for Anthony. Chaucer's alterations furthermore are as important as his omissions: This Cleopatra is wife to Anthony rather than mistress, and she follows rather than leads him in the flight from Actium that confirms their defeat and occasions their death. Wherever Chaucer may have found his Cleopatra among the several possible sources, and whatever he may have found her there to be, she enters English literature as a "good woman"—in the special sense of that term that obtains in this poem, a sense which he uses her legend, as first legend, to define.

If our interest, then, is in Chaucer's poem rather than in the Cleopatra of other books, these changes and omissions are of the first importance. But they do not contain their own explanation. They offer no clue as to why Chaucer should have gone to such lengths in order to include her in his legendary.[4] For that, I think we must look to Chaucer's largest single departure from the tradition: his version of her death. From a single detail recounted in all the sources, the tradition that Cleopatra killed herself with an asp, or with two, Chaucer invented a death scene that is wholly original and stunning in its power. It occupies the full final third of Cleopatra's legend and, if my reading is correct, offers one of two essential images meant to establish the meaning of the poem as a whole—a poem unfinished but conceptually complete, a poem whose larger "idea" (in the sense that Donald Howard has used the term) can still be reconstructed.[5]

So let us begin with what the earlier texts offered Chaucer concerning Cleopatra's death, and then look at that same subject within an associated tradition—its illustration in the medieval visual arts. For this is an example of "narrative imagery," as I define it in my book about imagery in *The Canterbury Tales*: a setting, or an event, or a property which Chaucer invites us first to visualize as part of the poem's literal action, and afterwards to recognize as bearing a suggestive likeness to (as displaying iconographic kinship with) certain other images known from elsewhere in medieval literature and the visual arts, some of which carry meanings that are stipulated and exact, generalized in their address, unmediated by the ambiguities of fiction or the accidents of history. The rhetorical elaboration of such images constituted for Chaucer one major way of winnowing "fruyt" from the "chaf" of fable, of discovering truth within the beautiful lie that is fiction. Their function in the story is made so essential, whether as architecture, landscape, costume, or event, as to confer upon them a certain "covered" quality: They are images discovered in, or uncovered by, the narrative as it moves naturally from its beginning to its end. They do not call attention to themselves in specifically symbolic ways, and the knowledge necessary to read them in their symbolic dimension is never essential to the surface coherence of the story. But those who wish to respond to Chaucer's narrative most fully will find that his art conceals within itself a powerful intellectual, artistic, and imaginative coherence, to which such images are central. In the present instance, Chaucer discovered within the Cleopatra tradition certain materials that could be made to address a truth more generalized than the particulars of chronicle or legend, and he worked them into a memorial center of meaning and meditative suggestion for the entire poem.[6] Cleopatra's death, in the Chaucer version, must be thought about iconographically if it is to be understood at all.

The tradition of her death that Chaucer worked out of (and ultimately counter to) can be represented in its essentials by the Roman historian, Florus: "Despairing of winning [a portion of her kingdom] from Caesar and perceiving that she was being reserved to figure in his triumph, profiting by the carelessness of her guard, she betook herself to the Mausoleum, as the royal sepulchre is called. There, having put on the elaborate raiment which she was wont to wear, she placed herself by the side of her beloved Antonius in a coffin filled with rich perfumes, and applying serpents to her veins thus passed into death as into a sleep."[7] In Boccaccio's *De claris mulieribus* as well, "Cleopatra, dressed in royal garments, followed her Anthony. Lying down next to him, she opened the veins of her arms and put two asps in the openings in order to die. Some say that they cause death in sleep."[8] Only in Boccaccio's *De casibus virorum illustrium* does one find even a partial hint of the nakedness with which Chaucer's Cleopatra will confront her death. There, though again

Figure 1. The death of Cleopatra. Engraving by Barthel Beham, ca. 1524. (The Warburg Institute, London)

Figure 2. The death of Cleopatra. Engraving by Augustin Hirschvogel, 1547. (The Warburg Institute, London)

Figure 3. The death of Cleopatra. Engraving by Hans Sebald Beham, ca. 1529. (The Warburg Institute, London)

Figure 4. The death of Cleopatra, with Cupid weeping. Engraving by Agostino Veneziano, 1528. (The Warburg Institute, London)

Figure 5. The deaths of Anthony and Cleopatra. London, Brit. Lib. MS. Royal 14 E. v, fol. 339, illustrating Boccaccio, *Des Cas des Nobles Hommes et Femmes,* trans. Laurent de Premierfait, ca. 1470–83. (Reproduced by permission of the British Library)

Figure 6. The deaths of Anthony and Cleopatra. London, Brit. Lib. MS. Royal 18 E. v, fol. 363v, an *Hystoire Tripartite* dated 1473. (Reproduced by permission of the British Library)

Figure 7. The deaths of Anthony and Cleopatra. Paris, Bibl. Natl. MS. fr. 12420, fol. 129v, illustrating Boccaccio, *Des Cleres et Nobles Femmes,* dated 1410. (Photo Bibliothèque Nationale, Paris)

Figure 8. The deaths of Anthony and Cleopatra. Paris, Bibl. Natl. MS. fr. 598, fol. 128v; same text as Fig. 7, MS. dated 1404. (Photo Bibliothèque Nationale, Paris)

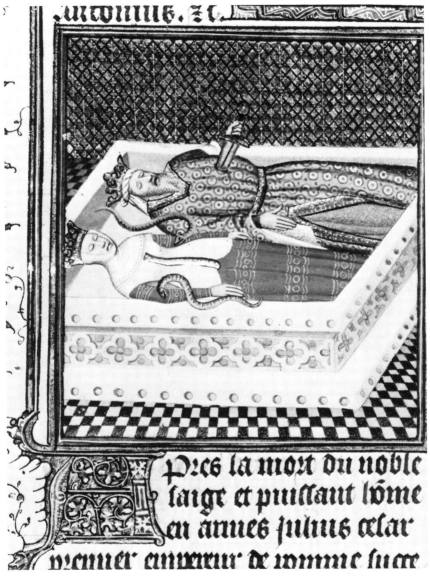

Figure 9. The deaths of Anthony and Cleopatra. Paris, Bibl. de l'Arsenal MS. 5193, fol. 272v, illustrating Boccaccio, *Des Cas des Nobles Hommes et Femmes*, ca. 1410. (Photo Bibliothèque Nationale, Paris)

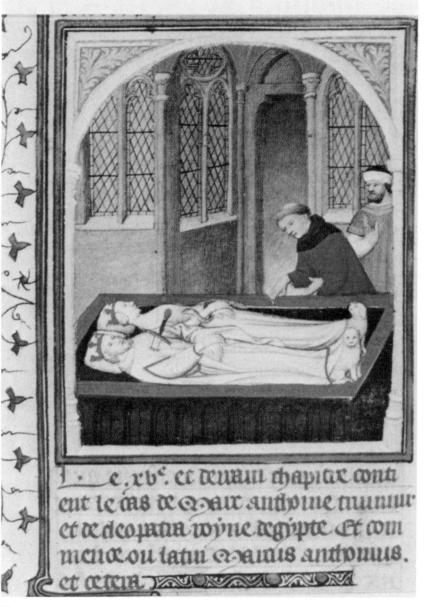

Figure 10. The tomb of Anthony and Cleopatra. New York, formerly Coll. Francis Kettaneh, no pagination; same text as Fig. 9, ca. 1415. (Reproduced from Millard Meiss, *French Painting in the Time of Jean de Berry: The Boucicaut Master,* London: Phaidon Press, 1968, fig. 392)

Figure 11. Anthony and Cleopatra dead. Paris, Bibl. Natl. MS. fr. 226, fol. 183v;
same text as Fig. 9, ca. 1415–20. (Photo Bibliothèque Nationale, Paris)

"anointed with perfumes and decorated with all her royal insignia," "she bared her breasts, and after placing serpents next to them, she lay down to die. As if in a quiet sleep her spirit was released."[9]

Renaissance engravings of Cleopatra's death, responsive to her full amorous history and perhaps specifically responsive to this latter text, customarily show her dying naked. In an engraving by Barthel Beham, for instance (figure 1), the asp coils around her arm almost like a bracelet, and the beauty of her body speaks more expressively than any idea of its mortality.[10] An engraving by Augustin Hirschvogel dated 1547 (figure 2), uses a recumbent pose to create a languorous mood; the frontal display of her body and the seductive rebuke of her glance suggest that the viewer has intruded upon her privacy rather than her death. The asp moving toward her breast emphasizes the picture's real subject—the female body as erotic icon. Cleopatra's death serves only as pretext, as presumptive occasion; it is not what the picture is about.[11] A fine engraving by Hans Sebald Beham (figure 3) differs significantly in choosing to show Cleopatra in a prison and at the moment of the serpent's sting: her face and body are contorted in anguish; it is the image of a heroic death.[12] But even here she dies semidraped and voluptuous, as she does also in an engraving by Agostino Veneziano, dated 1528 (figure 4), which locates her death within a classical setting, and creates an elegiac mood. Cupid weeps before a flaming altar as Cleopatra, resting against a pillar, slumps forward in death. The asp, twined round her arm, bites at the nipple of her breast.[13]

The medieval visual arts, in strong contrast, illustrate the written sources with a strict decorum, eschewing nudity of any kind—for the most part even in illustration of the *De casibus*, whose text specifies a baring of her breasts. Figures 5 and 6 represent two exceptions: I know of only three. The first, illustrating a French translation of the *De casibus*, shows Cleopatra in a fur-trimmed gown lowered to her waist, and was painted ca. 1470–83. The second illustrates an *Hystoire Tripartite*, and was made in Flanders in 1473.[14] I call attention to them because Chaucer's Cleopatra, like Cleopatra in the Renaissance engravings, will go to her death entirely naked, though with a different meaning. It is another of the ways in which she grows out of, but is distinguished from, the Cleopatra of tradition, even the *De casibus* tradition. For elsewhere in the medieval visual arts Cleopatra characteristically dies clothed, in royal robes and wearing a crown. In a miniature made in 1410 illustrating *De claris mulieribus*, for instance, a beautifully gowned Cleopatra dies upon a throne with serpents at her arms. Anthony lies dead before her in an ermine-lined robe, his hands still gripping the sword of suicide lodged in his breast (figure 7). The image is elegant and rather moving, but without iconographic resonance.[15] Like figure 8 (also illustrating a French translation of this text), it presents the minimum visual information necessary for us to identify and remember these personages: royal crowns, serpents, a sword.[16] In a manuscript of the French *De casibus*, made ca. 1410, the lovers lie side by side in a tomb of precious stones (figure 9); here too they are fully and royally dressed, the sword at his breast, the serpents at her arms.[17] They look almost like funeral effigies, which is what they have indeed become in figure 10, an illustration to the same text, made ca. 1415. Here two men, one of them a sacristan or monk, are shown visiting the lovers' tomb, a massive Gothic monument of black stone adorned with a golden rail. Their images are carved of alabaster or white marble, with gilded crowns and dagger; the single serpent is tinted a pale gray-blue, and a lion and dog are carved at their feet.[18] In figure 11, also illustrating the French *De casibus*, Anthony lies dead within a simple tomb or coffin that is open to the sky; Cleopatra lies beside him on the ground with enormous serpents feeding at the veins of her arms.[19] This picture, in distinguishing Anthony's final resting place from hers, comes a degree nearer to Chaucer's version of their ending than any illustration examined so far. But here the distinction signifies nothing beyond itself. If as critics we would accurately illustrate Chaucer's poem, or as readers accurately imagine it in our mind's eye, neither this nor any other image from the Cleopatra tradition will serve. Such images convey at most the essential elements of the tradition: the royal setting, whether throne or tomb; the dagger; the serpents. But knowing these images can help us to estimate better the brilliance and audacity with which Chaucer transformed that tradition within the first of his legends of good women.

The scene is so important to the poem as a whole that I must quote it here entire, and urge that it be read with attention to its full detail. After Chaucer has briefly noted Cleopatra's first grief over Anthony's death—"This woful Cleopatre hath mad swich routhe / That ther is tonge non that may it telle" (669–70)—he narrates her own death so:

> But on the morwe she wolde no lengere dwelle,
> But made hire subtyl werkmen make a shryne
> Of alle the rubyes and the stones fyne
> In al Egypte, that she coude espie,
> And putte ful the shryne of spicerye,
> And let the cors enbaume, and forth she fette
> This dede cors, and in the shryne it shette.
> And next the shryne a pit thanne doth she grave,
> And alle the serpentes that she myghte have,
> She putte hem in that grave, and thus she seyde:
> "Now, love, to whom my sorweful herte obeyde
> So ferforthly that from that blisful houre
> That I yow swor to ben al frely youre—
> I mene yow, Antonius, my knyght—

That nevere wakynge, in the day or nyght,
Ye nere out of myn hertes remembraunce,
For wel or wo, for carole or for daunce;
And in myself this covenaunt made I tho,
That ryght swich as ye felten, wel or wo,
As fer forth as it in my power lay,
Unreprovable unto my wyfhod ay,
The same wolde I fele, lyf or deth,—
And thilke covenant, whil me lasteth breth,
I wol fulfille; and that shal ben wel sene,
Was nevere unto hire love a trewer quene."
And with that word, naked, with ful good herte,
Among the serpents in the pit she sterte,
And there she ches to have hire buryinge.
Anon the nadderes gonne hire for to stynge,
And she hire deth receyveth with good cheere,
For love of Antony that was hire so dere.
And this is storyal soth, it is no fable.

(671–702)

Chaucer in these lines imagines for his Cleopatra a death far more strenuous and self-conscious than anything provided in the Cleopatra tradition. Instead of entering a mausoleum to put serpents to her veins and die beside her lover as in a sleep, she creates for Anthony alone a magnificent shrine, building it of precious stones (not corruptible as the flesh is corruptible), filling it with spices, and placing in it his embalmed corpse. Having thus arranged for her husband and lover what Petrarch might have called the Triumph of Fame over Death, she "graves" for herself a pit beside that splendid monument, fills "that grave" with all the serpents she can obtain, and descends into it "naked, with ful good herte." It is a powerful ending, even if one has no idea what it may have meant in its own time. But read iconographically and with an exercise of the historical imagination, it is more powerful by far. Although modern critics seem to have had difficulty in perceiving the intrinsic logic of this double image,[20] I think the attentive parish Christian of the fourteenth century would have understood it with ease.

For Chaucer's invention is based upon the fact that in medieval English the words *pit* and *grave* could be exact synonyms, as could the words *serpent* and *worm*, with the latter including not only earthworms and maggots, but snakes, dragons, toads, scorpions, and everything reptilian in between.[21] Cleopatra in her death dramatizes, and accepts with a fiercely stoic courage, the medieval commonplace that man's flesh was eaten by worms and serpents in the grave.

Some ancient psuedo-science lay behind this view of the body's corruption, as the medieval bestiary bears witness in its discussion of snakes:

Pythagoras says: "Serpents are created out of the spinal marrow of corpses"—a thing which Ovid also calls to mind in the books of the Metamorphoses, when he says:

"Some there are who believe that sealed in the grave, the spine rotting,
Marrows of humankind do turn themselves into serpents."

And this, if it is to be credited, is all very appropriate: that just as Man's death was first brought about by a Snake, so by the death of man a snake should be brought about.[22]

Hans Sebald Beham, in an engraving dated 1543 (figure 12), possibly draws upon this tradition in depicting the Temptation of Adam and Eve.[23] He shows the Tree of Knowledge, whose fruit will bring Death into the world, as a skeleton along whose spine there climbs the body of the serpent Tempter himself.

For reasons I shall soon explain, I do not think that Chaucer invented his version of Cleopatra's death in order to invite a specifically Christian interpretation, in which (let us say) the serpents that kill her are to be identified with the serpent of sin, or with sin's mortal consequence. Instead, I think Chaucer was working from and sought to go no further than a formulaic truth which medieval men and women heard all their lives long, and which they often saw depicted in funerary art: the truism that declares the human body to be ultimately nothing but food for worms. Among the traditional medieval meditations on death, no Warning from the Grave is more confident than "wermes fode þu salt be;" "wormes fode / is fyne of owre lyuynge."[24] Paintings that show the meeting of the Three Living and the Three Dead, for instance—a subject common upon church walls as well as in illuminated manuscripts—most often depict those personages as kings: three still alive and crowned, and three who confront them in the full, mocking beggary of death.[25] In the version included in the De Lisle Psalter (figure 13; English, ca. 1330–45), the living say in turn "Ich am afert. Lo whet ich se. Me þinke' hit beþ dueles þre," and the dead kings reply, "Ich wes wel fair. Such scheltou be. For godes loue be wer by me."[26] The living kings meet themselves, so to speak, in death: they encounter what they will ultimately become. We notice that the stomach of the first of the dead kings is being eaten by a carefully rendered company of worms.

But we are still at some distance from Chaucer's invention, though we are surveying traditions which he knew and upon which he depended for its legibility and cultural authority. A fifteenth-century debate poem entitled "A Disputacioun betwyx þe Body and Wormes," richly illustrated in its single extant manuscript, can take us directly to the scene's thematic center. Its narrator, moved to go on pilgrimage during a period of plague ("In þe ceson of huge mortalite"), stops at a church to pray. As he kneels "to ane ymage with gret deuocione"—an image (figure 14) depicting Christ on the cross—he notices at his side a newly made "towmbe or sepulture" (figure 15) adorned with "a fresche fygure fyne of a woman / Wele atyred in þe moste newe gyse."[27] He is so struck by this image that he falls into a slumber or swoon, and dreams that he hears a debate between the woman's body and the worms that are eating her—"betwyx þis body and wormes hyr fretynge." As her monument with its heraldic blazons, crown, and ermine robe clearly testifies, and as she herself is quick to remind the worms, the woman whose body speaks was nobly born: alive she was called "Lady and soferayne."[28] The worms boast in their turn that they have eaten "alle þat wer myghty passed forth and gone"—including emperors, kings, conquerors, the Nine Worthies, and women of great beauty and renown: Helen, Polyxena, Lucrece, Dido of Carthage.[29] Our lady of the debate is not the first to find her beauty mortal. Her figure is made royal, as so often in medieval death imagery, in order that its lesson may encompass all ranks, degrees, and conditions. Whatever the grandeur of her funeral monument, the truth of her present estate is imaged by the cadaver below, wrapped in its shroud, devoured by snakes and worms, toads, scorpions.[30] In the manuscript pages that follow, a series of marginal drawings, represented here by figure 16, depict over and over again the parties to the debate in their naked confrontation. Only the lady's headdress remains to indicate her body's gender; all other lendings have been lost.[31] This manuscript includes as well the story of the Emperor Antiochenus and his son— another Warning from the Grave—in which the son, surpassing even his father in wickedness, is led by a good steward to his father's golden tomb, where the corpse speaks from the grave to warn his son of what he will become in death, and how he ought to live in preparation for that end. Figure 17 reproduces the illustration to that story, in which (again) a magnificent monument is set in didactic relation to a grave and its serpent company.[32]

Chaucer, of course, could not have known these precise poems in this precise manuscript: it has been dated ca. 1435–40. But I wish to suggest that these poems and pictures, along with his version of Cleopatra's death, grow out of a common tradition. Chaucer has simply apportioned to Anthony the customary pomp and splendor of the tomb, and to Cleopatra the enactment of death's other meaning. In the speech she makes to Anthony's corpse just before her own descent into the grave, she recalls to him her marriage promise—"ryght swich as ye felten, wel or wo,/ . . . The same wolde I fele, lyf or deth"—declaring thereby that their two ends are essentially the same. The splendor of Anthony's tomb images their fame, while the horror of Cleopatra's serpent-ridden grave delineates that other truth which Fame can disguise or cover over, but never alter or deny. The two parts of the image are inseparable.

These starker aspects of death were often depicted in tomb sculpture of the fifteenth century, most powerfully in the so-called *transi* tombs, which represented the deceased as a corpse, naked or wrapped in a shroud, withered by death and often eaten by worms. The grandest of such monuments are double tombs, showing (above) the effigy of the departed as he or she was in life, lying in state, hands often folded in prayer, and (below, near floor level) the effigy of that same person in death.[33] The earliest known double tomb (figure 18) was commissioned by Cardinal Jean de Lagrange just before his death in 1402. His epitaph, carved above the *transi* figure, declares to the viewer the public purpose of such an image:

We have been made a spectacle for the world so that the older and the younger may look clearly upon us, in order that they might see to what state they will be reduced. No one is excluded, regardless of estate, sex, or age. Therefore, miserable one, why are you proud? You are only ash, and you will revert, as we have done, to a fetid cadaver, food and tidbits for worms, and ashes.[34]

(The debate poem whose pictures we have just examined may represent a meditation upon just such a tomb.) Henry Chichele, Archbishop of Canterbury, built for himself a similar tomb in 1424 (figure 19), and lived in the presence of those effigies for nearly twenty years—a most personal *memento mori,* instructive to other worshippers as well.[35] Another such tomb (figure 20), was built in Lincoln Cathedral by the Bishop Richard Fleming; he died in 1431.[36] The only surviving *transi*-tomb that may have been built before Chaucer's own death in 1400 is that of François de la Sarra in Vaud, Switzerland (figure 21). It has been variously dated from ca. 1370 to ca. 1400, although François died in 1363. Its single effigy—among the most remarkable in all medieval funerary sculpture—has toads at its eyes and at the corners of its mouth, with another covering its genitals; the entire body is eaten by long, thin, serpent-like worms (detail, figure 22).[37]

It is unlikely we will ever know whether Chaucer's double tomb for Anthony and Cleopatra anticipates this kind of tomb soon to become fashionable in funerary art, or simply works a brilliant variation upon it. Too much has been lost or destroyed, both in manuscripts and church sculpture, to allow a confident guess.[38] But as Kathleen Cohen has re-marked in her learned study of the *transi* tombs, the motifs from which such tombs and their characteristic epitaphs were invented had been commonplace in literature for several centuries. She cites, for instance, this passage from Innocent III's *De contemptu mundi,* a work that Chaucer had himself translated: "He who just now sat glorious on his throne, now lies in his tomb, looked down upon. Who just now was decorated with gleaming gold, now lies naked in the tomb. The man who just now dined upon delights in his living room, is now being dined on by worms in his grave."[39] If Chaucer's *Legend of Cleopatra* did indeed anticipate the art of the tomb-sculptor in this matter, it is worthy of note that his own grand-daughter, Alice de la Pole, Duchess of Suffolk, was buried at Ewelme in 1475 in an alabaster tomb of this kind (figure 23). The beauty of her effigy above (detail, figure 24)[40] establishes a relationship at once dialectical and elegaic with the *transi* that can be seen, though not effectively photographed, through the gallery of arches at floor level below. There her emaciated corpse, its hair loose about its shoulders, offers its separate truth. The Duchess' actual remains are interred in the chest that separates the two effigies and links their meaning.

Cleopatra's death in *The Legend of Good Women,* in short, bears a clear iconographic relationship to these Christian images of death. But the intention of Chaucer's image is not primarily the lesson of *memento mori,* as expressed, let us say, by the royal lady whose body is eaten by worms: "se what þou art and here aftyr sal be."[41] Nor does Chaucer invoke the image of a decaying corpse in order to persuade man to avoid the Seven Deadly Sins, as does his friend John Gower (near the end of the *Vox clamantis*), who devotes brief chapters to the mockery the grave makes of each.[42] Chaucer might have drawn upon the Cleopatra tradition to point either lesson—the admonitory horror of death, or the grave's rebuke to sin, here most probably the sins of pride and lechery—for the Middle Ages valued such lessons in literature, and in other places Chaucer too exercises his art in their service. But his larger purpose here is different. As I noted at the beginning of this paper, his Cleopatra is no figure of lechery, but is instead presented as Anthony's wife, faithful to him even unto the grave. She builds for herself no prideful monument, and she is not appalled by death even in its most horrible aspect. She goes into the grave alive and by her own will, to enact in advance, and by fierce analogy, the full horror and meaninglessness of the body's corruption in the grave. She creates and confronts that death "with ful good herte" and "with good cheere," as a means of *affirming* her life and love, not as a means of revaluing them.

As I shall soon explain, I think *The Legend of Good Women* significantly Christian in its meaning, but in ways more subtle and interesting than the formulaic lessons which Chaucer here passes over or leaves potential merely. He allowed Cleopatra, along with Dido, Medea, and all the other "good women" of his poem, a literary life essentially free of Pauline and Augustinian interpretation, in part because such standards are inappropriate to a fiction that concerns a company of pagan women, "hethene al the pak": their virtue, though real, was limited by their moment in history. But he did so also because his program for the poem as a whole provided a way of paying respect to Christian truth in a manner more tactful, humane, and ultimately more profound, in the legend intended for its conclusion. Just as the Legends themselves are experiments in plain and brief narration—"the naked text in English to declare / Of many a story, or elles of many a geste" (G 86–87)—so too his larger purpose, which is related to but not identical with the goals of Boccaccian humanism,[43] was to present the lives of pagan women "martyred" for love in a fashion free of extrinsic moralization. As the God of Love's commission would lead us to expect, Chaucer's image of Cleopatra's death is heroic rather than didactic: "For lat see now what man that lover be, / Wol doon so strong a peyne for love as she" (F 568–69). She strips for the grave, one might say, like an athlete preparing for a contest. Unlike the nudity celebrated in the Renaissance engravings of her death, the nakedness of this Cleopatra is austere, the nakedness of a corpse, not a courtesan. We hear from her at the end nothing comparable to Sir Philip Sidney's sonnet, valedictory to *Astrophel and Stella*, "Leave me, O love, that reachest but to dust." Chaucer's Cleopatra goes to ground with Anthony in proof that love and courage can coexist with despair.

In Chaucer's vision of the pre-Christian world there are tombs in plenty, but no answering image of Christ on the cross to whom one may pray (as does the narrator of the "Disputacioun betwyx þe Body and Wormes") in hope of heaven. Cleopatra's death, which Chaucer chose to begin his pagan legendary, offers a spectacle of courage, self-awareness, and self-definition, essentially untouched by authorial irony; but her martyrdom is also limited to those values. That it has no meaning be-yond itself *is* its essential meaning.

It is in this sense that Cleopatra's death offers a discreet preliminary gloss on the "naked text" of all the legends that follow. They end either in the creation of a death-spectacle, subtly varied for each, as in the case of Thisbe, Dido, Lucrece, and Phyllis; or in the bodiless reproaches of a letter (derived from Ovid's *Heroides*) written without expectation of an answer, as in the case of Hypsipyle, Medea, and Ariadne; or in no end-ing at all, just bleak continuance, as in the case of Philomela and Hypermnestra.[44] Their deaths and their suffering address no values higher than fame, the avoidance of shame, the preservation of good name—to echo a three-fold rhyme central to the verbal matrix of the poem. Cleopatra's death-scene, in which the asps of historical tradition become the mordant worms of the grave, is paradigmatic: it expresses the naked truth those other destinies bear at their center. Chaucer dis-plays the "good women" of his poem locked in a mortal coil in which dust embraces dust, whether in the marriage bed, through rape, or in a descent into the grave. Within such limits a poet can "make of sente-ment" [make verses about feelings] only (F 69), for the suffering that is Chaucer's present subject redeems nothing and is redeemed by nothing: It yields emotion, not meaning.

Although they were painted in the late fifteenth century, two French

illuminations of the death of Dido can express in visual terms what I take
to be (at its fullest range) the essential ethos of what Chaucer was able to
complete of his poem. In figure 25 a crowd of men watch solemnly and
at a distance as Dido, high upon a mountain path, falls forward upon a
sword, impaling herself and ending her life. One man, his arm draped
casually around the shoulders of a friend, points to her suicide; another
makes a gesture expressing wonder; others simply stare. Something is
happening; nothing is happening; such suffering causes nothing to
happen. Figure 26 shows Dido stabbing herself as she falls forward into a
sacrificial fire, while an attendant lady supports (or restrains) her, and as
a company of men make gestures expressing grief. Here the distance
between Dido's death and its observers is closed up both spatially and
emotionally, but the difference is not of great consequence. Dido's self-
sacrifice, with or without a ceremonial fire, is to no god more real than
the god of earthly love, and her death is meaningless outside his secular
theology. While responsive to the courage and pathos of her death, these
painters also imagined it in terms of the traditional iconography of despair: suicide with a sword or dagger.[45] Figure 27 projects the death of
Lucrece against the same archetype,[46] as do several of the miniatures
examined earlier that show Anthony dying by his own hand. Like the
martyrdom of Virginia in the Physician's Tale—the single Canterbury
tale that bears any thematic or generic relationship to these legends of
good women—such suffering is without purpose, and without redemptive potential: tragedy in a pagan world.[47]

And so it goes, in our present poem, from Legend to Legend; and so
the pressure grows, for poet and audience alike, to find escape from
these *topoi,* these commonplace truths that declare women can be faithful
in love, that men are deceivers ever, that erotic love (even when mutual,
as with Anthony and Cleopatra, or Pyramus and Thisbe) ends only in the
monument and the grave. Whatever the statistical claims of these *topoi* to
comprehensive truth (the twenty thousand women of the Prologue stand
ready to furnish further example[48]) they are finally no more than partial
and dispiriting. The poem as we have it is locked in a pattern from which
there is apparently no release. This becomes particularly clear in the
Legend of Phyllis, where the history of men false in love is declared not
only topological—commonplace, to be expected—but lineal. We have
heard "of Theseus the grete untrouthe of love" (1890) just two Legends
earlier, as he betrayed Ariadne for her sister Phedra, and now Chaucer
brings before us Demophoon, his son,[49] although Demophoon's history
can yield nothing new: "the same wey, the same path" (2463) for both.
The poet's discontent rises to its greatest intensity at this moment, as he
declares himself surfeited with such stories—"I am agroted herebyforn /
To wryte of hem that ben in love forsworn" (2454)—and wearied with
Demophoon (and his father) in particular:

Me lyste nat vouche-sauf on hym to swynke,
Ne spende on hym a penne ful of ynke,
For fals in love was he, ryght as his syre.
The devil sette here soules bothe afyre!

(2490–93)

Chaucer ran a certain risk in choosing this technique—a risk Yvor Winters termed in another context "the fallacy of imitative form"—and he pays a substantial price. In suggesting a personal antipathy to his subject and in recording an increasing weariness with its intrinsic limitations and its sameness, Chaucer offers a model of response difficult not to emulate: we become fretful and distanced in our turn. But the technique is not uncalculated, and it cannot be explained simply as a variation upon the rhetorical figure of *occupatio,* or as an experiment in the rhetorical technique of *abbreviatio.* Though I do not claim that an understanding of Chaucer's larger purpose can redeem in full the great unfinished middle of the poem—it often puzzles, and the tone is not managed successfully at every point—yet we must not judge the idea of the poem without paying some attention to where it was going. Its destination, quite simply, was Alceste.

One of the major curiosities of the criticism that has grown up around this poem consists in the fact that although hundreds of pages have been written concerning Alceste as a daisy figure (her identity in the Prologue) virtually nothing has been said about her legend, although it is her legend that has earned her that metamorphosis (apparently unique to this poem), and though it is her legend that is meant to bring the poem to its end. In the words of the God of Love:

But now I charge the, upon thy lyf,
That in thy legende thou make of thys wyf,
Whan thou hast other smale ymaad before.

(F 548–50)

We shall later have cause to note one honorable exception to this description of the extant criticism: in this matter, as in many others, D. W. Robertson, Jr., has adduced the information necessary to a fuller understanding of the poem.[50] But the essentials are furnished by Chaucer himself, in the God of Love's four-line abbreviation of her life:

"She that for hire housbonde chees to dye,
And eke to goon to helle, rather than he,
And Ercules rescowed hire, parde,
And broght hir out of helle agayn to blys."

(F 513–16)

Figure 12. The temptation of Adam and Eve. Engraving by Hans Sebald Beham, 1543. (Collection of The Art Institute of Chicago)

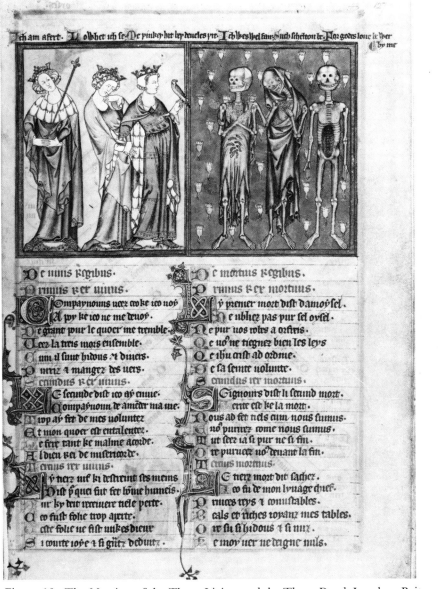

Figure 13. The Meeting of the Three Living and the Three Dead. London, Brit. Lib. MS. Arundel 83, fol. 127, ca. 1330–45. (Reproduced by permission of the British Library)

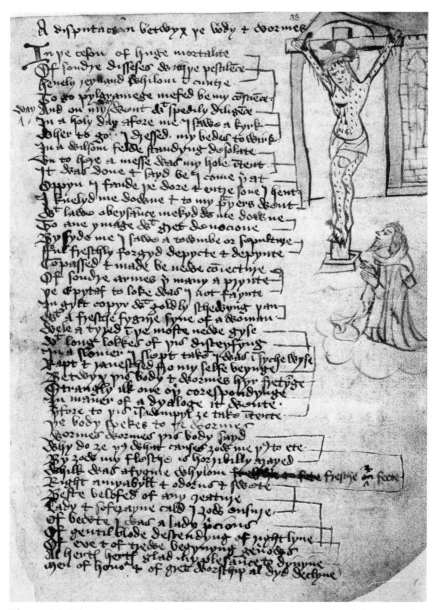

Figure 14. The narrator of "A disputacioun betwyx þe body and wormes" at prayer in a church. London, Brit. Lib. MS. 37049, fol. 33, ca. 1435–40. (Reproduced by permission of the British Library)

Figure 15. Tomb image illustrating the same poem. Ibid., fol. 32v. (Reproduced by permission of the British Library)

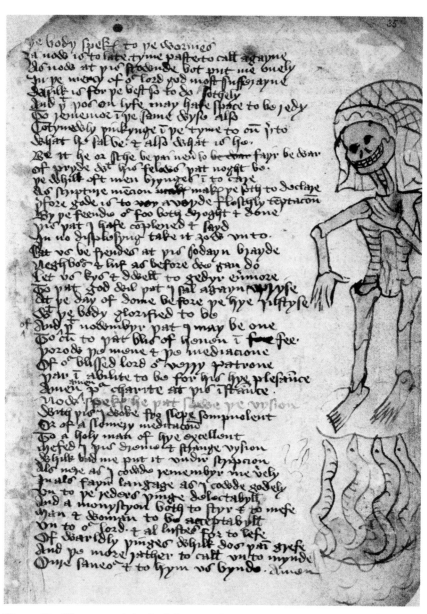

Figure 16. The woman's body debates with worms. Ibid., fol. 35. (Reproduced by permission of the British Library)

Figure 17. A warning from the grave; the tomb of the Emperor Antiochenus
visited by his steward and his son. Ibid., fol. 87. (Reproduced by permission of the
British Library)

Figure 18. The tomb of Cardinal Jean de Lagrange, 1402. Avignon, Musée Calvet. (Photo copyright Archives Photographiques, Paris. S.P.A.D.E.M.)

Figure 19. The tomb of Archbishop Henry Chichele, 1424. Canterbury Cathedral. (National Monuments Record, London)

Figure 20. The tomb of Bishop Richard Fleming, before 1431. Lincoln Cathedral. (National Monuments Record, London)

Figure 21. The tomb of François de la Sarra, ca. 1370–1400. Vaud, Switzerland.
(Archives de Jongh, Lausanne)

Figure 22. The tomb of François de la Sarra (detail). (Archives de Jongh, Lausanne)

Figure 23. The tomb of Alice de la Pole, Duchess of Suffolk, granddaughter to Geoffrey Chaucer, 1475. Ewelme. (National Monuments Record, London)

Figure 24. The tomb of Alice de la Pole (detail). (Photograph by courtesy of the Courtauld Institute of Art, London; © Canon M. H. Ridgway and Fred H. Crossley)

Figure 25. The death of Dido. London, Brit. Lib. MS. Add. 35321, fol. 43, illustrating Boccaccio, *Des Cas des Nobles Hommes et Femmes,* fifteenth century. (Reproduced by permission of the British Library)

Figure 26. The death of Dido. London, Brit. Lib. MS. Royal 14 E. v, fol. 77v, same text as Fig. 25, ca. 1470–83. (Reproduced by permission of the British Library)

Figure 27. The death of Lucrece. Ibid., fol. 121v. (Reproduced by permission of the British Library)

Figure 28. Hercules, with Cerberus on a leash, restores Alcestis to her husband Admetus. Rome, Via Latina, catacomb painting, fourth century. (The Pontifical Institute of Christian Archaeology, Rome)

Figure 29. Hercules rescues Alcestis from Hell. Rome, Vatican MS. Reg. Lat. 1290, fol. 5a v, illustrating the *Libellus de Imaginibus Deorum*, ca. 1420. (The Vatican Library)

Figure 30. Hercules rescues Alcestis from Hell-Mouth; Alcestis and Admetus (?) enthroned. Rome, Vatican MS. Palat. 1066, fol. 228, illustrating Ridevall, *Fulgentius metaforalis*, 1420. (The Vatican Library)

Figure 31. Geoffrey Chaucer: portrait with a daisy. London, Brit. Lib. MS. Add. 5141, fol. 1, sixteenth century. (Reproduced by permission of the British Library)

On the authority of these lines, and as the final argument of this paper, I wish to suggest that the poem as a whole, like the Prologue that introduces it, is essentially a quest to discover the identity and meaning of Alceste.

The Prologue's action begins with Chaucer's worship of a daisy in a field and makes of that devotion, so comically literal, a fiction at once preposterous and charming. The flower seems to elicit both his erotic love and his religious adoration:

> That blisful sighte softneth al my sorwe,
> So glad am I, whan that I have presence
> Of it, to doon it alle reverence,
> As she that is of alle floures flour.
>
> (F 50–53)

His obsession with the daisy leads him to sleep outdoors in a turfed arbor, where he dreams he sees the Queen of the God of Love dressed and crowned in such a way (green and gold and white) that she looks like that flower. In the ensuing action she stands between the poet and the anger of the God of Love, just as in her life (we remember, once we know who she is) she had stood between her husband Admetus and the god Apollo, when the god demanded his death. But for a long while we have no more idea than Chaucer-the-dreamer as to who she is: though he is moved by her beauty and grateful for her intervention, he can see in her only a deification of the daisy he worships in the field. When the God of Love identifies her in the four lines quoted above, and when Chaucer echoes her name—"And is this good Alceste, / The dayesie, and myn owene hertes reste?" (F 518)—the Prologue's quest on its most elementary level, the level of identification, is over. But the poem's larger quest—to realize the *meaning* of Alceste, to estimate properly the great difference between her and the twenty thousand other good women, a difference that has made her the God of Love's queen—that quest was to include, as essential stages along the way, the legends of nineteen other women who also died for love. I think it possible that Chaucer himself grew weary of the numbing repetition, the despair, the partial and (for Christians) superseded truths that characterize that preliminary series. But he was moving steadily toward the legend of a death that had served an end beyond its own fame: the legend of a lover willing to die so that another might live, and who earned her own release from death thereby.

Chaucer was not the first to put the legend of Alcestis to that use. It had served in the sarcophagus art of late pagan Rome to suggest the promise of a blessed afterlife,[51] and it had found occasional place in early Christian iconography as well. The fourth-century catacombs beneath the Via Latina in Rome include a notable chamber dedicated to

Hercules soter, which includes both a painting of Admetus on his death-
bed surrounded by family and friends, as Alcestis offers to die in his
place, and a painting in which Hercules leads Alcestis back to Admetus,
with Cerberus, the three-headed dog of hell, on a leash in his other hand
(figure 28).[52] They are scenes associated with one of the Labors of
Hercules, a cycle concerning the exploits of a mortal son of a god, and
thus find place in a program of imagery for the most part explicitly
Christian in motif and image. The paintings of Alcestis represent a transitional use of myth, a gesture of accommodation; but they had no
long-term Christian consequence. So far as I have been able to discover,
her legend survived into the later Middle Ages through mythographic
handbooks only. Because the importance that Chaucer assigns to Alceste
is otherwise without parallel in medieval art and literature, it is to those
handbooks and their illustrations we must turn, if we would guess usefully
at what Chaucer might have made of her story.

He would have learned at a minimum the story as it could then be
found in Fulgentius' *Mythologies:* "When Admetus fell ill and discovered
he was dying, he sought to avert it by entreating Apollo, who said he
could do nothing for him in his sickness unless he found one of his
relatives who would voluntarily accept death in his place. This his wife
undertook; and so Hercules, when he went down to drag away the
three-headed dog Cerberus, also freed her from the lower world."
Fulgentius, a Christian writing in the late fifth or early sixth century,
interprets the story chiefly in terms of Admetus, explicating it as an
allegory of mind: the test by which Admetus won Alcestis in marriage—
the successful yoking of a wild lion and a wild boar to a chariot—signifies
a marriage between "strength of mind" and "strength of body" that can
win one succour [*alce*] in the end, even from peril of death.[53]

This interpretation is repeated in essence by the three so-called Vatican mythographers, and again (with some variation) by Boccaccio in his
Genealogy of the Pagan Gods.[54] But it is not the kind of idea from which
Chaucer was making his *Legend.* On the basis of the 2723 lines that he
finished, I think we must judge wholly unlikely any movement into psychological allegory at the poem's end; and his focus is necessarily upon
Alceste rather than her husband. I think Chaucer trusted instead that
the superior dignity of Alceste could be made manifest even in a text as
"naked" as that of the other legends, because her story possesses a special
kind of suggestiveness. As Pierre Bersuire had noted in his introduction
to the *Ovidius moralizatus,* written in the early fourteenth century, Alceste
may be seen as a type of those "good women who love their husbands
perfectly so that on account of their love they will if necessary expose
themselves to death. They are worthy that Hercules, or Christ, rescue
them from Hell, or Purgatory, because of the conjugal faith they main-
tain."[55] Professor Robertson would follow Bersuire in putting his em-

phasis on that last clause—on Alceste's conjugal fidelity—and there is indeed evidence in the text that such emphasis is not inappropriate:

> For she taught al the craft of fyn lovynge,
> And namely of wyfhod the lyvynge,
> And al the boundes that she oghte kepe.

(F 544–46)

But Cleopatra is also a "faithful wife" within the Legend, as are others whose fate is equally unhappy; and pagan marriage does not normally carry sacramental value for a medieval poet. Because I think Chaucer was attracted to the legend of Alceste chiefly in its typological dimension, I would emphasize instead the "Hercules, or Christ" equation in Bersuire's commentary. In the death Alceste dies so that her husband might live, she adumbrates the redemptive history of Christ, just as her rescue by Hercules from Hades adumbrates the history of the virtuous soul rescued from Hell *by* Christ. Even "in naked text," the configurations of her story would have offered implicit commentary on every story that had gone before.

Her legend became so rare in later Christian centuries that I have been able to discover only two medieval pictures based upon it. The first is a line drawing from about 1420 illustrating the *Libellus de imaginibus deorum,* an abridged version of the first part of Bersuire's *Ovidius moralizatus* (figure 29).[56] It shows Hercules leading Alcestis from Hell (represented as a rocky landscape), with Cerberus on a leash going before, and reveals a clear iconographic affinity with images of Christ leading the patriarchs out of Limbo, even though no typology (in the sense of an authoritative theological tradition) existed to support such a reading. The second picture (figure 30) is more difficult to interpret, for it depicts several scenes simultaneously, and possibly conflates two of them into one. It illustrates the *Fulgentius metaforalis*—Fulgentius revised and further moralized by John Ridevall—and shows two persons seated together, whom I take to be Alcestis and Admetus, their hands joined in wedlock. On the right, Alcestis is shown twice, once just after her death, as she kneels to enter Hell, and again as she is being rescued from Hell-Mouth by Hercules, who drives a cart harnessed to a lion and a wild boar—the very feat that won Alcestis to Admetus as his wife. The Hell-Mouth is identical with that depicted on another page of this manuscript, where Pluto and Prosperina reign as King and Queen, with Cerberus at their feet.[57] Whatever the picture's obscurities, the foreground action is surely intended to depict the event that the God of Love describes so:

> "And Ercules rescowed hire, parde,
> And broght hir out of helle agayn to blys."

(F 515–16)

The movement of the poem as predicated in the Prologue and begun by the Legend of Cleopatra implies a clear progress from *topos* to *typos*, from a commonplace nineteen times rediscovered to a typological adumbration of transcendence. When the twenty thousand ladies who follow in Alceste's train kneel to do her honor as the one who "bereth our alder pris in figurynge" (F 298), they mean, I think, something quite technical and precise. They are saying that she surpasses them all in what she "figures"—in what she is a sign for.[58] Though her legend is myth rather than history, and though the Christian patterns of salvation discernible within it constitute a poet's or mythographer's figure rather than a theologian's "type," yet she alone among this vast company points toward Christ. She expresses through the pattern of her loving a possibility of release that Christ would later establish and make genuinely available—to any who would be, in this new and deeper sense, "trewe in love": "Ne shal no trewe lover come in helle" (F 553).

The legend of Alceste yields, in short, a pattern not of courtly loving but of the love that is charity. The *balade* that ushers her into the poem is virtually an advent lyric, summoning to memory the most famous and most beautiful ladies of the past, only to declare them dimmed by her radiance: "My lady cometh, that al this may disteyne," in the words of the refrain that closes each of the three stanzas (F 255, 262, 269). Chaucer glosses that line immediately thereafter—"For as the sonne wole the fyr disteyne, / So passeth al my lady sovereyne" (F 274)—because he is talking of something deeper than beauty and grace alone.[59] In the words of the God of Love:

> "Madame," quod he, "it is so long agoon
> That I yow knew so charitable and trewe,
> That never yit, syn that the world was newe,
> To me ne fond y better noon than yee."
>
> (F 443–46)

Her beauty and her deeds are at one: "she kytheth [makes known] what she ys" (F 504). Her legend alone, among the twenty originally intended, bears the impress of Christian martyrdoms to come. Her legend ends in joy.

                    *   *   *

If I have succeeded in these pages in reading the "idea" of the projected poem correctly, then that idea should cast back upon the Prologue itself some useful light. This interpretation confirms, first of all, what any attentive reading of the Prologue must suggest on its own: that Chaucer inhabits it from the beginning in a character of a poet, not a lover, and that his worship of the daisy represents a poet's choice of subject and muse rather than a lover's choice of carnal mistress. When Alceste assigns him a poet's penance, she clearly distinguishes him from those who serve love *paramours:* "Thogh the lyke nat a lovere bee, / Speke wel of love; this penance yive I thee."[60] But the precise extravagance of Chaucer's praise of the daisy near the poem's beginning has already established his identity as a poet, for he casts his "service of the flour" (F 82) in the rhetorical form of an invocation to his muse, hailing her first as "the clernesse and the verray lyght / That in this derke world me wynt and ledeth" (F 84–85); then as "the maistresse of my wit, and nothing I" (F 88); finally as one who plays upon him as a hand plays upon a harp, drawing forth the sound it chooses:

> *My word, my werk* ys knyt so in youre bond
> That, *as an harpe* obeieth to the hond
> And maketh it soune after his fyngerynge,
> Ryght *so mowe ye* oute of myn herte *bringe*
> *Swich vois,* ryght as yow lyst, *to laughe or pleyne.*
> Be ye *my gide* and *lady sovereyne!*
>
> (F 89–94; italics mine)

Though the so-called "Portrait with a Daisy" (figure 31) would fix Chaucer forever in relationship to a literal flower,[61] in fact he uses the daisy in his poem to point beyond itself, as a means of wittily reassessing the goals of his earlier poetry, and of declaring new poetic directions. The poet's fanciful devotion to the flower epitomizes (as a figure of synecdoche) his love of springtime and the beauty of the natural world, that beauty as it is reborn annually in seasonal cycle. His initial praise of the daisy grows into a greater poem, more than fifty-five lines long, that is virtually detachable from the rest of the dream-vision: a poem celebrating the season that has ended winter and all its cares.

> Forgeten hadde the erthe his pore estat
> Of wynter, that hym naked made and mat,
> And with his swerd of cold so sore greved;
> Not hath th'atempre sonne all that releved,
> That naked was, and clad him new agayn.
> The smale foules, of the sesoun fayn,
> . . . .
> . . . for the newe blisful somers sake,
> Upon the braunches ful of blosmes softe,
> In hire delyt they turned hem ful ofte,
> And songen, "Blessed be Seynt Valentyn,

> For on this day I chees yow to be myn,
> Withouten repentyng, myn herte swete!"
> . . . .
>   And Zepherus and Flora gentilly
> Yaf to the floures, softe and tenderly,
> Hire swoote breth, and made hem for to sprede,
> As god and goddesse of the floury mede.

(F 125–74)

As Chaucer hymns in these lines the beauty of spring, the graceful loving attributed to birds, the generative power of nature, and the feast day of Saint Valentine, he evokes memories of his earlier poems, most especially *The Parliament of Fowls,* in their essential ethos. (*The Canterbury Tales* will begin with such a poem, eighteen lines long, as part of its dialectical design.)

But Chaucer uses the daisy to point toward another part of his prior poetic making as well—toward the love poetry of fourteenth-century France that he had explored so brilliantly in his early poems, from *The Book of the Duchess* forward. Again the figure is one of synecdoche: that whole body of poetry is here represented by the "marguerite" poems— the French word for daisy—in which that flower is used to signify and (by convention) disguise the identity of the courtly lady whom the poet/ lover serves.[62] This usage points toward a different sort of flower indeed—a flower not literal, but no less mortal for that, no less bound to a natural cycle that moves from birth to death. Chaucer invokes the aid of his French contemporaries that he may praise the daisy suitably:

> Allas, that I ne had Englyssh, ryme or prose,
> Suffisant this flour to preyse aryght!
> But helpeth, ye that han konnyng and myght,
> Ye lovers that kan make of sentement;
> In this cas oghte ye be diligent
> To forthren me somwhat in my labour,
> Whethir ye ben with the leef or with the flour.

(F 66–72)

He disclaims any interest in the more fanciful part of their courtly games—the poetry of "the flour agayn the leef" (F 189)—for he has other purposes in mind: "This thing is al of another tonne, / Of olde storye, er swich stryf was begonne."[63]

In his bold identification of the daisy with good Alceste, a metamorphosis otherwise unrecorded in literature or myth, Chaucer (even in the Prologue proper) bypasses the ordinary use of that poetic figure among the French poets to whom his early poetry owes so much. *The Legend of Good Women* not only redresses the account of love offered in *The Ro-*

mance of the Rose and the *Troilus*—the two poems about which the God of Love specifically complains—but the versions offered in *The Book of the Duchess* and *The Parliament of Fowls* as well. Indeed, it is quite possible that the *balade* at the Prologue's center, "My lady cometh, that al this may disteyne," is an earlier poem interpolated here, much as Dante had incorporated his own early poems into the *Vita nuova*, creating for them a context in which their real meaning could be read for the first time, a prophetic meaning unclear even to Dante at the time of their composition. I think Chaucer's Prologue may have been meant to complete his otherwise conventional *balade* in a similar way, and to reorient (by implication) his future poetic oeuvre. While gracefully fulfilling the exigencies of a royal commission, he moves his fiction steadily toward the figure and the legend of Alceste, and through her toward patterns of dedication and release outside the poem.

Chaucer's praise of "good women" who lived before the time of Christ is never, I think, fundamentally ironic. Though he is sometimes amused, and even permits himself jokes that are tonally incongruous—"Be war, ye wemen, of youre subtyl fo, . . . / And trusteth, as in love, no man but me" (2559)—though he grows weary at times of the lessons these legends yield, and though he knows that the story of Alceste is finally no more than a myth concerning resurrection, yet his larger literary purpose is very different from satire. I think he would have said, as Boccaccio did in the Dedication to *De claris mulieribus*, "Whenever you read of a pagan woman having qualities which are worthy of those who profess to be Christians, if you feel that you do not have them, blush a little and reproach yourself that although marked by the baptism of Christ you have let yourself be surpassed by a pagan in integrity, chastity, or virtue." And I think he might have defended the categoric exclusions of his poem in the manner of Boccaccio's Preface to the same work: "I have neglected to include almost all Hebrew or Christian women among these pagans . . . because it seemed that they could not very well be placed side by side and that they did not strive for the same goal."[64] Surely, that is what the God of Love means in describing the good women from two distinct perspectives, both offering guidance to the reader: "Men schulde sette on hem no lak; / And yit they were hethene, al the pak" (G 298). Where Chaucer most differed from Boccaccio was in his wish to give the formal sequence of the work a meaning. From a profound respect for the pagan past, and for the dignity of women as fully human beings, Chaucer sought to suggest the shadow of a new dispensation to come, in which *AVE* would reverse *EVA*, and Mary Magdalene would see the resurrected Lord before any of the twelve apostles. Chaucer found a shadow of that "something-to-come" within the legend of Alceste, and intended to conclude with her for reasons as formally decisive as those which led him to begin with Cleopatra. He meant his poem to locate within pagan history certain possibilities of human loving that Christian history would later confirm and redeem.

The quest for a truer poetry begins or ends virtually all of Chaucer's major poems. In the version of this quest that begins *The Legend of Good Women,* Chaucer looks back upon much of what he has previously written, and presents himself (a few works excepted) as absurdly self-cast in the worship of that which is mortal and can only die. To the extent that his poems celebrate the coming of spring, the beauty of nature, and the potency of natural generation, they are themselves part of an order that ends in decay, corruption, and mortality, a poetry limited to cycles of death and rebirth, to tears for what is mortal. And in those of his poems which praise the lady as being beautiful as a flower—worshipping her, *fin amors,* for that beauty's sake—he sees his error compounded. For the flesh is *like* a flower[65] in another of the commonplaces central to the poem, and both flesh and flower end as food for worms. Cleopatra dies first in the poem in order to establish that fact. The God of Love's disdain when he first sees the poet kneeling alongside the literal flower—"Yt were better worthy, trewely, / A worm to neghen ner my flour than thow" (F 317)—intends no insult to worms. A literal worm near a literal daisy would draw no such rebuke. But that a poet should find his highest muse in the order of nature or the beauty of woman— that a rational creature possessed of an immortal soul should worship either flesh or flower—that is judged monstrous indeed. Behind the God of Love's comic misreading of Chaucer's prior texts, I think we are meant to hear the voice of the poet himself, rendering a deeper and more mordant judgment on his poetic career. It is spoken as part of a poem meant both to substantiate and to remedy that charge, a poem meant to move from the legend of Cleopatra, "fayr as is the rose in May" (613), through the legend of Dido, "of alle queenes flour" (1009), to Alceste, apotheosis of the daisy, only apparently and for a time mortal. Her body does not feed the worms, and her destiny transcends the grave. Whatever Chaucer's technical interest in the art of abbreviated narrative, it is the quest for Alceste, *in her deepest meaning,* that furnishes the essential narrative and thematic impulse of the poem. "Madame," the poet beseeches her, "yeve me grace so longe for to lyve, / That I may knowe soothly what ye bee" (F 459).

THE UNLIKELY NARRATOR:
THE NARRATIVE STRATEGY
OF THE *TROILUS*

BERNARD F. HUPPÉ

The *Troilus* contains an apparent disharmony which must be explained or candidly admitted as a basic flaw. The apparent disharmony involves, first, the proems, second, the discrepancy between the overriding comic mode of the *Troilus* and the solemnity of its conclusion, and third, the narrator. The problems presented by these three matters are interlocking; one cannot be solved without reference to the others.

The problem with the proems is quite simply that they belie the symmetry they promise. Book 1 begins with what is manifestly a proem, but without formal, external indication; Books 2, 3, and 4 begin with proems, formally indicated by *incipit* and *explicit*.[1] Book 5 appears to have no proem at all; even the two lines of reference to the angry Parcae do not function as proem but as a reminder of the absence of a proem. Further Books 1, 2, and in particular 3, end with formal transitional conclusions. Book 4 is not so concluded, but rather with no pause moves directly into Book 5.

Book 5, on the other hand, contains a very formal conclusion which begins, "Go, litel bok." The difficulty here is that it contains an embarrassment of finalities and a discordancy of sentiments. Thus the lines preceding the epilogue appropriately suggest that the narrative has been concluded. At the beginning of the poem the narrator had specifically limited his subject to the love story (1. 3–5, 53–55). Now in restating this limitation he declares that he has completed his tale, "I have seyd as I kan," (5.1765–70). This note of finality is enforced by the narrator's ensuing apology addressed to the ladies of his audience. Then having given his apology, he conveys his "litel tragedye" on its way to posterity. Although he has now dispatched his book, recalling apparently that his hero is not yet dead, and that his death is legitimately part of his love story, he returns to his narrative, "The wrath, as I bigan yow for to seye, / Of Troilus" (1800); further, in relating the overlooked death of his hero he goes Boccaccio one better by following Troilus after death, or more exactly by following him on the journey after death which Boccaccio had Arcite take in the *Teseide*. The death of the hero is thus not given until the narrative has been completed and the book sent on its way. In turn the postponed death leads to still another conclusion, one which for the first time condemns Troilus's love. This condemnation leads the narrator to the certainty that he has ended his tale, "And thus bigan his lovyng of Criseyde, / As I have told, and in this wise he deyde" (1833–34). This resumptive conclusion is then followed by a second stanza of address to his audience (1835–41), solemnly reminding them of the one true love, and is framed by a rhetorically violent stanza of further condemnation. This is followed by a redirection of his book, it now being conveyed under the correction of Gower and Strode and in the keeping of God, the ultimate and final conclusion now being achieved with a rendition of Dante's great prayer to the Trinity.

These unsymmetrical inconsistencies could be dismissed on the grounds that consistency is the hobgoblin of small minds and that absolute symmetry is a form of immoderate consistency. The omission of formal designation of the poem to Book 1 is a mere nothing, and an argument could be made for a higher symmetry in substituting a formal conclusion in Book 5 for the lesser symmetry of a formal proem. There is against such optimistic arguments the fact that Chaucer along with Dante, Petrarch, and Boccaccio assented to an aesthetic theory which gave formal symmetry an essential role. Even apart from theory, however, there remains an inescapable problem with the proem to Book 4 and the omission of a proem to 5. The proem to 4 quite clearly states that it is intended to introduce the final book:

> This ilke ferthe book me helpeth fyne,
> So that the losse of lyf and love yfeere
> Of Troilus be fully shewed heere.
>
> (4.26–28)

But Troilus's death is not shown until the epilogue to Book 5. Are we to conclude, then, that Chaucer so lost control of his poem that he intended to wind up the story in Book 4; then discovered that he had more material to handle than could be accommodated in a single book, and was thus forced to tack on a fifth book to which, as indicating a merely arbitrary division, a formal proem would be inappropriate, as would a formal conclusion to Book 4? Such arrangement would not suggest mere inconsistency, but complete loss of control over his materials. In consequence, unless the inconsistency is only apparent and is designed to reveal a deeper symmetry, a serious question of Chaucer's mastery over his poetic design must be raised. In short, are we looking through a window into a concealed design, or are we simply facing the blank wall that a careless and unserious poet has thrown up? It is clear that if the window be there, it should be found in some principle of ordered symmetry which involves deliberate inversion of order in the service of a higher level of order.

There is reason to doubt that Chaucer, at the point which he had reached in his rendition of the *Filostrato,* could have thought that one book would suffice to complete his work, for by the end of Book 3 he has covered only three cantos of the nine which comprise Boccaccio's work. The narrator of the *Troilus,* of course, claims not to be following the *Filostrato* but an unknown work by an unknown Lollius. Perhaps Lollius might have filled the narrator with a false optimism about what Book 4 would cover; the *Filostrato* could never have done so to Chaucer. Moreover, the design of the opening of Book 5 is not really haphazard, for its lack of a proem is balanced by the lack in 1 of any formally marked proem, and interlocking of design is also involved. Thus in the first book one of the Furies, Tisiphone, is invoked. In the proem to Book 4 all three are invoked by name; further, in the concluding stanza of 4, Troilus is placed in hell on earth. Book 5 in its first stanza makes reference to the other three fatal sisters, the Parcae. Books 2 and 3, to the contrary, invoke Clio and Calliope, the Muses of history and epic poetry respectively. The invocations not only appear patterned, but also appear entirely appropriate to the books they introduce. Book 1 under invocation to Tisiphone tells of Troilus's dark sufferings when he fell in love. Book 2 under the invocation of Clio gives the history of how Troilus gained his love. It is a busy book, full of goings and comings, the manipulations of that master of historical events, Pandarus. Book 3 under invocation to Calliope celebrates the fulfillment of Troilus's love—the epic moment in a love story if not in an epic. Here, however, apparent appropriateness disguises a more basic incongruity; for the rhetoric of the form (epic) is at variance with the content (love), a fact which may provide a clue to the reason for other incongruities.[2] In Book 4, Troilus awaits the loss of his love, an anguish of deprivation, in terms of fate, more profound than the anguish of desire. Appropriately all the Furies are here invoked. Book 5 tells of the final resolution of events as they are governed by the implacable forces which reveal to Troilus the emptiness of his faith in Criseyde; fittingly the Parcae introduce, although without formal, proemic invocation, the unwinding of the destiny of a fated man in a fatal love. Design is thus involved, but design which either employs inconsistency and incongruity, or conversely is marred by them.

Further examples of rhetorical symmetry involving apparent inconsistencies appear in the conclusions to the five books. Books 1, 3, and 5 have highly formal conclusions. Book 1 concludes with four stanzas; the first is transitional to Pandarus's activities in the following book, "And caste his werk ful wisely or he wroughte" (1071); the second two stanzas describe Troilus's reformation through love and provide an appropriate conclusion to the book which shows him falling in love; the final stanza formally marks a pause in the action, and thus serves the function both of conclusion and transition, "Now lat us stynte of Troilus a stounde" (1086). Book 3 ends with seven concluding stanzas: the first five describe Troilus's complete transformation through love, the next consists of a very formal address of thanksgiving to almost anybody within poetic earshot—Venus, Cupid, and not only Calliope but all the nine Muses—and the final stanza, as in 1, marks a formal pause in the action, "My thridde bok now ende ich in this wyse" (1818). Book 5, as noted, ends most formally of all, with a conclusion of insistent finality, where in the first two stanzas the book is sent on its way, then in four stanzas the death of the hero is told, followed by two stanzas containing an elaborately contrived apostrophe on true love addressed to the audience. These two stanzas are framed by two stanzas of rhetorical violence in condemnation of the events of his book, and in the final two stanzas the book is again sent on its journey under the guidance of Gower and Strode and in the hands of the Trinity.

Although Book 2 ends with a formal stanza of transition and Book 4 ends without much index of formal transition, the resemblance between the conclusions is stronger than the difference. As Books 1, 3, and 5 are marked by the formal rhetorical solemnity of their conclusions, Books 2 and 4 are entirely lacking in concluding elaboration. Book 2 leads directly to 3 by asking "lovers" to participate sympathetically in Troilus's suspense as he awaits Criseyde's appearance. The effect of the request for sympathy is transitional; Troilus's unendurable suspense links one book with the next, the time sequence being instantaneous, however comically Troilus himself is stretched on the rack. Book 4 prepares for the doom of Book 5 somewhat more solemnly but with an inverted variant of the request for sympathy of 2, "For mannes hed ymagynen ne kan, / . . . The cruel peynes of this sorwful man" (1695–97).

Such suggestions of interlocking design as in the references to the Furies and Fates are supported by a design of allusion found in the proems and formal conclusions. Thus the "weeping verse" of the first stanza of the poem, ultimately derived by way of Boccaccio from the opening of Boethius's *Consolation,* is recalled along with the reintroduction of Tisiphone in Book 4, "My penne . . . / Quaketh for drede" (13–14). This introductory allusion to Boethius is the first of the many allusions to the *Consolation* in the *Troilus.* Further, the inclusion in the proem to Book 1 of the figure of Tisiphone and of the thematic phrase, "the double sorwe," neither of which is in the *Filostrato,* interweaves allusions to the *Thebaid* and the *Divine Comedy,* which will also echo throughout the poem. Tisiphone is an inhabitant of Dante's Hell and is the chief demonic force precipitating the fratricide which leads to the Fall of Thebes. The double sorrow appears to reflect *Purgatorio* 22.45, where the reference is to the sorrows of Jocasta in Statius's *Thebaid,* which Criseyde is hearing read, 2.100–04. Again, the steerless boat of Troilus's Canticus in Book 1, at the opening of Book 2 becomes the hard-to-steer boat of the narrator's poetic voyage in a passage derived from *Purgatorio,* 1.1–3. In turn, Book 3 ends with thanks to Venus and the rest for guiding the narrator to the happy port of his triumphant Book 3. The image of the boat thus serves to establish a relation between the literary journey and that of his hero; indeed it cannot escape notice how involved the narrator is with his characters; he shares Pandarus's joy in the manipulation of events; he admires and feels for Troilus, and is attracted to Criseyde.

This intricate relation between narrator and poem may be subtly established at the beginning of the poem in the statement of theme; for the allusion to Jocasta's double sorrow echoes Virgil's address to Statius in the *Purgatorio.* A powerful set of relations is here established. In a poem narrating the road to salvation, Dante, an agent of grace, depicts the pagan Virgil, who wrote of the Fall of Troy, addressing the unavowed Christian, Statius, who wrote of the Fall of Thebes and who acknowledges his indebtedness to Virgil. In turn Dante acknowledges his indebtedness to both by having each in turn act as his guide. If the *Consolation of Philosophy,* the *Thebaid,* and the *Divine Comedy* echo for Chaucer at the beginning of his poem, the echo might suggest to him a set of resemblances: as Statius is to Virgil, so Dante (or Boethius) is to the fallible persona of the narrator whose journey leads out of error to revelation. Might this set have suggested to Chaucer a strategy in the handling of his own narrator?

The parallels suggested by the Dante allusions do appear to reverberate in the organization of the narrative, for the form of the *Divine Comedy* seems to be reflected, awryly to be sure, in the first three books of the *Troilus.* In the Proem to Book 1 the narrator establishes a universe of Cupid, complete with its saints, its suffering, and its damned. The narrator is himself far "from his help in derknesse" (18); he begs Cupid's saints to intercede for suffering lovers like Troilus, that they may come "in hevene to solas" (31), and for Cupid's damned, who "never nyl recovered be," that they be granted "soone owt of this world to pace" (41). In short, this universe is the imaginary, mirror image of Dante's real world of Heaven, Purgatory, and Hell. The story of Troilus's rise from his suffering because of the onset of love not only fits the Dantesque framework, but the resemblance is supported by a set of suitably awry allusions to the *Divine Comedy.* Clearly Troilus begins in Hell. The invocation to Tisiphone in the proem to Book 1 establishes that. In Book 2 Troilus emerges from Hell in his steerless boat to begin his Purgatory of waiting, and the proem begins suitably with a rendition of the opening of the *Purgatorio*, "Owt of thise blake wawes for to saylle, / O wynd, O wynd, the weder gynneth clere," and with the invocation to a muse (8) as in *Purgatorio*, 1.9, although awryly not to Dante's Calliope, but to Clio, who is invoked at the beginning of the *Thebaid*, 1.41. Calliope is invoked in the proem to Book 3, and it is in this third book that Troilus reaches his heaven, as its proem suggests in the elaborate address to Venus, the third planet, the sphere which caused Dante to exclaim in *Paradiso*, 8.1 ff.: "The world used to believe to its peril that [Venus] turning in the third epicycle radiated mad love."[3]

Of course, since Troilus's journey is a reversed, mirror image of the truth, he only apparently journeys upward, but in reality descends. He does not arrive at Dante's destination, the eternal stillness, so that the narrator's design has a fatal flaw. Nothing can follow after Dante's rise to the truth; it is only after Troilus's rise to false felicity that the knowledge of truth can come to him in bitterness. Thus, as we have seen, and it is not surprising, the symmetrical structure falls apart with the proem to Book 4, although the structural interlacement of allusions continues. That is why when in Book 4 Troilus falls back into a deeper pit of the lover's hell, the single fury Tisiphone of Book 1 is joined by her sisters, the three appearing together as in the *Inferno*. Further, Book 4 is dominated throughout by the image of the journey to Hades in the thoughts and conversations of Troilus and Criseyde (viz. 302–09, 473–76 [with echo of *Inferno* 9.43 ff.], 743–46, 784–91, 1143–44, 1152–56, 1175–76, 1187–1211, 1554). Finally, in the temple scene (4.946–1078), Troilus, in Boethius's words but not his understanding, accepts the doctrine of fatalism, "Of thynges that ben wist bifore the tyde, / They mowe nat ben eschued on no syde." In effect, this declaration of a false faith leads directly to Book 5, which depicts the final resolution of events under the implacable operation of Fate and reveals to Troilus too late the emptiness of his faith in earthly love. Fittingly, another set of three sisters, the Parcae, introduce, although without formal invocation, the unwinding of the fated man in a fated love.

Design is involved, that is clear. But it is equally clear that the design appears frequently to be contradictory in its effect. The evidence of structural planning in the proems cannot explain away a seeming failure in execution—unless it is not failure, but the triumph of subtle design, of significant rhetorical structure.

This takes us to our second problem, the contrast between the comic and the tragic in the poem. For the proems, if they are part of a meaningful inner design, must function to carry off a supreme *tour de force* in securing from the comic treatment of Troilus's love a conclusion of the highest solemnity. If the form of the proems is defensible it must be because they are part of an inevitable movement in the whole poem toward the conclusion, "Go, litel bok, go, litel myn tragedye." Only if the conclusion has been carefully prepared can it achieve the silence of stasis.

On the other hand, Chaucer does call his prevailingly comic poem a tragedy. Even though tragedy did not mean for Chaucer what it does for us, the question still nags as to whether he wanted to write a tragedy, but because he lacked "high seriousness" could not manage anything but comedy. Or is it wrong to find any comedy in the *Troilus* except for allowable comic relief? To answer this question and illustrate the pervasive comic mode of the poem it is necessary only to adduce one fairly obvious motif, that is, Chaucer's treatment of his hero—the supreme example in all literature of the horizontal hero. When we first meet him he is vertical, strutting like a peacock, in the temple, and we see him later creating a vertical impression on Criseyde as he rides his horse out of battle, in considerable glory. Then too he is permitted to speak in the words of Boethius on the high problem of Predestination, even though he misses the point, not surprising in a pagan; further, he is given passages of high poetry, as in his address to the temple without its deity, that is, Criseyde's abandoned palace (5.546–53); and of romantic sensitivity in his perceiving a breeze as Criseyde's sighs (5.668–79). Finally his death, suspended until the epilogue, is given special dignity with the verbal entwining of the dead Troilus's view of time and eternity with those of Scipio Africanus and Dante.

Chiefly, however, we see him stretched out on a bed, moaning, groaning, weeping. Indeed it is difficult to think of Troilus apart from bed, the horizontal hero. It makes no difference that he sometimes inhabits a bed with Criseyde—his supine horizontality is always emphasized. When she meets him in person for the first time he is stretched out in bed, a sick boy. When he is brought to bed to her, a precise description of what happens, he kneels at the bedside and faints, leaving handy Pandarus to pick him up, throw him in, and leave the initiative to her.

It is hard to believe that Chaucer's risibilities were less sensitive than ours, that he didn't find all this heroically horizontal love-making comic, that he didn't in fact make the most of it. Yet this does not mean that Troilus is not given a very real dignity, even a quality of heroic tragedy. It is counterpoint that gives to the *Troilus* the status of comedy. Its comedy is uproariously funny—and very serious, with implications of the tragic to exercise the reflective mind. In achieving this effect the proems may be shown to play an important role; their awryness is apparently deliberate and serves a function in the overall design. But to perceive this design it is necessary to understand the narrator in his ambiguous and ambivalent role.

For there is something awry about the narrator, too, however simple his role may appear at first glance. At the beginning of the poem the narrator is presented as

> the sorwful instrument,
> That helpeth loveres, as I kan, to pleyne,
> . . . .
>
> For I, that God of Loves servantz serve,
> Ne dar to Love, for myn unliklynesse,
> Preyen for speed.
>
> (1.10–17)

He cannot himself aspire to Love's service for his "unliklynesse,"

> But natheles, if this may don gladnesse
> To any lovere, and his cause availle,
> Have he my thonk, and myn be this travaille!
>
> (1.19–21)

The whole is couched in highly religious terminology, except that it has reference to the worship of Cupid. Curiously, the narrator assumes a papal title, the servant of the servants of God, yet this high priest because of his "unliklyness" is in the exterior darkness, far from the God of Love's help. As we have seen, he treats successful lovers as the blessed of the New Jerusalem (22 ff.), asking them to intercede for suffering lovers of the cupidinous church militant:

> And prieeth for hem that ben in the cas
> Of Troilus, as ye may after here,
> That Love hem brynge in hevene to solas;
> And ek for me prieeth to God so dere
> That I have myght to shewe, in som manere,
> Swich peyne and wo as Loves folk endure,
> In Troilus unsely aventure.
>
> (1.29–35)

Unless one takes this as mere words, the effect of the narrator's request is to leave an obvious question: How will it promote the reign of the God of Love to exemplify in his poem the pain and torment that lovers suffer? In view of such insensitivity it is not surprising that he should be in Cupid's exterior darkness. Or again note the blank literal-mindedness of the narrator's plea to Cupid's saints that they pray even for those in despair. "So graunte hem soone owt of this world to pace, / That ben despeired out of Loves grace" (41–42). Let them, in short, have an end to their sorrows, a sad life and a short one. In the mirror of the narrator's mind, suicide, which is condemned in the confessional manuals as the consequence of despair, becomes the merciful outcome of despair; since lovers live for love, if they despair of love's solace, in mercy their life should end. Again when the narrator asks for prayer to God, it is not certain which God is to be invoked. Obviously the rhetoric in celebration of the lover's life is undermined by the ambiguity and misapplication of a religious terminology which forces the reader to look in the direction opposite to that toward which the rhetoric points. This is most obvious in the penultimate stanza of the first proem:

> For so hope I my sowle best avaunce,
> To prey for hem that Loves servauntz be,
> And write hire wo, and lyve in charite,
>   And for to have of hem compassioun,
> As though I were hire owne brother dere.
>
> (1.47–51)

The word *charite* tolls like the monk's chapel bells and contradicts the entire purport of the preceding rhetoric.

The narrator's "unliklyness" for love is compounded of the obvious physical aspect and of a spiritual aspect, his desire to live by another love than Cupid's, that is, charity. This spiritual aspect as a bar to *amor* the narrator tends to disregard, and he does not seem to include it as contributing to his unlikeliness for love. And the special relation he establishes between himself and lovers, and by definition with the protagonists of his poem, contains a similar unresolved combination of contradictions. What is the nature of his brotherly compassion? Is it Epicurean? Christian? Romantic? Does it spring from comprehension or sentimentality?

The same set of contradictions appears in the narrator's role as the translator of "Lollius," so that the device which is supposed to secure credibility seems at every point to undermine the narrator's claim to authenticity. The reader cannot take him or his claim of faithful rendition seriously; because he appears too earnest to be a liar, however, he must be a fool, self-deceived, a believer in the truth of fiction. Thus the very first allusion to Lollius appears in Book 1.394; as the narrator is about to "translate" Troilus's first song, he pauses to assert that he is giving not only "the sentence, / As writ myn auctour called Lollius," but the actual words of the song, "save oure tonges difference." His insistence on historical authenticity serves, in fact, simply to underline his departure from the never-mentioned, actual source of the *Troilus*, Boccaccio's *Filostrato*, for Troilus's song is not a rendition of anything there, but of Petrarch's Sonnet 88. Thus the first mention of Lollius, which is reasonably characteristic of the remaining references, clearly involves a silent gesture to the *literati* in the audience, a gesture which reveals the narrator as himself a comic creation.

Again and again the narrator insists on his earnestly pedestrian concern with the historical authenticity of his narrative; he is literal or he is nothing. Thus in the proem to Book 2 he supports his claim by insisting that his function is that of the artless translator, dispassionate in his transcription. May Clio help him, he prays:

> To ryme wel this book til I have do;
> Me nedeth here noon other art to use.
> Forwhi to every lovere I me excuse,
> That of no sentement I this endite,
> But out of Latyn in my tonge it write.
>
> (2.10–14)

He is merely a rhymer; his "sentement" is not involved. If lovers are annoyed with what they find (an obtuse reminder that they should be) the substance is that of the solemn Latin writer, Lollius:

> Wherefore I nyl have neither thank ne blame
> Of al this werk, but prey yow mekely,
> Disblameth me, if any word be lame,
> For as myn auctour seyde, so sey I.
>
> (2.15–18)

Indeed his sentiments about love would be inappropriate because of his unlikeliness:

> Ek though I speeke of love unfelyngly,
> No wondre is, for it nothyng of newe is;
> A blynd man kan nat juggen wel in hewis.
>
> (2.19–21)

Although Lollius is apparently one of the ancients and his story comes from long distant times, yet it remains valid for moderns who understand the story. As for the narrator, he transmits the story, nothing more, "Myn auctour shal I folwen, if I konne" (49).

In the remaining proems (that is, to Books 3 and 4) this same literary role is maintained. In Book 3, however, the narrator tends to soar to meet the height of his subject, the achievement of love's solace. His "destresse" (46) now springs from the problem of how he may "telle anonright the gladnesse / Of Troilus." He needs all the help that Calliope and Venus can bring. When he has completed his third book, however, he obviously "points with pride" to an achievement which he feels has demonstrably surpassed his "modest" claims to a purely pedestrian talent. Thus he finds it necessary to thank Venus, Cupid and all the nine Muses for their aid. In Book 4, as we have seen, he returns to the "weeping pen" image of 1, and asks all the Furies as well as Mars to help him finish the poem in that book. Apparently, unlike Venus and the Muses, they do not oblige him.

The narrator also plays a role in the narrative proper, but it is an unobtrusive one, for the narrative art of the *Troilus* is primarily dramatic, with much of the action presented in dialogue or interior monologue. Indeed the poem may readily be divided into scenes connected by brief transitional passages (see Appendix A). In this dramatic action the narrator intrudes occasionally with three kinds of interjection. The first, consistent with the proems, comprises allusions to the "auctour," in effect further investing the narrative persona with the role of "translator," a literal-minded instrument for transmitting his source on the level of sense. This has already been illustrated in the first reference to Lollius in Book 1. Frequently his pose as "translator" by demanding interpretation from the reader serves to enhance the drama of the narrative. For one example of many, he insists on scholarly historicity, saying of Criseyde that he does not know "wheither that she children hadde or noon, / I rede it naught, therefore I late it goon" (1. 132–33); however, since Boccaccio says clearly that she had none, his statement is false and arises from the fallibility of his pose as transcriber of the letter. The effect is to involve the reader by forcing him to conjecture, and to conclude with Boccaccio, that she had no children. Raising the question actually serves to call attention to a characterizing detail (e.g., the Wife of Bath). His pose of laborious authenticity also permits the "translator" frequent expression of his feeling for Criseyde by excusing her conduct. This expression of feeling arises in Book 5. 1051–99 to infatuated apology for her betrayal of Troilus. There he explains, "the storie telleth us" no woman was sorrier; furthermore, "ther is non auctour telleth" how long it took her to fall (although inadvertently he has just told us himself, 842 and 1030); finally he exclaims that he cannot chide her "forther than the storye wol devyse," and that, beyond this, he would still excuse her because of her grief and his own pity.

The second way that the narrator interjects himself into the story is by comment and explication. Where these exist independently of the role of the translator, they tend to suggest a further role as narrative commentator. These explications frequently have the ambivalence of the proems, thus further developing this aspect of the narrator, as in his comment when discussing Criseyde's pleasure in thinking of her capture of Troilus: "But al passe I, lest ye to longe dwelle; / For for o fyn is al that evere I telle" (2.1595–96). The "o fyn" suggests the literary doctrine of sentence as the end of poetry, but here it may simply refer to the narrator's concern with the effectiveness of his narrative as such. Certainly many of his narrative interpolations suggest a sympathetic involvement with his characters; thus when he assigns reasons for Criseyde's acceptance of Troilus, he is careful to put her conduct in the best light: "So wis he was, she was namore afered,— / I mene, as fer as oughte ben requered" (3.482–83).

The third type of narrative interjection consists of rhetorical interpolation and apostrophe, often lengthy and elaborate and involving personal judgment and interpretation, evoking themes like that of fortune. Such set pieces of rhetorical interpolation, although not frequent, taken in conjunction with the formal proems and conclusions, provide a rhetorical frame for the narrative. They place the whole, at least up to the epilogue, in the context of a special viewpoint, that of the narrator whose sympathy for the characters of his story is as evident as is his ambiguous relation to them, and as evident as his ineptness.

Although the fictional persona, then, has great significance for the narrative art of the *Troilus,* his role as narrative commentator is fairly unobtrusive. All three types of interpolation discussed are reasonably infrequent; indeed it is possible to list briefly all significant occurrences (see Appendix B). Such an overview serves to establish very clearly the character of the narrator as persona playing his own role in the conduct of the poem, as does his appearance in the proems and conclusions. Dramatic as the narrative is, it is nevertheless conveyed to us colored by the ambiguous character of the narrator. On the one hand, he claims to be a mere translator, capable of rhyming, but not of comprehension. He professes himself unable to get beyond his source to explain the motivations of his characters, except that each protestation of ignorance underlines a clue to the reader. He can declare his desire to celebrate love and his unsuitability for the task, although inspired in Book 3 to a height of celebration which requires that he thank everyone he can think of. He can proclaim his noninvolvement in love and his determination to live in charity, yet declare he would give his immortal soul to experience a love he cannot describe: "Why nad I swich oon with my soule ybought, / Ye, or the leeste joie that was theere?" (3.1319–20). He is very curious about Criseyde, is attracted to her, exhorts the ladies in his audience to follow her example in taking Troilus: "For love of God, take every womman heede / To werken thus, if it comth to the neede" (3.1224–25). Yet finally there is no ambiguity. At the end of Book 5 after the book is first dispatched and the hero has died and seen his folly too late, then the author speaks of the "fyn" of his hero's life and works, and draws the unambiguous Christian moral.

But this moral clarity is precisely what raises the central question of discordant elements in the *Troilus,* because on the face of it, we cannot reconcile the stern moralist with the complaisant narrator. The latter admires Troilus, is one in spirit with Pandarus, and holds Criseyde up as an example; the latter condemns all that the narrator enjoys. Yet, in effect, the passing reference in Book 2.1596 to the "fyn" which is the narrator's guide is given life and full meaning by the stanza which follows the death of his hero.

> Swich fyn hath, lo, this Troilus for love!
> Swich fyn hath al his grete worthynesse!
> Swich fyn hath his estat real above,
> Swich fyn his lust, swich fyn hath his noblesse!
> Swich fyn hath false worldes brotelnesse!
> And thus bigan his lovyng of Criseyde,
> As I have told, and in this wise he deyde.
>
> (5.1828–34)

Here the worth of any life, however regal, which is governed by "worldes brotelnesse" not by true reality, the "estat real above," is made inescapably clear.

The apparent contradiction of narrative voices, along with the ambiguity of the proems and the contrast between comic and tragic, are too interwoven, too omnipresent not to be part of a design. Perhaps the fact of the narrator as character, however ambivalent, may provide the clue to Chaucer's strategy of design, a strategy responsive to his own experience as a poet in the Augustinian tradition.

Central to this tradition is the distinction between sense and sentence, a distinction which created for the poet a special tension. On the one hand he is governed by the "fyn" of his work, an unambiguous sentence; on the other he is completely involved in the convolutions of the fiction which conveys the sentence. Put at its simplest, the poet must enjoy his fiction, must feel sympathy for his characters to whom he gives literary life. He must rejoice in finding the rhetorically effective phrase. In short he must actively participate in his own fiction. Yet all this that fully occupies him cannot be an end in itself; it is the shell to be discarded for the kernel. Brilliant contrivance and careful design exist to be transcended. The reality of the fiction leads to the discovery of a reality which belies its simulacrum.

Jean de Meun, among many others, was concerned with this problem of fictional reality, and in the *Roman de la Rose* gave it brilliant expression in his tales of Apelles' and Pygmalion's attempts to imitate nature. Apelles recognized his limitations; Pygmalion fell prey to the ultimate delusion of believing in the reality of his own creation. The distinction, as suggested in passing by Saint Augustine, is between author and guide.[4] The poet who audaciously believes he is himself the author of reality is the victim of his lie; there is but one Creator. However, in realizing that he serves only through faith as a guide to reality, the poet may find a valid role. That is, he cannot play God, but he can imitate a temporal reality in order to help his audience perceive eternal reality. Jean was also alive to the role of the poet as narrator. In the gloriously comic beginning of his portion of the poem, he continues Cupid's speech to the lover by posing a very curious problem. Cupid in addressing the narrator found himself in the predicament of having the narrator's auctorial actuality die. A narrator has an existence independent of the author, but only in words already written; Cupid, however, has a fictional life beyond that of a particular narrator, and in the fictional present in which he lives is aware that Guillaume's work will be continued by Jean. On the one hand, in actual time, Jean was not yet born; on the other, in the fictional present, which has nothing to do with time—or with eternity—Jean is ready to guide the narrator to his conquest of the rose.

Chaucer was to continue to develop this and other comic realizations of the role of the narrator as conveyor of the sense, from *The Book of the Duchess* through *The Canterbury Tales*. The *Troilus* provides no exception to this interest; indeed, the narrator of the *Troilus* may well be the most subtle and provocative of all Chaucer's fictional alter egos. For if the surface structure of the *Troilus* appears ambiguously complex and puzzlingly ambivalent, the recognition of its dazzling interior design is clearly revealed when the role of the narrator is understood.

The source of Chaucer's conception of his narrator must come from the donnée in the situation. He has set out to "translate" Boccaccio's *Filostrato*. In making the Italian poem his own he had first to deal with the problem of Boccaccio's persona, in his fiction the lover of a lady who has left Naples. This persona has his own comedy. He writes his poem to reveal his suffering at his loss of his beloved's presence; that is to say, Troilo is to "Boccaccio" as Criseida is to his lady. The analogy pleases Boccaccio's persona, who is sufficiently dense not to see that it might not equally please the lady whose favor he is presumably trying to win.[5] Since the narrator thus conceived had to be altered to suit Chaucer's manner, what more obvious than to realize him in his role as "translator." As such he could share in the *Filostrato* narrator's dullness of perception; thus the *Troilus* narrator fails to perceive that many of his statements are self-contradictory, or that Troilus's love is folly. As "translator" he must also stand in a purely literary relation to his hero and could not play the role of Boccaccio's narrator as lover; thus his posture of being merely an onlooker at the game of love, living, as the first proem would have it, in the outer darkness of love's universe.

This literary role also implies the profession of unworthiness, of unlikeliness for poetry as well as love, as suggested by the standard *topos* of self-depreciation. Such display of modesty, however, does not preclude rhetorical display as long as suitable acknowledgment of indebtedness is made. Throughout the *Troilus* the comedy inherent in the rhetorical pose is exploited. Thus the narrator indulges in rhetorical interpolation and apostrophe, oblivious to their inappropriateness, as when he declares, "Blissed be Love, than kan thus folk converte!" (1.308) to mark the beginning of Troilus's descent into the torment of love; or again when he concludes Book 2 with expression of great sympathy for Troilus as he waits in agony for Criseyde to enter. The narrator's sympathy for his hero results in prolonging his hero's agony as he concludes Book 2 with a formal "demaunde" to his audience on the subject of Troilus's suspense, and follows this by the long rhetorically embellished proem to Book 3 before ending Troilus's suspense with which his rhetoric is all in sympathy. This same proem to Book 3 provides, as we have seen, the supreme example of the narrator's misplaced rhetorical flight. By the end of the Book he has been so impressed that in modesty he must thank Venus, Cupid, and all the nine Muses for granting him so far to exceed his own powers. All the time, however, the reader is aware that the narrator has consistently misapplied his references, for example, in using Dante's prayer to the Virgin to celebrate Venus in the proem and in invoking the Muse of epic poetry to celebrate a willing capitulation in bed.

As Chaucer's narrator is of a type totally different from Boccaccio's, the work he is translating must also suffer a change; thus the fiction that he is translating the work of Lollius, clearly more authentic than any modern Italian poem. His search for authenticity has, however, the unexpected result of making him blandly gullible, as when, for example, he takes Petrarch's sonnet as the authentic language of Troilus's song. This posture results from his being concerned primarily with the integument, the level of sense, of story. And the posture has the effect of making him, though at a literary distance, visualize and realize his characters, to become involved in their story and increasingly feel not a general but a particular fellow-feeling and sympathy for them, to participate in Troilus's suffering and his joy, to feel something of his blind love for Criseyde, and as manipulator of words to participate admiringly in Pandarus's manipulation of fictional events. Thus the narrator who in Book 1 declares his intention to live in charity in Book 3 has become so involved that he wishes to share Troilus's joy even at the expense of his immortal soul; and he cannot bear to think evil of Criseyde even when she is manifestly false.

Conversely, his involvement with the sense places him in a special relation to the sentence to which it is the function of the sense to lead. But as the pedestrian translator he claims to be, he has no advantage over the casual reader in perceiving the sentence until the poem is complete and the "fyn" made clear. That is why the narrator, although he knows he writes for "o fyn," is not sure what it is. Indeed he has planned a rhetorical strategy which involves acceptance of values which the sentence of his work will disprove. Thus he begins with Love's universe as reality, following the structure of the *Divine Comedy* to frame the ascent of his hero from cupidinous sinner to cupidinous saint. What he fails to realize is that Love's universe belongs to the world of the narrator, that is, the world of fiction. If Troilus's story were also the narrator's fictional creation, his rhetoric might have worked, and Troilus and Criseyde could have lived in bed happily thereafter. Unfortunately, he is only a translator, not a creator, and the fate of his hero demands a descent from the eternity of the moment. Thus the narrator's dilemma when he comes to Book 4 and desires to bring his tale to an end quickly. In this expectation, despite his rhetoric, he will be defeated by the demands of the sentence which governs the story he is translating.

   In all Chaucer's major works the "I" narrator plays a primary role. Unless this role is understood the shape and meaning of any of these poems may be missed. This is obviously true of the *Troilus,* where the narrator plays a role of major importance in providing the clue to the significance of the ambiguities of its surface structure. Through him is realized the central problem of the poet who must create believable fiction, while knowing that its appearance of reality is merely a means toward the perception of a higher reality. Exploitation of the role of the narrator leads to the shock of recognition, the facing of ultimate meaning which occurs at the end of the poem. It is the same effect for which Boethius strove in his retelling of the story of Orpheus and Eurydice, which he concludes thus: "But who can give lovers a law? Love is a stronger law unto itself. As they approached the edge of night, Orpheus looked back at Eurydice, lost her, and died." Nothing could be more warmly human, more sympathetic to lovers, nothing more cognizant of the power of love, its grandeur, and its tragedy. Wagner's *Liebestod* provides the fitting accompaniment to the words. And the evocation in the reader of such feeling is precisely what Boethius is after. He wants him to feel the overpowering allurement of love so that he may be shocked into a keen awareness of the true meaning of the fable, for Boethius continues: "This fable applies to all of you who seek to raise your minds to sovereign day. For whoever is conquered and turns his eyes to the pit of hell, looking into the inferno, loses all the excellence he has gained."[6]

   What Boethius does here in miniature Chaucer does on the large canvas of the Fall of Troy. In the *Troilus,* as the narrator becomes involved with his characters so does the reader, but the deeper this involvement the greater the shock of recognition when Troilus laughs at his own funeral observances. It is toward the condemnation and affirmation which follow this laughter of the dead that the poem has been moving as its "fyn." Toward this high solemnity we have, thanks to the narrator, been moved through comedy, and yet with sympathy for Troilus until his empty laugh awakens us to an eternal reality. The author-rhetorician has become the guide to truth and raised our "minds to sovereign day."

SIGNS, SYMBOLS, AND CANCELLATIONS

JOHN GARDNER

It was once more common than it is among the present generation of Chaucerians to dismiss certain of Chaucer's works as "bad" or to excuse them as "early." Before its subtlety came to be understood, *The Book of the Duchess* was considered merely imitative, the work of a young poet sharpening up his tools. *The Parliament of Fowls*, the *Anelida and Arcite*, the Physician's Tale, and various other works were treated in the same way. Then came the revolution, largely the work of the misnamed "historical" critics—misnamed, to my way of thinking, because they gave emphasis to long-dead writers like Augustine, making Chaucer seem a sternly pious seventh- or eighth-century Christian poet, and for the most part ignored the quality and character of Chaucer's actual historical moment, a moment that included the magnificent, merrily pagan parade for Edward's mistress Alice Perrers, "the Lady of the Sun"; included the presence in Chaucer's audience of such prominent adulterous lovers, besides Alice Perrers, as Katherine Swynford and Princess Joan; and included the profound influence of thinkers like Roger Bacon, father of modern science and of the frightening idea that when you come right down to it we can know nothing.

Bacon had been asked by the pope to figure out what kind of knowledge we can trust, so that the hounding of heretics might be fair-minded. It was the new, scientific approach to translation, a movement in which Bacon was heavily involved, that had begun all the trouble. It would lead indirectly to the closing of Oxford University, hothouse of dangerous rationalist ideas ever since Abelard had arrived there from Paris with his skeptical new way of looking at old texts. The new translators had already cast doubt on the authority of scripture and thus on the whole exegetical tradition. Bacon was convinced that the problems raised by the first tentative gropings toward higher criticism would soon be ironed out; but dismissing for the moment that chief source of authority, now temporarily in doubt, and studying closely all that remained of the two great pillars of medieval thought, authority and experience—

the authority of logic and philosophical tradition and "experience" in the sense of scientific method—he reached and communicated to the pope the conclusion we have reached once again in the present century, that, in philosophical questions not involving firetrucks, certainty is beyond our means.

These matters—Bacon's doubts, the rise of rationalism, Alice Perrers' parade, Richard's towering, step-ladder throne, King John the Good's inordinate love of candy, Oxford student riots, and so forth—give us the tone of medieval life and thus of its art. True "historical" criticism, it seems to me, must take into account both the fourteenth-century intellectual's esteem for early Christian writers and his real historical situation—his delight, allegorically justified but also physically savored, in love and war, in the arts and sciences (which now, thanks to Bacon, he could study with spectacles), and, above all, in the contrast between the old and the new, a contrast no longer felt to be alarming, though one might still tease a horse-faced goose of an outriding monk who, in his humorless, witless self-admiration, went too far. More often than not, historical criticism, focusing mainly on the writings of sober-minded people like the Church fathers, has led to gross misunderstandings of Chaucer, for instance the scholastically arguable but tonally lunatic notion that the Miller's Tale is a "Christian meditation." This is not to deny that the effect of the so-called historical critics has been beneficial: we have come to see *The Book of the Duchess,* for instance, for what it is, an immensely intelligent, highly original work of art, which, starting with Robertson, critic after critic would now like to prove not early but late.

Tone is the historical critic's disaster area. Think of Koonce's reading of *The House of Fame.* Even if all his observations were correct—most are, some are not—the whole reading is undermined, if not made to seem preposterous, by his stubborn refusal to notice the poem's single most obvious feature, its bubbling, unbungable humor—a feature that partly cancels the signs and symbols in much the way King Edward, struggling to run his necessarily huge bureaucracy under an outmoded code, would occasionally throw a large party, give a few presents, and cancel the strict construction of inconvenient laws.

Poetic cancellation of one kind or another must become, and is becoming, a matter of increasing concern for historical critics of the poetry of Chaucer. I am not dismissing out of hand the work done so far. As I have said, the historical critic's study of signs and symbols has redeemed many of the works of Chaucer that used to be called bad, by showing in them a richness and depth beyond the obvious. Numerological critics have opened up new vistas in *Anelida and Arcite* and *The Parliament of Fowls,* to say nothing of the *Troilus.* Critics interested in biblical exegesis have found gold even in what seemed the leaden Monk's Tale and *The Legend of Good Women.* I think no one who has seriously studied the works of Chaucer will deny that, discounting small mistakes, what these critics have pointed out is indeed there. The carpenter John in the Miller's Tale really is, as any fool can see, a mystery-play Noah-carpenter and a John who, like John of the Apocalypse and Noah before him, has been given a vision—in this case fake—of the end of the world; Nicholas, whether or not he has to do with the Nikolatanie, really is, like St. Nicholas in the plays, a guest who brings surprises; and the thunder and stench of the tale's famous fart really are closely parallel to the work of God's angels on the Last Day. None of this makes the tale a sober-minded meditation, but neither is any of it irrelevant. Each character's sly and private "purveyaunce," his self-absorbing role in the Theater of the World, proves a puzzle-piece in the totality of God's providence—to no one's surprise in the fourteenth century. Even jokes exist inside God's providence, as everyone in Chaucer's day had at some time or another been told. What doesn't exist within the total order? What humor can there be except reality misunderstood, as devils misunderstand it in the mystery plays? When the Miller's Tale was read, the whole court roared with laughter, we may be sure, not because they missed the tale's "philosophy," but because they caught it. And they did not catch it because they were the sober-minded persons Professor Robertson has, I think, wrongly identified as the key members of Chaucer's audience.[1] All the hard evidence we have suggests that Chaucer, all his life, wrote mainly for the feminine leaders of the court: Lady Blanche, Queen Anne, Princess Joan, and so on. When Richard went to fight in Scotland, Chaucer was called to the king-abandoned court and paid exactly what Froissart used to be paid for the entertainment of Queen Philippa; and at that time he wrote a poem, *The Legend of Good Women*, honoring Alceste, usually identified as Princess Joan, a regular visitor to Anne's house. It seems unlikely that Clanvowe, Stury, and the others Robertson cites would have been there, though they may have been. But it does not seem unlikely that the audience Chaucer wrote for would have gotten the jokes.

Professor Robertson, though a brilliant unearther of important facts, is not as satisfying when it comes to reading poetry. He tells us England was the "New Troy" and asks us to understand that Troilus is clearly meant to be recognized as a bad example for Englishmen in a nation under threat.[2] But however Troilus may groan, the fact is that he is a superb fighter, and love makes him fight better and better. If Chaucer had meant what Robertson wants him to mean, he would have had no choice but to make him a *bad* fighter, a threat to his kingdom. Again, he tells us that, because clothmakers employed women, the Wife of Bath is an exploiter and thus no feminist.[3] He neglects to notice that, first, if Chaucer had intended to make the Wife a figure of exploitation he would have mentioned, at least in half a line, the Wife's exploitation of women; second, the women Robertson considers exploited did not by any means consider *themselves* exploited; third, militant feminism and female preaching were indeed common in Chaucer's day, and were taken seriously, whatever Augustine might have thought (Augustine, remember, lived longer before Chaucer than Chaucer lived before us); fourth, we have no reason to doubt that in her misuse of Paul and others the Wife is joking, even mocking herself, as smart ironists do; so that in fact the only strong argument we have for condemnation of the Wife is that she's a money grubber and a sexual incontinent. But nearly all the pilgrims are money-grubbers, even the Clerk, whose library is made up mostly of expensive books by Aristotle (clad in black and red), a secular writer and one known chiefly, up to Chaucer's day, as an alchemist. The only clear exceptions are the Knight, with whom no one has yet been able to find fault, and the Parson, who, among other things, dislikes women and Jews, as he would not, we know both from certain *Canterbury Tales* and from the tradition he alters in his interminable sermon, if he were smarter. As for the Wife's sexual incontinence, I will say only this: given the personal affairs of certain key members of Chaucer's audience, Chaucer, whatever he may privately have believed, was not in a good position to make much point of sexual incontinence.

Chaucer's jokes, in the Miller's Tale and everywhere else, were funny to his audience because those jokes and their premises were understood—at least insofar as difficult art is ever understood by its audience—insofar, for instance, as Beckett was understood when his works were first performed, or William Faulkner when his fiction was first published. All funny jokes have philosophical premises. Think of the assumptions behind the Polack joke—remarkably similar in some respects to those behind Chaucer's humor—namely, that human energy as expressed in the Polack can be stopped by nothing in heaven or on earth, though in all he attempts the poor low-minded Polack must get everything wonderfully wrong. And it is worth noticing that for the Polish themselves, as for sensitive and intelligent people everywhere, the jokes carry also a second assumption: that the Polish are in fact anything but stupid, though the immigrant generation may have seemed it to dull-witted outsiders. The comparison with Chaucer's base of humor seems obvious. The eternally optimistic, myopic narrator of *The House of Fame* and the prattling eagle who serves as his guide may both seem pretty silly in a universe of baffling conflicts; but the eagle really does come from Jupiter, so that all he says really can be taken, on one level, "in ernest"; and, as for Geffrey, as he says to the man at his back, he knows pretty well where he stands when it comes to writing verse.

When he fails to observe the cancellations and sometimes, as in *The House of Fame*, the double cancellations, the historical critic makes necessary but minor things major; he confuses background and foreground. He is like the intelligent agnostic, Buddhist, or Jew musing on the blasphemous jokes about Jesus told by Jesuits or Anglican bishops. So the Monk's Tale is for the most part doctrinally sound, though some early historical critics doubted it; yet the tale is cancelled by the Knight because in fact it is, at least to the Knight, sententious and boring, or at least tiresomely one-sided.

This kind of oversight by critics, the failure to notice comedy's cancellations or gentle undercutting, should pose for us no real problem. Reading *A Preface to Chaucer,* the sensible Chaucerian can take the fruit and throw away the chaff. Serious is serious and funny is funny, whether or not the author of that book seems to know it. And however wrong-headed the interpretations, the facts are facts; we cannot reach a true interpretation of the poetry without them. Nothing seems to us more misguided now than Talbot Donaldson's wail, in Dorothy Bethurum's collection, that Chaucer is just merry Chaucer. I take it as proved, mainly by Robertson and Huppé, helped by their disciples, that Chaucer makes serious and continual use of Christian scholastic and exegetical ideas, and that even in his lightest, most bawdy jokes he has people like Boniface in mind. I take it as known by all sensible Chaucerians that the Miller's Tale is a comic masterpiece wherein Christian symbolism and allusion make the comedy funnier and more joyfully obscene. The misreadings can be corrected without fuss by anyone able to feel a poem's tone.

But one major problem still remains: What do we do with the obviously serious and aesthetically successful works that Chaucer cancels? The Monk's Tale is not all that bad. Yet when the Knight cries "Whoa!" breaking off the Monk's Tale, we are amused. We are slightly more surprised by the interruption of Sir Thopas, since the parody has abundant bounce and joy-of-life. Then there are cancellations still more puzzling, for instance, the *Melibee.* Lydgate loved it, and though he was a monk with too much time on his hands, his opinion was not all wrong; yet Chaucer, in his introduction, sets up the tale as a joke, the longest, most tiresome quotation collection in all literature, but one which Harry Bailey and the Pilgrims have no choice but to endure to the bitter end, since the sentence of it sooth is and since Chaucer has mock-pitifully presented himself as, though stupid perhaps, a feeling creature; "And therfore herkneth what that I shal seye, / And lat me tellen al my tale, I preye."[4] Then again there is the intellectually and lyrically beautiful *Legend of Good Women,* which Chaucer undercuts with his grousing about having to write on an impossible subject, "virtuous women." How seriously should the reader take what Chaucer takes back?

We are not dealing here, it is important to notice, with intentionally bad, even stupid poems like the Physician's Tale or the Manciple's Tale. Though medievalists reviewing my recent book *The Poetry of Chaucer* have not been quick to agree with me (medievalists being what they are), it seems to me obvious beyond a shadow of a doubt that the Physician's Tale was conceived and wrought as a tale told by an idiot signifying nothing. Eager to convince us that Virginia was a real girl and that the tale is "historical," and no fable, the pompous Physician introduces his heroine in terms grotesquely artificial and pseudo-poetic. Notice the repetition of terms suggesting artifice, exactly the kinds of terms a realist should avoid—"forge," "bete," "grave," "peynte" and so on—in the opening speech the Physician gives to that stiff old artifice Dame Nature on the real and historical young lady:

> Lo! I, Nature,
> Thus kan I forme and peynte a creature,
> Whan that me list; who kan me countrefete?
> Pigmalion noght, though he ay forge and bete,
> Or grave, or peynte; for I dar wel seyn,
> Apelles, Zanzis, sholde werche in veyn
> Outher to grave, or peynte, or forge, or bete,
> If they presumed me to countrefete,

> (11–18)

and so on. The motivation for the story in Gower's version, to say nothing of Livy's, is all stripped away in the Physician's version, and the moral the Physician finds is—as Harry Bailey notices at once—pure nonsense. The chief culprit is charitably forgiven in a piece of sugary piety on the father's part, and all those who consented in this cursedness—conspirators the Physician has neglected to mention—are furiously, righteously hanged. To claim, as many Chaucerians have done, that the Physician's Tale is an example of Chaucer not at his best is like saying, two or three centuries from now, when confusion has set in, that "Little Boy Blue," by Eugene Field, must be one of Robert Lowell's youthful works. Either Chaucer did not write the Physician's Tale, which obviously he did, or he was kidding.

Chaucer did write intentionally bad poems, exploring, as I have argued elsewhere, the idea of poetry's limitations as a vehicle of truth, an idea to which I will return in the conclusion of my argument. John Finlayson has pointed out that even the Parson's Tale is limited by the teller: Chaucer left his sources to bring in hardshell opinions (no surprise when we think of the Squire's comic attempt to imitate his father, misapplying his father's mighty lines, or the Prioress's comically ignorant attack on Jews—alas, more comic in Richard's court than later—or the Manciple's crackpot speech against all speech). But the poems which self-destruct are again not the problem; we can handle them, they make clear dramatic sense. The problem, or, at any rate, the problem to which I address myself, has to do with those poems which, the better we understand them, the more we admire, but which Chaucer nevertheless cancels, as he cancels everything we love in his retractions. The most interesting case, it seems to me, is the Second Nun's Tale.

It would be barbaric to suppose that Chaucerians do not know the beauty and intellectual cunning of the Second Nun's Tale. But it is obviously the case that, at least in a sense, the tale is canceled by the Canon's Yeoman's Tale which follows it in Fragment 8 and is explicitly linked with it. Both tales have been shown to be alchemistical. The first treats true alchemy, analogous to Cecilia's purification of those around her, through exemplary suffering, faith, and wisdom; the second treats false alchemy, motivated by cupidity rather than by charity, and in the tale's unfolding undercuts the first tale's sober message.

In the Canon's Yeoman's Tale the Canon's Yeoman, a man engaged in the false "bisyness" of duping people through alchemy, is led by his own reason and Harry Bailey's curiosity to a renunciation of his evil pursuit. In the sober old tradition whose figurehead is Augustine, intellectual curiosity is not highly praised; but after the Yeoman's sly hints that his master is more than he seems—and could indeed turn this whole world up-so-doun—Harry Bailey asks questions more and more direct until the Yeoman confesses all, driving his wicked master from the Christian company. In the process, right at the end of his recitation, the Yeoman gives the Pilgrims a passage from Arnold of the Newe Toun on the philosopher's stone. Rightly interpreted, the passage reveals that the philosopher's stone is none other than Christ, by extension the Pearl of Price, and so on, exactly as Cecilia's tale says it is. The stone is Titanos, Magnasia, the Lodestone, the "root" of a "water," that is, Christ as font, who in coming to this world was incarnated in "elementes foure." Thus it is better that the Yeoman can say, parroting but not understanding his betters, since he has failed to see that the stone is Christ,

> Lat no man bisye hym this art [alchemy] for to seche,
> But if that he th'entencioun and speche
> Of philosophres understonde kan;
> And if he do [understand], he is a lewed [unlearned] man.
> (1442–45).

If one has faith, one needs no science; if one has science, one finds that it leads back to faith. Ironically, the Yeoman, misunderstanding what he quotes, rejects the text and does exactly what the text advises—turns from science to faith, becoming one of the Pilgrims. Thus the Yeoman's stupidity, if that word is not too harsh, leads exactly where Cecilia's clear vision leads, toward salvation. Let me restate the cancellation to make sure my point is clear. The Second Nun's Tale openly advises that wise, clear-sighted people like Cecilia go to heaven, whereas blind ignoramuses like Almachius, her judge, or the bleary-eyed Canon's Yeoman do not. The Canon's Yeoman's Tale argues by dramatic implication that the foolish and ignorant too may be heaven-bent.

Until quite recently (the mid-1960s) neither of the tales was much liked by Chaucerians. Now, it seems to me, the party line goes this way: The Second Nun's Tale is a beautifully constructed, old-fashioned work, but archaic in its devices and essentially no more than a set-up for the Canon's Yeoman's Tale, which gives us Chaucer's true belief: God's providence is merciful without limits. This seems not only the general argument of Joseph Grennen,[5] who mistakenly imagined all alchemists to be fools, but also of Bruce Rosenberg, who understands about holy alchemy but maintains wrongly that "only through juxtaposition does the life of St. Cecile gain complexity, subtlety, and a richness beyond its seemingly facile surface. And only when linked to The Second Nun's Tale does The Canon's Yeoman's Tale acquire religious overtones."[6] The truth is that with or without the Second Nun's Tale, the religious implications of the Canon's Yeoman's Tale are as visible as the plot; only our blindness to the tale's huge neon signs and symbols made us miss the fact. As for the integrity of the Second Nun's Tale, we have no reason to doubt that the work (this work and not some other—for instance, one written in prose and known by the same name) was written in 1378 or shortly thereafter, when Chaucer asked for a deputy to relieve him of his custom-house duties to write a royally requested "Lyf of St. Cecyle." If this is so, the poem was written nearly ten years before Chaucer worked out the conceit of *The Canterbury Tales*. No critic has persuasively argued that the legend was revised for inclusion in the collection. The speaker in the poem talks explicitly of writing (not oral composition), and the matter is not incidental; to revise these lines out would be to cut to the heart of the poem's intellectual structure. Whatever Chaucer may have hoped to make someday of his "Lyf of St. Cecyle," altering it to make it fit in with the conceit, the theme of the poem as it stands is translation; and in one of the word's multiple senses—the transfer of statements from one language to another—translation is a hard thing to do extemporaneously while riding to Canterbury on a horse.

So the poem as we have it had once been and thus still is a complete work, probably a royally commissioned work so difficult to accomplish that the poet had to ask for time off from his regular job. It was a poem sufficiently important to earn mention in Chaucer's prologue to *The Legend of Good Women,* and a work that draws on some of the greatest writers Chaucer knew, including Dante. Why is it, then—this is the problem—that years after writing it Chaucer drew this work into *The Canterbury Tales* only to undo it with the tale of the Canon's Yeoman? Let us dismiss out of hand as far-fetched and, in Longinus's sense, frigid, the possible argument that Chaucer's intent was to wreck the tale as he wrecked the traditional tale of Virginius and Virginia.

The Second Nun's Tale is a work no poet in his right mind would take back. It was an artifice, of course. No one in the court of Richard II, I suspect, took hagiography seriously, that is, took it for undeniable historical fact, though many, like Gloucester and Warwick, to say nothing of the king himself, kept large, gloriously illuminated collections, and no one denied the possibility of miracles and magic. At least in England, no one had written hagiography as history since the ninth century, and by the thirteenth the saint's-life legend had already become an essentially fabulous literary genre, figural to the core, except, of course, in the immediate environs of shrines where the legends brought in money, and cures sometimes worked, as they still do. It was a genre that celebrated passionate devotion and piety, like that of black-gowned Gloucester, patron of many chapels; if the genre favored miracles and grim executions, as Paul M. Clogan reminds us, these were not taken at face value but only as expressions of certain great truths, the eternal verities of the good Christian life: One need not get one's head chopped off, but one ought to be willing to suffer and sacrifice for others.[7] It was commonly acknowledged well before Chaucer's day that some of the saints whose literary existence was most celebrated may never have existed in the flesh. Of these Cecilia was one.

In writing the Second Nun's Tale, then, or rather, in translating it from Jacobus de Voragine or someone else, Chaucer engaged himself in an exercise already out of date or, at any rate, considered "mere art" among his Oxford friends, old-fashioned, nonscientific *translatio* with all its stiff rules of amplification, reduction, paraphrase, rhetorical heightening, and comment—the kind of thing he treats comically, again and again, in *The House of Fame*.[8] Yet the "Lyf of St. Cecyle" was of course not just a joke, not just (as I have too hastily described it elsewhere) an exercise in pure art. He seems perfectly serious, and is in full accord with Christian literary tradition, when in the poem's first section he speaks of translation as a kind of "feithful bisyness," a way of escaping that sinful "ydelnesse" which can lead to "roten slogardye," a corruption of the irascible soul, and "greet confusioun," a corruption of the rational soul. As Russell Peck has pointed out, in translating the old text Chaucer seeks a kind of translation, that is, purification, of himself; rather than sink into the slothful life wherein the body thinks only of eating and drinking "al that othere swynke," that is, the fruits of others' "leveful bisynesse," he will work at his book. If he was joking, or at any rate partly joking when he set himself to writing in *The Book of the Duchess* and *The Parliament of Fowls*, no such reading is possible here. Whereas the *Book of the Duchess* narrator is prohibited by the laws of courtly love from making the plain-speech confession that the poem itself, through the shrift of the Knight, has proved requisite, so that the narrator's poem can no more relieve his sufferings as a lover than did the Knight's forest lyrics earlier (although writing may perhaps relieve other sufferings), and whereas the *Parliament* narrator seems doomed to dissatisfaction, comically hungering for knowledge (that is, facts), exactly as lesser lovers hunger for each other, the narrator of the "Lyf of St. Cecyle" has good reason to hope for success. This narrator—Chaucer or the Nun, as you like—is not boxed in by any private "purveyaunce" but seeks relationship with God's total order. Here in this world, the realm of the "tryne compas" ruled by the one tripartite God, spiritual health must rise from the proper work of the three faculties or "sapiences" Cecyle mentions to Tiburce, "memorie, engyn [or will], and intellect." Translation of a saint's life, whether one takes it figurally or literally, is a willed exercise in Christian memory which can lead to or reinforce wisdom, that is, knowledge and faith. And not only does translation lead the writer to communion with the holy, it also encourages the reader to join that communion and thus to be "translated" in turn. As the body of Mary, "sonne of excellence," "translated" divinity to humanness, clothing God in "blood and flessh," and as the narrator, "unworthy sone of Eve"—a verbal play too long obscured by academic disputation on the sex of the speaker— now fleshes out the legend by "dressing" it in English verse (if we accept Clogan's slightly forced reading of "dresse" as a pun), so the reader is enjoined to flesh out or "translate" the poem he is reading and thus to translate himself upward, as Enoch was translated, according to Trevisa's *Polychronicon.* Thus the poem is made the center of the ultimate Christian mystery, the translation of spirit to flesh and of flesh to spirit.

This central idea Chaucer ornaments in several ways at once. He introduces the alchemistical sense of translation from base metals to higher through the efficacy of the philosopher's stone, which he identifies with Cecyle herself, with Mary, with honest work, and with the New Jerusalem. This is the point of the transposed and thus greatly emphasized passage from Jacobus, a passage Chaucer has altered only slightly, mainly by insertion of the key word *philosophres:*

And right so as thise philosophres write
That hevene is swift and round and eek brennynge,
Right so was faire Cecilie the white
Ful swift and bisy evere in good werkynge,
And round and hool in good perseverynge,
And brennynge evere in charite ful brighte.

(113–18)

It is for the same purpose that he gives new emphasis to the colors red and white, which Grennen identified as key elements in the "chemical wedding," the "whippe of lead" that Almachius wields (lead because that is the heaviest element and thus the one farthest from the Empyrean fire), and also the reason he introduces his various jokes on multiplication, as when, according to St. Cecyle, Almachius "multiplies," asking two questions where a clearer, less hair-splitting mind would see only one. Chaucer also heightens the tale, of course, with touches of his famous comic realism, as when Cecyle, suggesting that Almachius is blind, light-heartedly urges Almachius not to look at, but to feel his idols and see that they are stone.

Chaucer ornaments the tale in other ways. Heightening the form's archaicism, he introduces words obsolescent in the London dialect, such as *heryen, wemmelees, flemed,* and *lotynge,* and he makes heavy use of old-fashioned church paradoxes. The word *ydelness,* Paul Clogan points out, has a double sense: It means sloth, which "busynesse" must counteract, but as "porter of the gate . . . of delices" it may call to mind Mary, porter of the gate to heavenly delights, and thus may suggest *passio* in the sense of voluntary suffering in a right cause, which may in turn call to mind the Christian mystery at the heart of the poem, the mystery Bernard of Clairvaux expressed in his paradox of Christ's "passive action" and "active passion." Paradox and doubling were regularly employed in old-fashioned religious verse, for example English poetry in Cynewulf's day, to express, as Professor Clogan puts it "the paradoxical dual nature of certain religious doctrines which could not otherwise be expressed or explained: the mystery of God-man, the hypostatic union of divine and human; of a Creator and creature; logos and flesh; virgin and mother; passion and glory; death and resurrection."[9]

The work's single most peculiar device is one Chaucer has woven through the whole texture of the poem: In line after line the narrator allows himself exactly such doubling as Cecyle mocks in Almachius. I am not speaking now of antithesis or paradoxical doubling, but of what we would normally call flab. Chaucer calls idleness "the ministre and the norice unto vices"—why both? To achieve salvation, he says, "Wel oghte us werche and ydelnesse withstonde"—why both? And we must "bileve aright and knowen verray trouthe"—why both? These are just a few instances among many, and if we add traditional doublings like "mother and maid," or " 'Almighty Lord, O Jhesu Crist,' quod he," verbal doubling, most of it linguistic fat, becomes one of the most notable features of the poet's style. Nowhere else in Chaucer can we find such padding, if we choose, uncautiously, to call it that. Why does Chaucer use it? I think we can only answer subjectively, from the effect. It heightens the effect of the poem as antique, a piece as stiff, awkward, and curious to Chaucer's audience as eighteenth-century machinery seems to us. Perhaps it does more. If Cecyle is right about clear-sightedness and confusion, God's simplicity and the foolish multiplication of squinters like Almachius, then Chaucer has built into his poem—intentionally—the same befuddled humanness the poem, or the truth that stands behind the poem, is meant to burn away.

Whether or not this reading of the doubling is right is unimportant; it is something that, one way or another, interpretation must explain. What *is* important is the ingenuity and seriousness of the poem, its clear aesthetic value—and the fact that, bringing it to *The Canterbury Tales,* Chaucer canceled the poem's message with what we might call, anachronistically, the gothic-comic realism and the spiritual happy ending of the Canon's Yeoman's Tale. Why did he do it?

I think the right answer is the same right answer we must give to the question, What is Chaucer doing in *The Canterbury Tales* as a whole? or, still more grandiosely, What is the basic vision behind all Chaucer's work? The new, scientific approach to translation, to which Chaucer had lent himself in his translation of the *Consolation of Philosophy,* had thrown open all doors, torn up the very floor; nothing was any longer out of doubt. Plato and Aristotle had not said at all what people had for centuries believed they said; neither had Jerome or even Jesus. And the possibility of doubt was increased on every hand: Aquinas had recognized that logic, however rigorous, could prove things mutually exclusive and so had dropped his great project, the *Summa,* to become a mystic. Ockham had argued with some cogency that we can never understand each other, since ideas come only from experience and our experiences differ—the nominalist position Thomistic philosophers hated but could never quite refute. Bacon had shown, in his writings on optics, that experience (in the old sense) often lies. Siger of Brabant and many others, probably including the Oxford rationalists, had made faith secondary to reason. Wycliffe was having doubts about some of the sacraments, and Chaucer's friend and patron John of Gaunt was willing to send his army to break up a heresy trial.

Chaucer was not one to shrug off these new doubts and affirmations. He made comedy of them, as in *The House of Fame,* or he cheerfully admitted dissension even where he knew well what he believed. No sensible person would deny, he would have said, the cosmic order set forth or (as rhetoricians put it) "clothed" in the Knight's Tale; but it is a fact that the Miller does not see things as the Knight does—his experience has led him to a less noble world view—and neither does the Reeve. Chaucer, though no nominalist, smiles and lets them have their say, avoiding the dogmatism that Robertsonians would impose. When we begin to ask, Then what authority can we trust? Chaucer, again with nominalist befuddlement in mind, disingenuously trots out the Man of Law, with his sonorous tale of true constancy, the authority of God, pope, husband, and so on, to which the Wife of Bath instantly and quite rightly objects. So it goes throughout the Tales, even to the Parson's Tale; if Finlayson is right, except in the retractions, no one gets the absolutely last word. I do not mean that Chaucer is a man without opinions, only that his world is a roomy one in which all opinions, both the better and the worse, get speaking time. Poetry, like all other implements of knowledge, can reach toward but never quite grasp the truth. However inspired, it is always limited, as we see clearly in the Physician's Tale, by the humanness of its creator. Chaucer does not cancel the Second Nun's Tale because he seriously doubts the "sentence" of its antique piety; he cancels it because even this noble statement may not be—surely *cannot* be, in this infinitely various, infinitely mysterious universe—the whole truth. Cecyle's great virtue, charity, is the same virtue Harry Bailey reveals, however clumsily and tentatively, in asking sharp questions of the Canon's Yeoman; the same virtue the Yeoman comes to as he talks himself into renouncing his master's nasty tricks. Charity can be trusted, however devious its ways. After that truth, well, things get confusing for blear-eyed fallen man.

NOTES

Introduction

1. *The Life and Times of Chaucer* (New York, 1977), p. 3.
2. *MLN*, 69 (1954), 470–72.
3. Modern English translation by the editors.
4. Paul E. Beichner, ed., *Aurora: Petri Rigae Biblia versificata*, University of Notre Dame Publications in Medieval Studies, 19 (Notre Dame, Indiana, 1965).
5. Alan S. Downer, ed., *English Institute Essays, 1950* (New York, 1951), pp. 3–31.
6. Heiko A. Oberman, "Fourteenth-Century Religious Thought: A Premature Profile," *Speculum*, 53 (1978), 86.
7. "Some Medieval Literary Terminology, with Special Reference to Chrétien de Troyes," *Studies in Philology*, 48 (1951), 689.
8. "The Nun's Priest's Tale and Boethius' *De musica*," *Modern Philology*, 68 (1970), 188–91; "The Music of the Spheres and *The Parlement of Foules*," *Chaucer Review*, 5 (1970), 32–56.
9. "Chaucerian Tragedy," *ELH*, 19 (1952), 1–37.

Simple Signs from Everyday Life in Chaucer   D. W. ROBERTSON, JR.

1. *De doctrina Christiana*, 1.2.2; 2.1–4; 2. 16, 40. Cf. Peter Lombard, *Sententiae*, 1.1.1.
2. Cf. Erwin Panofsky, "Iconography and Iconology," in *Meaning and the Visual Arts* (New York, 1955), pp. 26–54.
3. *The Allegory of Love* (Oxford, 1936), ch. 2. A modern "symbol" is not the same thing either as a sacrament or as a figurative attribute. It is, rather, in Crocean terms, an intuitively perceived inner reality based on feeling that can be expressed only as a symbol. We are inclined to think of many of the ideas implied by figurative signs as "abstractions." But the idea that generalized concepts of all kinds are derived from the observation of a series of related particulars is Aristotelian and did not profoundly influence European thought until after the thirteenth century. Even then, "abstractions" were often treated as external realities whose existence might be discovered through experience. Generally speaking, "reality" has moved rapidly inward since the late eighteenth century. The term "personified abstractions" applied to certain figures in works like the *Roman de la Rose* is misleading, a fact clearly indicated by our tendency to think of them as "psychological" even when some of them, like *Bien celer*, are clearly strategic rather than "psychological." They actually belong to a moral rather than to a psychological realm. One of the last great English works to employ allegory in the ancient manner is Pope's *Rape of the Lock*, where the sylphs and gnomes represent outer realities that may or may not be reflected in Belinda,

depending on her choice of whether she harbors an "Earthly Lover" (3.144) in her heart or maintains "good sense" and "good humour" (5. 16, 30).

4. "The Question of 'Typology' and the Wakefield *Mactacio Abel*," *American Benedictine Review*, 25 (1974), 157–73.

5. Earl E. Miner, ed., *Literary Uses of Typology* (Princeton, 1976), Preface, where *typology* becomes synonymous with *allegoria* in its exegetical sense, from which *types* and *antitypes* are actually derivative, and comes perilously close also to embracing the sacraments.

6. As Boethius sagely observed, *Consolatio*, 5. pr. 6, "omne quod scitur non ex sua sed ex comprehendentium natura cognoscitur." On conventional figurative signs in the Middle Ages, see E. Mâle *L'Art religieux du XIIIᵉ siècle* (Paris, 1923), Introduction, ch. 1. It was generally thought that a failure to understand figurative signs in the Scriptures was extremely reprehensible. See Saint Augustine, *De doctrina Christiana*, 3.5.9. The idea persisted throughout the Middle Ages. Cf. Erasmus, *Enchiridion*, 3. With reference to poetry, the same author observes (*Enchiridion*, 14) that it may be better to read a poetic tale allegorically than to read the Scriptures literally. Petrarch and Boccaccio recognized the fact that some might fail to understand figurative signs in poetry. See C. G. Osgood, trans., *Boccaccio on Poetry* (rpt.; New York, 1956), pp. 58–62 (*Genealogia deorum gentilium*, 14.12.).

7. A pioneer study now often neglected is A. Goldschmidt, *Der Albani-Psalter* (Berlin, 1895).

8. "Iconography and Delusion," delivered 23 Nov. 1976 at the Courtauld Institute, London. She is preparing a book on the subject of iconographic research for which she is likely to propose extremely high standards. Cf. the recent study by Peter Hyland, "Number Symbolism in *The Canterbury Tales:* Some Suggestions," *The Annual Reports of the Faculty of Arts and Letters, Tohuku University*, 26 (1976), 1–11.

9. Specious argument was much relished as a source of irony in the Middle Ages. See, for example, my "Two Poems from the *Carmina Burana*," *American Benedictine Review*, 27 (1976), esp. 45–60; "Chaucer's Franklin and his Tale," *Costerus*, n.s., 1 (1974), esp. 12–17; Roy J. Pearcy, "Investigation into the Principles of Fabliau Structure," in Paul G. Ruggiers, *Versions of Medieval Comedy* (Norman, 1977), esp. pp. 97–100. J. A. W. Bennett, *Chaucer at Oxford and Cambridge* (Toronto, 1974), p. 83, refers justly, I think, to "that delight in specious argument for its own sake which characterizes the later fourteenth century," although Chaucer uses it for satiric comment on the speaker. For an amusing example from everyday life, see the hypothetical defense offered by a manorial tenant for stealing fish in F. W. Maitland and W. P. Baildon, *The Court Baron*, Selden Society, 4 (1891), 54–55.

10. "Clio and Venus: An Historian's View of Medieval Love," in F. X. Newman, ed., *The Meaning of Courtly Love* (Albany, 1968), pp. 28–29, 37. If a fairly orthodox audience is being addressed we can be reasonably certain that the definition is valid. Professor Benton, for example, believes that it "deserves a place at the beginning of every edition of [Chrétien's] *Lancelot.*" Along with the quotation from John of Salisbury in note 12 below it might well have a place at the beginning of every edition of Chaucer.

11. The first part of the Wife of Bath's Prologue offers an excellent illustra-

tion, but the technique flourished long before Chaucer. See the article on the *Carmina Burana* mentioned in note 9 above, and for another striking illustration the Old French play, *Courtois D'Arras*. For Chaucer, see also Gail Gibson's article in this volume.

12. Letter to Martin Dorp (no. 337, 1515) often printed in early editions of *The Praise of Folly.* For a similar use of Horace (*Sermonum,* 1.1.24–25) with the conclusion that "nothing forbids telling the truth with a laugh and representing in fabulous narratives, which philosophy does not reject, that which may be prejudicial to morals" see John of Salisbury, *Policraticus,* ed. Webb (Oxford, 1909), 8.11.753a. Cf. Richard de Bury, *Philobiblon,* ed. A. Altamura (Naples, 1954), 13. 15–25, and Chaucer, Cook's Prologue, 4356.

13. Mâle, *L'Art religieux,* pp. 186–97, and Bernard Rackham, *The Ancient Glass of Canterbury Cathedral* (London, 1949), p. 63 and pl. 19.

14. Reproduced from a MS in the Princeton University Library in my *Literature of Medieval England* (New York, 1970), p. 479.

15. E.g., Charles Rufus Morey, *Mediaeval Art* (New York, 1942), pl. 112.

16. See my *Preface to Chaucer* (Princeton, 1962), p. 243 and fig. 39.

17. George F. Farnham and A. Hamilton Thompson, "The Manor of Noseley," Transactions of Leicestershire Archaeological Society, 12, pt. 2 (1921–22), 242. For another example, see the description of the "garden of the Church" in Bishop Bransford's visitation notification of 1339, printed by R. M. Haines, *The Administration of the Diocese of Worcester in the First Half of the Fourteenth Century* (London, 1965), p. 85 (n. 3).

18. *Chaucer and the Tradition of Fame* (Princeton, 1966), pp. 125–29.

19. Theoretical psychology is essentially a feature of the modern universe of discourse (not necessarily of "the nature of things") which is unsuited to the study of authors whose analysis of human conduct is basically moral. The fragmentation of modern theoretical psychology into "schools" does not speak well for its credibility, and modern practical psychology must face social and cultural circumstances entirely different from those of the Middle Ages and, consequently, entirely different kinds of people. On this last point Dr. J. H. van den Berg of the University of Leiden has been insisting for some time. See most recently his *Divided Existence and Complex Society* (Pittsburgh, 1974).

20. See F. R. H. Du Boulay, "The Historical Chaucer," in Derek Brewer, *Geoffrey Chaucer* (London, 1974), p. 37. Cf. my "Some Disputed Chaucerian Terminology," *Speculum,* 52 (1977), 572.

21. "The *Troilus* Frontispiece and Chaucer's Audience," *Yearbook of English Studies,* 7 (1977), 73–74.

22. The standard article on this subject is W. T. Waugh, "The Lollard Knights," *Scottish Historical Review,* 11 (1913–14), 55–92, who regarded Lollardry among persons of rank with general skepticism. A more favorable attitude toward possible Lollardry among Chamber knights was advanced by K. B. McFarlane, *Lancastrian Kings and Lollard Knights* (Oxford, 1972), part 2. McFarlane also corrected certain errors of fact in Waugh's account and added new biographical information. He may, however, see "Lollardry" (specifically sympathy for Wyclif's doctrines) in reforming attitudes having other origins. Thus Du Boulay, "The Historical Chaucer," p. 46, observes that "it remains possible that as a group they showed in exaggerated form the sentiments felt by many

orthodox contemporaries." On Clanvowe, see V. J. Scattergood, *The Works of Sir John Clanvowe* (Totowa, N.J., 1975). Clifford's membership in the Order of the Passion, which envisaged a new crusade, and the participation of Clanvowe and Neville in a crusade are hardly consistent with Wyclif's teachings. A worldly person might hurl the epithet "Lollard," which was originally a term of opprobrium, at any unworldly person. See my *Chaucer's London* (New York, 1968), pp. 152, 211. The word "Lollard" was apparently applied to followers of Wyclif by Henry Crump, Regent in Sacred Theology at Oxford, in 1381, an act that led the Chancellor of the University, Robert Rigg, to charge him with breaking the peace. See the discussion in Joseph Dahmus, *William Courtenay* (University Park and London, 1966), ch. 6. We may compare the tone used by Henry of Wakefield, Bishop of Worcester, in a pastoral letter of 1387 concerning followers of Wyclif in his diocese wherein he speaks of "quidam tamen eterne dampnationis filii Antichristi discipuli et Machomete sequaces instigatione diabolica conspiratori in collegio illicito et a iure reprobato nomine seu ritu Lollardorum confederati." See W. P. Marett, *A Calendar of the Register of Henry of Wakefield, Bishop of Worcester, 1375–1395*, Worcester Historical Society, n.s., 7 (1972), 150. Harry Bailey's remark, "I smelle a Lollere in the wynd" (Man of Law's Tale, Epilogue, 1173) is probably indicative of his own worldliness and rude speech rather than of any weakness on the part of the Parson, who is idealized in the General Prologue in highly conventional terms. As John Barnie indicates, *War in English Medieval Society* (Ithaca, 1974), p. 103, English reverses during the seventies and eighties "were explained as a punishment visited by God on the sins of his people." A moral stance among responsible courtiers and officials was thus to be expected.

23. The information here is derived from the studies of Waugh and McFarlane mentioned in the previous note unless otherwise indicated.

24. See John Hatcher, *Rural Economy and Society in the Duchy of Cornwall* (Cambridge, 1970), p. 127.

25. Printed by Karl Young, *The Drama of the Mediaeval Church* (Oxford, 1933), 2:225–45; for a translation, see Robert S. Haller and M. Catherine Rupp, O.S.M., *Figurative Representation of the Presentation of the Virgin Mary in the Temple* (Lincoln, Nebraska, 1971). Documents for the Order of the Passion have been published by Abdel Hamid Handy, "Philippe de Mézières and the New Order of the Passion," *Bulletin of the Faculty of Arts*, Alexandria University, 18 (1964), 1–104; Philippe's *Songe du vieil pèlerin* has been edited by G. W. Coopland (Cambridge, 1969), and the same editor has published (with a translation) Philippe's *Letter to Richard II* (Liverpool, 1975) urging Richard to join the Order. The standard biography of Philippe is N. Jorga, *Philippe de Mézières, 1327–1405, et la croisade au XIVᵉ siècle* (Paris, 1896). For the influence of Philippe's order in England, see J. J. N. Palmer, *England, France, and Christendom* (London, 1972), pp. 181, 186–91, 198.

26. The usual modern allegations rest on the unfounded assumption that the recognizance by John Grove of 2 July 1380, two months after Cecily's release of Chaucer, represented hush money supplied by the poet. For the documents, see Martin M. Crow and Clair C. Olson, *Chaucer Life-Records* (Oxford, 1966), pp. 343–47. If Chaucer had raped Cecily or anyone else, it is probable that he would have been forced to purchase a pardon, as Henry of Wakefield was forced to do

for this offense, to be presented before the King's Bench. Rape was a felony punishable by death. Du Boulay, "The Historical Chaucer," p. 46, lists the modern tendency to see Chaucer as a rapist among "rash dramatizations" concerning the poet's life.

27. Cf. *Chaucer's London,* p. 2. The idea was still current in 1605, when the story of Brutus was reenacted in a pageant by Anthony Munday, *The Triumphes of Re-United Britannia.* See David M. Bergeron, "Civic Pageants and Historical Drama," *Journal of Medieval and Renaissance Studies,* 5 (1975), 103–04.

28. Eleanor Searle, *Lordship and Community: Battle Abbey and Its Banlieu* (Toronto, 1974), p. 345. In 1377 there were raids along the south coast, assaults on the Isle of Wight and Yarmouth, and Rye and Hastings were burned. At Southampton the burgesses petitioned the king in 1376 to take the town into his own hands and to assume its defenses. Henry Yevele, whom Chaucer undoubtedly knew, was commissioned in 1378 to build a new keep for the city. There were further invasion scares in 1383 and in the period between 1385 and 1388. See Colin Smith, *Medieval Southampton* (London and Boston, 1973), pp. 127–28. J. J. N. Palmer observes, *England, France, and Christendom,* p. 5: "Almost every parliament of the 1380s made plaintive reference to the innumerable enemies surrounding the kingdom: all of them rich, powerful and active; all intent on the utter destruction of the country; all inseparably bound together by firm alliances; and all possessing separate and highly dangerous advantages over their isolated and dismayed opponent." On the general invasion scare of 1386, see ibid., ch. 4. In view of the conventional association of England with Troy and the actual situation in which England found itself at the time Chaucer wrote his poem, the usual romantic, sentimental, psychological, or "courtly love" interpretations now fashionable among academic critics amount to nothing more than accusations that Chaucer and his friends at court were frivolous and irresponsible, and these are hardly supported by the facts as we know them. But such interpretations have little or no support in the text, which, as its closing stanzas clearly indicate, should be read as a warning.

29. For Hodge, see *Chaucer's London,* p. 104.

30. Frances M. Page, *The Estates of Crowland Abbey* (Cambridge, 1934), p. 77.

31. *Chaucer's London,* p. 47.

32. *Chaucer's London,* p. 106. Cf. Ruth Melinkoff, "Riding Backwards," *Viator,* 4 (1973), 153–76. In this article it seems to me that attacks against the Old Law as it appears among Christians are sometimes mistaken for literal attacks against Jews.

33. Douglas Jones, *The Church in Chester 1350–1540,* Chesham Society, 3d ser., 7 (1957), 35–36.

34. E.g., see the Archbishop's injunctions to the monastery of St. Peter's Gloucester (1301) in William Henry Hunt, *Historia et cartularium monasterii Sancti Petri Gloucestriae,* 3 (Rolls Series, 1867), esp. lxiv (on dress), lxii (on behavior outside the cloister), lxvii (on sporting dogs, reserved for the abbot alone). Abbots and priors sometimes entertained noblemen by hunting with them on their estates and thus had need of dogs.

35. On population decline see Jones, *The Church in Chester,* p. 11. And for the same problem in the south, cf. Eleanor Searle and Barbara Ross, *The Cellarer's Rolls of Battle Abbey, 1225–1513,* Sussex Record Society, 65 (1967), 15. Abbeys

found difficulty in supporting their many visitors in midcentury. See H. J. Hewitt, *Mediaeval Cheshire,* Chetham Society, 2d ser., 88 (1929), 128. For decay of monastic fare elsewhere, see Marett, *Calendar,* p. 160. Monastic houses were generally less well supported after the middle of the fourteenth century. See Dorothy Owen, *Church and Society in Medieval Lincolnshire* (Lincoln, 1971), p. 53. Abbots, like lay lords, often resorted to the device of leasing their demesnes after the Black Death, and there was a natural tendency for them to engage in profitable worldly enterprises.

36. The "literacy of the nobility" in the later Middle Ages is still an obscure subject, perhaps because literacy, like other characteristics, varied enormously from one nobleman to another. For an illustration of the kind of books that might be treasured by a member of the higher nobility, see the evidence from the will of Eleanor de Bohun, Duchess of Gloucester (1399), cited by K. B. McFarlane, *The Nobility of Late Medieval England* (Oxford, 1973), p. 236. Among her books were Psalters, one glossed, a copy of the Golden Legend, St. Gregory's *Cura pastoralis,* a book of decretals, a book of French history, and a French Bible. For the complete list, see N. H. Nicolas, *Testamenta Vetusta* (London, 1826), pp. 147–48. The will of Alice, Lady West, the wife of a knight, leaves to her daughter-in-law all her books in Latin, English, and French (McFarlane, p. 137). Women may have been more bookish than men. In any event, there is some evidence for a general revival of interest in the classics among laymen during the later fourteenth century. Chaucer's Knight may represent an "ideal" in this respect, just as he does by his campaigns under Peter of Lusignan, his worthiness, his wisdom, and his humility.

37. In general, violence as a manifestation of social disruption seems to have become frequent around 1360, again in the mid- to late seventies, and again after the revolt of 1381. See E. B. Dewindt, *Land and People in Holywell-cum-Needingworth* (Toronto, 1972), ch. 4; J. A. Raftis, *Warboys* (Toronto, 1974), pp. 216–21, and idem, "An English Village After the Black Death," *Mediaeval Studies,* 29 (1967), esp. 163–65. The records of the Durham Halmotes show a temporary unrest in 1360 and then after 1378 cases of beating and drawing knives become more frequent. See W. H. Longstreet and John Booth, *Halmota prioratus Dunhelmensis,* Surtees Society, 82 (1889), 36–37, 145, 146, 147. A few measures illustrating efforts to prevent contention may be listed here from this source. It was forbidden to call a man a "rustic" or a "native" (pp. 33, 40–41, 141), to call a woman a "whore" (p. 144), to defame another in any way (pp. 151–53), to permit a stranger to start a fight (p. 147), to raise knives or clubs (p. 154), to play at dice (p. 166), to arrange football contests between villages (p. 171). Women were especially restrained from shrewish speech (pp. 144, 169, 171). Eavesdropping, false raising of the hue and cry, and harboring strangers were common transgressions. Fornication and adultery (thought to give rise to contention) could bring fines in local courts to bondwomen, although men and free women were left to the mercies of the ecclesiastics. A man guilty of fornication might be whipped around his parish church or market place, or, if he persisted in fornication with the same woman, might be forced to marry her. See R. H. Helmholz, *Marriage Litigation in Medieval England* (Cambridge, 1974), pp. 172–75, 182. Cf. the Harley lyric beginning "No mai no lewed lued libben in londe."

38. E.g., see the wills printed by Marett, *Calendar*, pp. 15, 25–27.

39. On dyes, and kermes in particular, see Eleanora Carus-Wilson, "The Woolen Industry," in *The Cambridge Economic History of Europe* (1952), 2:375–77.

40. Cf. Owen, *Church and Society*, p. 125.

41. C. R. Cheney, *Medieval Texts and Studies* (Oxford, 1973), p. 354.

42. Except where indicated the following information about the cloth industry is based on the article in *The Cambridge Economic History* cited in note 39 and on E. M. Carus-Wilson, "Trends in the Export of English Woolens in the Fourteenth Century," *Economic History Review*, 3d ser., 2 (1950–51), 162–79; E. M. Carus-Wilson and Olive Coleman, *England's Export Trade, 1275–1547* (Oxford, 1963); Herbert Heaton, *The Yorkshire Woolen and Worsted Industries*, Oxford Historical and Literary Studies, 10 (Oxford, 1920).

43. See the important article by Norah Ritchie, "Labour Conditions in Essex in the Reign of Richard II," in E. M. Carus-Wilson, ed., *Essays in Economic History* (London, 1962), 2:91–111. On the stimulus to wages provoked by the cloth industry, see A. R. Bridbury, *England and the Salt Trade in the Middle Ages* (Oxford, 1955), p. 36–37.

44. See F. R. H. Du Boulay, *An Age of Ambition: English Society in the Late Middle Ages* (London, 1970). A concomitant phenomenon was, naturally enough, higher prices. E.g., see the blanket condemnations of various tradesmen for overcharging at Nottingham in 1395 and 1396 in W. H. Stevenson, *Records of the Borough of Nottingham* (London, 1882), 1: 296–73, 317–19.

45. L. F. Salzman, *English Trade in the Middle Ages* (Oxford, 1931), pp. 337–38.

46. Cf. *A Preface to Chaucer*, p. 321.

47. Cited by J. Z. Titow in *Essays in Agrarian History* (Newton Abbot, 1968), 1:45.

48. Clerks who married widows were declared *bigamus* and denied benefit of clergy. See Pollock and Maitland, *The History of English Law*, 2nd ed. (Cambridge, 1952), 1:445.

49. See the amusing cases testing male impotence, cited by Helmholz, *Marriage Litigation*, pp. 88–89, and the belief cited by Benton, "Clio and Venus," p. 32, to the effect that women enjoy twice the pleasure experienced by men in intercourse.

50. See the discussion by Barnie, *War in English Medieval Society*, p. 63.

51. J. W. and E. F. Jones, *The Commentary on the First Six Books of the Aeneid of Vergil Commonly Attributed to Bernardus Silvestris* (Lincoln, Neb., 1977), p. 12.

52. The nature of this paradise is well illustrated in the Merchant's Tale.

53. The Wife, who is a vivid representation of Old Law attitudes characteristic of "the children of wrath" (Eph. 2:3) represented in her Prologue by Mars, provokes a wrathful quarrel between the Friar and the Summoner, who are also, in Old Law fashion, blind to spiritual realities and interested primarily in material gain. The Friar, who, as we learn in the General Prologue, cares nothing for the repentance of those who come to him for confession, but only for their money, amusingly suggests that summoners repent. And the Summoner, a minister of God's "wrath" or justice, wrathfully tells a tale illustrating the folly of exactly the kind of wrath from which he suffers. The two tales are comic and exaggerated revelations of the corruption in the administration of God's mercy and justice in a society where many are, like the Wife, interested only in the

satisfaction of the senses, or private rather than common good. The activities of men like the Friar and the Summoner could lead only to widespread impenitence, compounding the problem.

54. The "sect" of the Wife should probably be seen as a comment on the widespread pursuit of greater profits and more ostentatious self-indulgence becoming manifest among both the laity and the clergy after the Black Death, which disrupted established communities and led to a breakdown in mores. For some fairly typical examples among ordinary people see Rosamund Sillem, *Records of Some Sessions of the Peace in Lincolnshire, 1360–1375*, Lincoln Record Society, 30 (1936), 21 (case of Robertus Raulyn), 173–74 (case of Hugo Beaumares and similar cases), 198–99 (case of Henricus Souter). Concerning the last, cf. G. O. Sayles, *Select Cases before the Court of the King's Bench*, 7 (Selden Society, 1971), 61–62. It would be possible to cite many similar cases from other areas, including the boroughs. The rolls reveal numerous erring ecclesiastics, especially chaplains, but even a bishop might stray. Thus Bishop Henry of Wakefield was indicted for extortion and even rape. See Elizabeth Gurnsey Kimball, *Some Warwick and Coventry Sessions of the Peace, 1377–1397*, Dugdale Society, 16 (1939), 105–06, and Sayles, *Select Cases*, 7:53–54. Some local lords were notorious. For example, Lord John Fitzwalter of Essex regularly practiced extortion, illegal distraints, and outright theft. See Elizabeth Chapin Furber, *Essex Sessions of the Peace, 1351, 1371–79*, Essex Archaeological Society, Occasional Publications, 3 (1953), 61–62. There were obvious reasons why Chaucer and his audience at court should be concerned about moral decline.

55. E.g., see Norah Ritchie's observations, "Labour Conditions," p. 95, on the effects of the flourishing cutlery trade at Thaxted.

Chaucer's Thematic Particulars   EDMUND REISS

1. All quotations from Chaucer are according to *The Works of Geoffrey Chaucer*, ed. F. N. Robinson, 2d ed. (Boston, 1957).

2. On "nyne and twenty," see my "Pilgrimage Narrative and *The Canterbury Tales*," *Studies in Philology*, 67 (1970), 303–05.

3. See, e.g., the note in Robinson, pp. 675–76; see also the Prologue to the *Legend of Good Women*, F 503, G 491.

4. The cardinal's hat was especially associated with Jerome in the late fourteenth century after the composition of the *Hieronymianus*, a collection of all texts pertinent to the saint, by Giovanni d'Andrea (Johannes Andreae).

5. Jerome, *Epistola adversus Jovinianum*, 1 (*PL*, 23:222 ff.); cf. Wife of Bath's Prologue, D 1–162.

6. For a full study of the ironic parallels between Jerome and the Wife, see my forthcoming study, "The Wife of Bath's Hat and St. Jerome."

7. On the pelican, see, e.g., Florence McCulloch, *Mediaeval Latin and French Bestiaries*, University of North Carolina Studies in the Romance Languages and Literatures, 33 (Chapel Hill, 1962), pp. 155–56. On Dante's image of the pelican, see *Paradiso*, 25.112 ff.; on the dry tree, see, e.g., *Purgatorio*, 32.38 ff.

8. See Joyce E. Peterson, "The Finished Fragment: A Reassessment of the Squire's Tale," *Chaucer Review*, 5 (1971), 70–72.

9. Peter of Blois, *Epistola* 61 (quoted in D. W. Robertson, Jr., *A Preface to*

Chaucer [Princeton, 1962], p. 192); Gower, *Mirour de l'Omme.* ll. 901 ff.; Isidore, *Etymologiae,* 12.7.55–56; Ambrose, *Hexaemeron,* 5.18.59. See also McCulloch, *Bestiaries,* pp. 123–24.

10. *Plowman's Tale,* 11. 1309–10, 1312; *The Complete Works of Geoffrey Chaucer,* vol. 7, *Chaucerian and Other Pieces,* ed. W. W. Skeat (Oxford, 1897), p. 188; *Piers Plowman,* B 5.438; C 8.44.

11. Ovid, *Metamorphoses,* 6.426–674. On the association of the swallow with spring, see McCulloch, *Bestiaries,* p. 175.

12. Cited in Louis Charbonneau-Lassay, *Le Bestiaire du Christ* (Bruges, 1940), pp. 530–31.

13. Boccaccio, *Decameron,* 5.4; ed. Charles S. Singleton, Scrittori d'Italia, 97 (Bari, 1955), 1:369: "molte volte faccendo cantar l'usignuolo." On the nightingale in medieval literature, see especially Thomas Alan Shippey, "Listening to the Nightingale," *Comparative Literature,* 32 (1970), 46–60.

14. Gower, *Confessio amantis,* 5.6049–52; 8.2583–86; *The English Works of John Gower,* ed. G. C. Macaulay, EETS, e.s. 82 (London, 1901).

15. Boccaccio, *Teseida,* 4. 54, 73.

16. Dante, *Purgatorio,* 9.13–15; ed. Natalino Sapegno, 2d ed., Scrittori Italiani (Florence, 1968): "Nell'ora che comincia i tristi lai / la rondinella presso alla mattina, / forse a memoria de' suo' primi guai."

17. Petrarch, "Sonetto 310," l. 3; *Il Canzoniere,* ed. Mario Marcazzan (Milan, 1966): "e garrir Progne e pianger Filomena."

18. In the fourteenth-century verse *Ovide moralisé* Philomena is said to signify "amour decevable et faille" (6.3756; ed C. de Boer, Verhandelingen der Koninklijke Nederlandse Akademie van Wetenschappen, Afdeling Letterkunde, 21 [Amsterdam, 1920], 368); in the fifteenth-century prose version she signifies "amour, desordonée et decepvant des biens mondains," 6.12, ibid., 61.2 (1954), 198.

19. *The Owl and the Nightingale,* ll. 1449–50.

20. Boccaccio, *Teseida,* 11.9; cf. 12.6.

21. Plutarch, *Lives,* "Theseus," 22; ed. Bernadotte Perrin, Loeb Classical Library (London, 1914), 1:45; Catullus, "Poem 64," ll. 241–44; ed. F. W. Cornish, Loeb Classical Library (London, 1913), p. 115. See also Apollodorus, *Epitome,* 1.10; ed. James G. Frazer, Loeb Classical Library (London, 1921), 2:137; and the summary in Robert Graves, *The Greek Myths* (Baltimore, 1955), 1:343.

22. Boccaccio, *Genealogiae deorum gentilium,* 10.48.

23. See, e.g., Louis Charbonneau-Lassay, *Le Bestiaire du Christ,* pp. 848–49; and Dorothea Forstner, *Die Welt der Symbole,* 2d ed. (Innsbruck, 1967), pp. 318–20.

Musical Signs and Symbols in Chaucer: DAVID CHAMBERLAIN
Convention and Originality

1. D. W. Robertson, Jr., *A Preface to Chaucer* (Princeton, 1962), pp. 121–35 et passim; Edmund Reiss, "The Symbolic Surface of the *Canterbury Tales:* The Monk's Portrait, Part I," *Chaucer Review,* 2 (1968), 258–62; Bernard F. Huppé and D. W. Robertson, Jr., *Fruyt and Chaf* (Princeton, 1963), ch. 2; Chauncey Wood, "The Significance of Jousting and Dancing as Attributes of Chaucer's Squire," *English Studies,* 15 (1971), 116–18; James I. Wimsatt, *The Marguerite*

Poetry of Guillaume de Machaut (Chapel Hill, 1970); John Gardner, *The Life and Times of Chaucer* (New York, 1977), pp. 93–97.

2. Introduction to the Man of Lawe's Tale, B¹ 92, ed. F. N. Robinson, *The Works of Geoffrey Chaucer* (Boston, 1957), 2d ed., p. 63. All references will be to this edition. The Pierides are nine proud maidens who challenge the Muses and sing derisively about the gods. They are turned into magpies. See Ovid, *Metamorphoses*, 5. 294–331, 662–78; and for one mythographer, John of Garland, *Integumenta Ovidii*, ed. Fausto Ghisalberti (Messina-Milano, 1933), ll. 275–76.

3. Lines A 672–74. See P. Baum, "Chaucer's Puns," *PMLA*, 71 (1956), 232; D. Biggins, "Chaucer's G. P., A 673," *Notes and Queries*, 204 (1959), 435–36; B. D. H. Miller, "Chaucer's G. P., A 673: Further Evidence," *Notes and Queries*, 205 (1960), 404–06; Emma Dieckmann, "The Meaning of *Bourdoun* in Chaucer," *Modern Philology*, 26 (1928–29), 279–82.

On the Wife of Bath, see D 457–65: "'How koude I daunce to an harpe smale, / And synge, ywis, as any nyghtyngale, / Whan I had dronke a draughte of sweete wyn! / . . . / And after wyn on Venus moste I thynke . . .'" The erotic interpretation of nightingales grows partly out of Ovid's story of Philomela (*Metamorphoses*, 6.531–670) and is vivid in such works as Alan of Lille, *De planctu Naturae*, prosa 1; *Ovide moralisé*, 6.3755–60, 3839–40, ed. C. de Boer, 5 vols., *Verhandelingen der Koninklijke Akademie van Wetenschappen te Amsterdam*, Afdeeling Letterkunde, New Series (Amsterdam, 1915–38), 2:367–69; and Boccaccio, *Decameron*, 5.4, where "molte volte faccendo cantar l'usignuolo" and similar expressions are figures for intercourse (ed. Vittore Branca, *Tutte le opere*, 4 [Milano, 1976], 474–76).

On the Miller (A 565), see Edward A. Block, "Chaucer's Millers and Their Bagpipes," *Speculum*, 29 (1954), 239–43; George F. Jones, "Wittenweiler's *Becki* and the Medieval Bagpipe," *JEGP*, 48 (1949), 209–28; and E. Winternitz, *Musical Instruments and Their Symbolism in Western Art* (New York, 1968), chs. 4 and 10.

4. Line 472. See the Parson's Tale on "Accidia," especially 725–27, to justify the connection.

5. "Hoold thou thy pees, thou poete Marcian, / That writest us that ilke weddyng murie / Of hire Philologie and hym Mercurie, / And of the songes that the Muses songe!" (E 1732–35). See Martianus Capella, *De nuptiis Philologiae et Mercurii*, ed. Adolfus Dick (Stuttgart, 1969), bk. 2, paragraphs 117–26, for the separate songs of the nine muses, each praising Philology for a branch of learning, and for a common refrain justifying her deification. The allusion is unusual.

6. See Ovid, *Fasti*, 3.833 and 6.695–710; Claudian, *In Eutropium*, 2.255–58; Albericus of London (Mythographus Vaticanus Tertius), ed. G. Bode, *Scriptores rerum mythicarum Latini tres* (Cellis, 1834), pp. 225–26, among others.

7. Especially the *De nuptiis*, other works of Boccaccio, and Middle French allegories by Machaut, Froissart, and others, such as Thibaut's *Li romanz de la poire*, ed. F. Stehlich (Halle, 1881); *La fablel dou Dieu d'Amours*, ed. D. O. Lecompte, *Modern Philology*, 8 (1910), 63–86; and Jean de Condé's *Messe des oiseaux*, ed. Jacques Ribard (Geneva, 1970).

8. Physician's Tale, 72–82; *Romaunt*, 4284–90 (re the "olde vekke"); also *Troilus*, 3.694–700 ("But Pandarus, that wel koude ech a deel / The olde daunce, and every point thereinne, / . . . He thought he wolde upon his werk bigynne, / And gan the stuwe doore al softe unpynne").

9. See also Criseyde's frisky allusion to "loves daunce" (2.1103–06), and

Pandarus's blander allusion to "the daunce / Of hem that Love list febly to avaunce" (1.517–18).

10. *Policraticus*, bk. 1, ch. 6, ed. C. I. Webb, 2 vols. (Oxford, 1909), 1:39–44.

11. See the general remarks about literary sources and art by Emile Mâle, *The Gothic Image*, trans. Dora Nussey (New York, 1958), pp. 16–27, 98–108, 131–39. With respect to music, see Reinhold Hammerstein, *Die Musik der Engel: Untersuchungen zur Musikanschauung des Mittelalters* (Bern and Munich, 1962); idem, *Diabolus in Musica: Studien zur Ikonographie der Musik im Mittelalter* (Bern, 1974); and H. M. Brown and J. Lascelle, *Musical Iconography: A Manual for Cataloguing Musical Subjects in Western Art Before 1800* (Cambridge, 1972), pp. 5–12. An exception to art's slight influence on literature may exist with respect to popular instruments like the bagpipe. See the discussion of bagpipes in *A Preface to Chaucer*, pp. 128–31.

12. See my "Music in Chaucer: His Knowledge and Use of Medieval Ideas about Music," Ph.D. dissertation, Princeton University, 1966, ch. 2.

13. Augustine, *De musica*, 6. 29, 33, 34, 36; ed. Guy Finaert and F.-J. Thonnard, *Oeuvres de Saint Augustin*, 7 (Paris, 1947), 430–38.

14. For instance, by Cassiodorus, Isidore of Seville, Aurelian of Reôme, Hugh of St. Victor, Alexander Neckam, Jerome of Moravia, Vincent of Beauvais, Bartolomaeus Anglicus, Jaun Gil de Zamora and many others. See my "Music in Chaucer," ch. 3.

15. See Otto von Simson, *The Gothic Cathedral*, 2d ed. (Princeton, 1962), pt. 1; Gerhard Pietzsch, *Die Klassifikation der Musik von Boetius bis Ugolino von Orvieto* (Halle, 1929); Robertson, *A Preface to Chaucer*, ch. 2.

16. *Jacobi Leodiensis Speculum musicae*, bk. 1, ch. 2–3, ed. Roger Bragard, *Corpus scriptorum de musica*, 3 (Rome, 1955), 15–16. See also bk. 1, ch. 5.

17. Bk. 5, ch. 1–3, ed. Albert Seay, *Corpus scriptorum de musica*, vol. 7, pt. 3 (Rome, 1963), 87–98.

18. *The Parliament*, 111, and implicitly 59–63; the Merchant's Tale, 1732, and *House of Fame*, 985; the Nun's Priest's Tale, 3294, and implicitly in *House of Fame*, 765–80.

19. "The Nun's Priest's Tale and Boethius' *De musica*," *Modern Philology*, 68 (1970), 188–91. For an opposing view, see Peter Dronke, "Chaucer and Boethius' *De musica*," *Notes and Queries*, 13 (1966), 92.

20. See my article, "The Music of the Spheres and the *Parlement of Foules*," *Chaucer Review*, 5 (1970), 32–56.

21. Cassiodorus implies God's music in *Institutiones*, ed. R. A. B. Mynors (Oxford, 1937), 2.5.9; and in *De anima*, *Patrologia Latina* (hereafter *PL*), 70:1303; *Scholia enchiriadis* (ca. 860), ed. Martin Gerbert, *Scriptores ecclesiastici de musica sacra potissimum* (St. Blasien, 1784), 1:195a, mentions Augustine's *numeros divinos;* Bartolomaeus Anglicus (ca. 1240), "De musica," in *De proprietatibus rerum*, 19.145, ed. Hermann Müller, Riemann-Festschrift (Leipzig, 1909), p. 255, mentions divine exemplars of music; Magister Lambertus, *Tractatus de musica*, ed. Edmond de Coussemaker, *Scriptorum de musica medii aevi nova series* (Paris, 1867), 1:270a–70b, sees the Trinity as exemplar of music; Juan Gil de Zamora (ca. 1270), *Ars musica*, ed. Gerbert, *Scriptores*, 2:377b, sees God as the "harmonia" of the soul.

22. *Speculum musicae*, bk. 1, ch. 12, also ch. 5.

23. "O martir, sowded to virginitee, / Now maystow syngen, folwynge evere in

oon / ... Biforn this lamb, and synge a song al newe, / That nevere, flesshly, wommen they ne knewe," Prioress's Tale, 1769–75. See Chauncey Wood's essay in this volume for the general fleshliness of the Prioress herself. For the celestial "Osanne," see Man of Lawe's Tale, 642, and Second Nun's Tale, 69.

24. Robert Hollander, *Boccaccio's Two Venuses* (New York, 1977).

25. Huppé and Robertson, *Fruyt and Chaf*, p. 46.

26. *Chaucer and the Tradition of Fame: Symbolism in "The Hous of Fame"* (Princeton, 1966), pp. 212–14.

27. Compare Psalm 15:8–9: "I set the Lord always in my sight . . . therefore my heart hath been glad and my tongue hath rejoiced: moreover my flesh shall rest in hope" (Douai-Rheims), quoted in Acts of the Apostles, 2:25–26.

28. *Speculum musicae*, bk. 1, ch. 13; *Consolation*, 4. meter 6.17, 19; 2. meter 8.15, 29. The subdivisions of *mundana* in Jacques are the "motion, nature, and location" of the spheres and the "qualities and location" of the elements. Jacques spends much of his time denying a sonorous music of the spheres. In the next century, both Ugolino of Orvieto (bk. 1, chs. 1, 4, and Prohemium) and Georgius Anselmus Parmensis, *De musica*, ed. G. Massera (Florence, 1961), pp. 97–106, among others, affirm a sonorous melody.

29. "The Music of the Spheres and the *Parlement of Foules*," *Chaucer Review*, 5 (1970), 48–51.

30. *De nuptiis*, ed. Dick, pp. 11, 19–20, 70–76; *Anticlaudianus*, ed. R. Bossuat (Paris, 1955), pp. 116–21.

31. *The Poetry of Chaucer* (Carbondale, 1977), p. 183.

32. *Speculum musicae*, bk. 1, ch. 14.

33. Augustine, *De musica*, 6.38–50; Chalcidius, *Timaeus a Calcidius translatus commentarioque instructus*, ed. J. H. Waszink, *Plato Latinus*, 4 (London, 1962), 272, and 246–47; Macrobius, *Commentarii*, ed. J. Willis, 2.16.25; Cassiodorus, *Institutiones*, 2.5.2; Rabanus Maurus, *De institutione clericorum*, 3.24, *PL*, 197:401; Roger Bacon, *Opus majus*, ed. J. H. Bridges, 2 vols. (Oxford, 1897), 1:179.

34. Adelard of Bath, *De eodem et diverso*, ed. Hans Willner, *Beiträge zur Geschichte der Philosophie des Mittelalers*, 4.1 (1903), 26.16–19; Honorius Augustodunensis, *De animae exsilio et patria* or *De artibus*, 4, *PL*, 172:1244; Alfredus Anglicus, *Patrica artis musicae* (A.D. 1271), cited in Pietzsch, *Die Klassifikation der Musik* (Halle, 1929), p. 97; Alan of Lille, "Expositio prosae de angelis," ed. M.-T. d' Alverny, *Alain de Lille: textes inédits* (Paris, 1965), p. 196.

35. *Didascalicon*, ed. C. H. Buttimer (Wash., 1939), 2.12; Richard of St. Victor, *Liber exceptionum*, 1.10, ed. J. Chatillon, (Paris, 1958), p. 108; Jerome of Moravia, *Tractatus de musica*, ed. S. Cserba (Regensburg, 1935), p. 26.

36. See "accorde . . . and have pees," "concord and pees" (b² 2864–65), and "of pees and of accord" (2988, also 2972, 2483), also *Consolation*, 2.m.8 and 4.m.6. In other tales of fragment b², there is the abundant singing "accordynge with the note" in the Prioress's Tale (1737) and the "sweete accord" of Chauntecleer and Pertelote (4069). Chaucer's statement that the four Gospels "alle accorden as in hire sentence" (b² 2137) evokes the traditional "concordia" and "consonantia" of the Bible, which is well analyzed by Henri de Lubac, *Exégèse médiévale: Les quatres sens de l'Écriture*, 1 (Paris, 1959), 330–41.

37. For analysis of other irony and humor in the musical passages of the Miller's Tale, see Jesse Gellrich, "Parody of Medieval Music in the 'Miller's Tale,'"

JEGP, 73 (1974), 176–88; also, "Nicholas' 'Kynges note' and 'Melodye,'" *English Language Notes*, 8 (1971), 249–52; and Fletcher Collins, "The 'Kynges note,' the Miller's Tale, line 31," *Speculum*, 8 (1931), 195–97.

38. For a recent discussion of this rather old idea, see David L. Higdon, "Diverse Melodies in Chaucer's 'General Prologue,'" *Criticism*, 14 (1972), 97–108. See also the articles by Reiss and Wood in note 1, and P. Baum, "Chaucer's 'Faste by the Belle,' C.T. A 719," *MLN*, 36 (1921), 307–09.

39. A 565–66. For a possible pun in the Miller's bringing them "out of towne," see Samuel McCracken, "Chaucer's Cant. Tales. A 565–6," *Explicator*, 23 (1965), 5. The lines for the other pilgrims are Pardoner A 710–14, 672; Monk 170–71, also B² 3984; Friar 235–37, 265; Squire 91, 95–96; Prioress 122–23; Summoner 673–74. The Clerk's preference for books to "robes riche, or fithele, or gay sautrie" (296) also contributes mildly to music as a sign of cupidity in the General Prologue. The only seemingly neutral musical detail is the Yeoman's "horn . . . the bawdryk was of grene" (116).

40. *Speculum musicae*, bk. 1, ch. 18.

41. Ibid., ch. 19, also chs. 1, 3, 4, and especially 5.

42. "Prolacions," not in Boethius, suggests that Chaucer was interested in technical aspects of music. See J. Hollander, "'Moedes or Prolacions' in Chaucer's Boece," *MLN*, 71 (1956), 397–99. For other ideas about music that Chaucer may have seen in the *Consolation*, see my "Philosophy of Music in the *Consolatio* of Boethius," *Speculum*, 45 (1970), 80–97.

43. *Duchess*, 47–86, 1155–62, 1173–82.

44. For instance, in Froissart's *Paradys d'Amours*, in *Oeuvres*, ed. Scheler (Brussels, 1870), vol. 1, where lines 75–202 are an elaborate "complainte de l'amant," lines 1079–1354 a "lay" (pleading for pity), 1423–44 a "virelai" (praising Amours), and 1627–53 a "balade" (celebrating the marguerite). Chaucer borrowed details from this poem for the *Duchess*, so the contrast in songs is especially relevant.

45. Among all these works some of the most influential are Augustine, *Enarrationes in Psalmos*, *Corpus Christianorum* (hereafter *CC*) 38, 39, 40 (Turnholt, 1956); Cassiodorus, *Expositio Psalmorum*, *CC*, 97, 98 (Turnholt, 1958); Rabanus Maurus, *Commentaria in Cantica quaedam . . .*, *PL*, 112:1089–1166; Peter Lombard, *Commentarii in Psalmos Davidicos*, *PL*, 191: 55–1296; *Glossa ordinaria*, *PL*, 113:841–1080, 1125–68 (on Psalms and Canticles); Honorius Augustodunensis, *Expositio in Canticum Canticorum*, *PL*, 172:347–518, and *Gemma animae*, 551–738; Gulielmus Durandus, *Rationale divinorum officiorum* (Venice, 1581).

46. *The Psalter or Psalms of David . . . by Richard Rolle*, ed. the Rev. H. R. Bramley (Oxford, 1884), who did not realize it was a translation of Lombard.

47. *Speculum musicae*, bk. 1, ch. 12; Augustine, *De Trinitate*, 4.2.4, 4.3.5–6, 4.6.10; Johannes Tinctoris, *Tractatus de musica*, ed. Coussemaker, *Scriptores*, 4154a; Rupert of Deutz, *Commentaria in Cantica Canticorum*, *PL*, 168:839; John Algrin, *PL*, 206:21; Philippe de Harveng, *PL*, 203:270; Peter Lombard, *PL*, 191:811 (also Augustine, *CC*, 39:1209.31–40); Bersuire, *Repertorium morale*, s.v. "cantare," *Opera omnia* (Moguntiae, 1609), 3. On his miracles, beatitudes, and testaments, see Lombard, *PL*, 191:531; *Glossa*, *PL*, 113:927–28; Augustine, *CC*, 39:706.33–38; *Allegoriae in Vetus Testamentum*, 6.1, *PL*, 175:692; Rupert, *De sancta*

Trinitate et operibus ejus, PL, 168:1389; *Didascalicon,* 5.2; *Glossa, PL,* 113:642; Rabanus, *PL,* 109:346: See also "Music in Chaucer," pp. 542–56.

48. Rolle, *The Psalter* . . . , Psalm 20:13, p. 76; Augustine, *CC,* 40:1536; Cassiodorus, *CC,* 97:187; Lombard, *PL,* 191:224 (re the title of psalm 87). Rolle omits the Lombard's interpretations of the titles, but they go back in the west to Hilary of Poitiers (*Tractatus super Psalmos, PL,* 9:245) and are commonplace. See Rabanus Maurus,*De universo, PL,* 111:496; Honorius Augustodunensis,*Expositio selectorum Psalmorum, PL,* 172:269, etc.

49. Rolle, pp. 490.3, 493.5, 492.2, 347.6, 298.2, 114.2, 247.6; *De universo, PL,* 111: 499, 500; Augustine, *CC,* 39:1374–75, 38:251; Lombard, *Sententiae, PL,* 192:825.7, 191:327; *Allegoriae in Sacram Scripturam,PL,* 112:1067; Augustine,*CC,* 39:1207–08, 40:1926–27, *Confessiones*, 4.15.

50. For detailed interpretation of these songs, see "Music in Chaucer," pp. 512–38. For the range and vividness possible in one exegete, see my article, "Wolbero of Cologne (d. 1167): A Zenith of Musical Imagery," *Mediaeval Studies,* 33 (1971), 114–26.

51. Jerome, *Commentarium in Isaiam, PL,* 24:84, repeated by Remigius, *PL,* 116:748, 749, and by the Glossa,*PL,* 113:1241; Bersuire,*Repertorium morale,* s.v. "carmen," "melodia," "sonus," *Opera omnia,* 3:1503a.

52. Exodus 15, Judges 5, Judith 16, Luke 1:46, 68, and 2:29. Other such songs are those of Deuteronomy (32), Hannah (1 Kings 2), David (2 Kings 22), Isaiah (12), Ezekiel (38), Habakkuk (3), and the Three Children (Daniel 3:52–88).

53. Amos 6:4–6, Ezekiel 26:13, Job 21:12–13; Ezekiel 33:12; Psalms 68:13, Lamentations 3:14, Job 30:9; Isaiah 23:16, Apocalypse 18:22. For exegesis, see "Music in Chaucer," pp. 460–75.

54. Bersuire, "Cantus," *Repertorium morale, Opera omnia,* 3:385; Lotario dei Segni (Pope Innocent III), *De miseria condicionis humane,* 1.20 and 2.20, ed. Robert E. Lewis, The Chaucer Library (Athens, Ga., 1978), pp. 129, 169.

55. See Mortimer J. Donovan, "Sir Thopas, 772–774," *Neuphilologische Mitteilungen,* 57 (1956), 237–46.

56. "Chaucerian Tragedy," *ELH,* 19 (1952), 25.

57. "'Kyrie,' so 'kyrie,'" ed. R. H. Robbins, *Secular Lyrics of the Fourteenth and Fifteenth Centuries,* 2d ed. (Oxford, 1955), p. 21.

58. On this unusually elaborate sign of cupidity, see John F. Fleming, *The "Roman de la Rose": A Study in Allegory and Iconography* (Princeton, 1969), pp. 81–89.

59. *Fulgentius the Mythographer,* trans. L. Whitbread (Columbus, 1972); Boccaccio,*Genealogie deorum gentilium,* ed. V. Romano, 2 vols. (Bari, 1951); John Ridewall, *Fulgentius metaforalis,* ed. H. Liebeschütz (Leipzig, 1926); Pierre Bersuire, *Ovidius moralizatus,* Werkmaterial 2, ed. J. Engels (Utrecht, 1962), *De formis figurisque deorum,* Werkmaterial 3, ed. J. Engels (Utrecht, 1966); Thomas of Walsingham, *De archana deorum,* ed. Robert van Kluyve (Durham, 1968).

60. Ovid,*Metamorphoses,* 10. 86–108, 143–47, 11. 1–5, 44–53;*Policraticus,* 1.4; *De planctu Naturae,* prosa 4, *PL,* 210:447–48: "Solus homo meae moderationis citharam aspernatur; et sub delirantis Orphei lyram delirat." Also, *Roman de la rose,* ed. Langlois, 19640–54; *Ovide moralisé,* 10.2494–2539.

61. Ovid, *Metamorphoses*, 1.515–24, 2.676–85; *Remedia amoris*, 75–78, 251–52, 703–06; Statius, *Thebaid*, 6.355–64; Albericus of London (Myth. Vat. Tertius), ed. G. Bode, *Scriptores rerum mythicarum*, pp. 202–03, 210, 211.

62. Ovid, *Metamorphoses*, 5. 294–331, 662–78; 6.382–400; *Aeneid*, 6.162–74. On the nightingale, see note 3 above and add John of Garland, *Integumenta Ovidii*, ed. Ghisalberti, 6.292–93; Giovanni del Virgilio, *Allegorie librorum Ovidii . . .*, 6.32, ed. Ghisalberti, *Il giornale dantesco*, 24 (1931), 3–110. On the muses, see especially Boethius, *Consolation*, 1.pr.1; Boccaccio, *Genealogie . . .*, 14.20; *Hous of Fame*, 1395–1405.

63. The sirens' sensuality is a commonplace, but see Boethius, *Consolation*, 1.pr.1; Fulgentius, *Mitologiae*, 2.8; Albericus of London (Myth. Vat. Tert.), ed. Bode, *Scriptores*, pp. 233–34; Boccaccio, *Genealogie*, 7.20; Brunetto Latini, *Tresors*, ed. F. J. Carmody, 1.136; Dante, *Purgatorio*, 19.7–63. For Bacchus, see mainly Statius, *Thebaid*, 1.661–68, 4.667–68, 7.168–73, 8.218–39. For Hymen, *Metamorphoses*, 6.429, 10.4–5, 9.762–97; Claudian, "Shorter Poems," Loeb ed., 31.1–32, *Epithalamium . . . Honorii*, Preface, 9–22, 202–27, *Epithal. Paladii* (Shorter Poems 25), 30–33, 45–55, 95–110; Martianus Capella, *De nuptiis*, 9.902–03; Alan of Lille, *De planctu Naturae*, pr.8, m.9.

64. *Ars amatoria*, 3.311–28; *Genealogie*, 2.547; *De consulatu Stilichonis*, 2.131–42.

65. *Parliament*, 59–63; *Boece*, 3.m.9.41, 3.pr.10.16, 3.m.12.2; 4.m.6.41, 5.m.5.6.

66. See J. M. Steadman, "Venus' *Citole* in Chaucer's *Knight's Tale* and Berchorius," *Speculum*, 34 (1959), 620–24. Meg Twycross, in *The Medieval Anadyomene: A Study in Chaucer's Mythography*, Medium Aevum Monographs, n.s. 1 (Oxford, 1972), is strangely reluctant to agree with Steadman (and Robertson) on the carnal nature of Venus in the Knight's Tale (pp. 67–70), even though she offers a wealth of detail to show (1) that Chaucer probably used Berchorius, (2) that the libidinous Venus was associated with stringed instruments (pp. 42, 51–63) even when she might be "astrological," and (3) that the conch shell of Venus, besides having erotic implications (p. 78) and musical ones, can also be associated with the comb and mirror of Venus, Luxuria, and the Sirens (pp. 82–96). Linda Tatelbaum, in "Venus' *Citole* and the Restoration of Harmony in Chaucer's Knight's Tale," *Neuphilologische Mitteilungen*, 74 (1973), 649–64, is wrong in thinking that the cithara and other stringed instruments are not associated with the carnal Venus, for which association more evidence could be cited than even Twycross provides.

67. For instance, *De planctu*, PL, 210: 434, 443, 453, 448, 472; *Anticlaudianus*, ed. Bossuat, 3.386–468, 4.345–483, 2.213–324.

68. In the harmony of birds and leaves, the singing and dancing of Matilda, the singing of the twenty-four elders and the angels ("Hosanna," "Ave Maria," "Canticles," etc.), and the dancing and singing of the seven virtues (*Purgatorio*, cantos 28–33). See "Music in Chaucer," pp. 669–92. Also, Reinhold Hammerstein, "Klang und Musik in Dantes Jenseits," *Die Musik der Engel* (Munich, 1962), pp. 145–91.

69. Ed. Langlois, 65–77, 478–96, 643–80, 701–11 (birdsong); 727–76, 831–64, etc., 1291–96 (carole); 16949–54 (spheres); 20350–56, 20655–59 (Shepherd's Park); 21021–58 (Pygmalion).

70. For instance, Machaut, *Rémède de Fortune*, *Le Dit de la harpe*, and *Le Prologue*; Boccaccio, *Teseida*, *Comedia delle ninfe fiorentino* (*Ameto*), and *Amorosa visione*; for Froissart and others, see notes 7 and 44.

71. D. Riessler, *Altjüdisches Schrifttum ausserhalb der Bibel* (Augsburg, 1928), p. 1028; *Hexaemeron*, 5.12.36 and 5.24.84, *PL*, 14:237C, 254B; *De universo*, *PL*, 111:241–42; Bersuire, "Cantus," *Repertorium morale;* etc.

72. *La Fonteinne amoureuse*, ed. Hoepffner, SATF, 3 (Paris, 1908), ll. 1355–60; *Le Paradys d'Amours*, ed. Scheler, pp. 42–47, 209–12; *Roman de la rose*, see note 69; Claudian, *Epithalamium . . . Honori*, 62–64.

73. Knight's Tale, 2197–2207, 2483–87; Squire's Tale, 263–305; Franklin's Tale, 925–30, 947–50; the important connecting links of the *Decameron*.

74. C. C. Olson, "Chaucer and the Music of the Fourteenth Century," *Speculum*, 16 (1941), 64–91; R. M. Smith, "'Mynstralcie and Noyse,' in the *House of Fame*," *MLN*, 65 (1950), 521–30; John Hollander, *The Untuning of the Sky* (Princeton, 1960), pp. 62–66. All these studies fail to relate Chaucer's musical imagery to medieval traditions.

75. Ed. E. J. Arnould, Anglo-Norman Text Society, 2 (Oxford, 1940), 77–78. The Physician (hypocritically) has Virginia show the same view: "she wolde fleen the compaignye / Wher likly was to treten of folye, / As is at feestes, revels, and at daunces, / That been occasions of daliaunces" (63–66).

76. Sir John Bourchier, Lord Berners, trans., *The Chronicle of Froissart*, intro. by W. P. Ker, 6 vols. (London, 1901), 5:422–25.

77. H. T. Riley, ed. *Liber custumarum*, in *Munimenta Gildhallae Londonensis*, Rolls Series, 12, vol. 2, pt. 1, 229, 225.

78. E 1712–35, with its allusions to the "melodye" of Orpheus and Amphioun (effeminizing), the "mynstralcye" of Joab and Thiodamas (violent), the "daunce" of Venus (erotic), and the "songes" of Capella's muses (virtuous—see note 5).

79. *Physiologus Latinus, versio y*, ed. F. J. Carmody (Berkeley, 1941), pp. 113–14. Chaucer equates mermaids with sirens (*Boece*, pr. 1, where the Latin has "Sirenes"); *Romaunt*, 682–84. In addition to my note 63, see John B. Friedman, "The Nun's Priest's Tale: The Preacher and the Mermaid's Song," *Chaucer Review*, 7 (1973), 250–66.

80. Nigel de Longchamps, *Speculum stultorum*, ed. John H. Mozley and Robert Raymo (Berkeley, 1960), pp. 59–64. For more relevance to the Nun's Priest's Tale, see Richard J. Schrader, "Chauntecleer, the Mermaid, and Daun Burnel," *Chaucer Review*, 4 (1970), 284–90.

81. I offer here new evidence for the general interpretation of Charles Dahlberg, "Chaucer's Cock and Fox," *JEGP*, 53 (1954), 277–90. This tale's relevance to the Monk's Tale suggests, however, that monastic as well as secular clergy may be the target.

82. Thomas Cantimpratensis, *Liber de natura rerum*, 5.57, ed. H. Boese (Berlin, 1973), p. 206.

83. Augustine, *Enarrationes in Psalmos*, CC, 40:1776.1.1–7, 1789.5.1–11, 1825.1.1–4, 1856.1.12–18, 1785.9.2–13, 1889.1.1–14; Cassiodorus, *Expositio Psalmorum*, CC, 98:1139–40, 1212–13 (the fifteen steps); Rolle, *Psalter*, p. 437 ("The tityll of these fyfteten psalmys is sange of degres, that is, ioy of thoght in gastly steghynge in whilke luf stirs the fote. forthi the mare that any lufis god the

heghere he clymbis"); Lombard, *PL*, 191:1133–34; *Glossa, PL*, 113:1041–53. Both the *Glossa* and Lombard elsewhere express the commonplace idea that seven signifies this life and eight the resurrection, so "fifteen" teaches "to live in the seven of this life so that in the octave of the resurrection we may wear the robe of glory" (*PL*, 113:843; 191:56, 1294; also Remigius, *PL*, 131:136; Augustine, *CC*, 40:2190–91.

84. See notes 33 and 34.

85. See Robert M. Correale, "Chaucer's Parody of Compline in the *Reeve's Tale*," *Chaucer Review*, 1 (1967), 161–65.

86. The wedding itself (1715–35), January's dawn song or lauds (1844–50), and his abuse of Canticum (2138–44). See Paul A. Olson, "Chaucer's Merchant and January's 'Hevene in erthe heere,'" *ELH*, 28 (1961), 203–14.

87. See the Cook's fragment: "For thefte and riot, they been convertible, / Al konne he pleye on gyterne or ribible" (4396), and Miller's Tale, "And pleyen songes on a smal rubible" (3331). See also Henry Holland Carter, *Dictionary of Middle English Musical Terms* (Bloomington, 1961).

88. A 169–71, 710–14; D 1724–28; B² 4386–93; Absalom's "chaunting" (A 3360–67), etc.

89. A 872, 3097; E 271; G 134–37; H 113–15.

90. A 3213–17, 4162–72; F 268–92; E 2038–41.

91. 2:64–70, 899–903, 918–24. This interpretation of Tesiphone is in Fulgentius, *Mitologiae*, 1.7, and Boccaccio, *Genealogie*, 3.9.

92. For contrary arguments, see Charles A. Owen, Jr., "The Design of the *Canterbury Tales*," *Companion to Chaucer Studies*, ed. Beryl Rowland, 2d ed. (Oxford, 1979), pp. 192–205.

93. *Metamorphoses*, 2.542–632; *Confessio amantis*, 3.783–817. See also Machaut, *Livre du voir-dit*, ed. P. Paris (Paris, 1875), pp. 317–50; and *Ovide moralisé*, 2.2143–2455.

94. See note 61 and also Boccaccio, *The Book of Theseus (Teseida delle nozze d'Emilia)*, trans. Bernadette M. McCoy (New York, 1974), glosses to 4.77, 10.13, 11.62–63. Apollo's playing, not his singing, surpasses anyone else's.

95. Implicitly in A 931–1032, 1328–33; *Inferno*, 33.79–90; *Thebaid*, 1.214–17, 7.206–21; Fulgentius, *Super Thebaiden*, ed. Helm, pp. 182–86, trans. Whitbread, pp. 239–43.

96. *Hous of Fame*, 1091–1109; Franklin's Tale, 1031, *Troilus*, 1.69–72, 1.730–35; Wife of Bath's Tale, D 952–82.

97. *Metamorphoses*, 2.676–85; Boccaccio, *Genealogie*, 5.3, ed. Romano, pp. 236–37; *Teseida*, 4.46 and gloss (slightly different version); Walsingham, *De archana deorum*, 2.5, ed. van Kluyve, p. 57; *Ovide moralisé*, 2.3466–582.

98. Psalms 2:13, 7:13–14, 17:15, 29:6, 37:3, 44:6, 64:7, 75:8, 76:18, 77:31, 89:7,9, etc.

99. 2.2549–2622, ed. de Boer, 1:226–28; interpretation is repeated in 2.3301–15 (p. 242).

100. Paul A. Olson, "Le Jaloux and History," Ph.D. dissertation, Princeton University, 1959. The musical evidence will be developed more fully in a forthcoming article.

101. See Alcuin, "De luscinia," ed. Dümmler, *Poetae Latini Aevi Carolini*, 1:274; Sedulius Scottus, *Carmina*, 3.2, ed. Traube, *Poetae Latini* . . . , 3; *Ecbasis captivi*, ed.

E. Voight, *Quellen und Forschungen*, 8 (Strassburg, 1875), p. 121; Ambrose, *Hexaemeron*, 5.85, *PL*, 14, 254; John Pecham, *Philomena*, ed. Clemens Blume and Guido Dreves, *Analecta Hymnica*, 50 (Leipzig, 1907); Rabanus Maurus, *De universo*, 8.6, *PL*, 111:247.
102. *The Psalter*, p. 459.2, 4; p. 485.10.

Chaucer's Use of Signs in   CHAUNCEY WOOD
His Portrait of the Prioress

1. *The Works of Geoffrey Chaucer*, ed. F. N. Robinson (Boston, 1957), Parson's Tale, 993; General Prologue, 225–26.
2. *On Christian Doctrine*, trans. D. W. Robertson, Jr., The Library of Liberal Arts (New York, 1958), p. 34.
3. "The Horsemen of the *Canterbury Tales*," *Chaucer Review*, 3 (1968), 29–36.
4. *The Prioress and the Critics* (Berkeley and Los Angeles, 1965), p. 16.
5. Charles Joret, *La Rose dans l'antiquité et au moyen âge* (Paris, 1892), pp. 231–58, 281–84, 308. Ernest P. Kuhl, "Chaucer's Madame Eglantine," *MLN*, 60 (1945), 325–36 notes the relationship to the crown of thorns, but R. T. Davies, "Chaucer's Madame Eglantine," *MLN*, 67 (1952), 400–02 proves that Kuhl misquotes his source, Mandeville's *Travels*. Thus the "good" reading of Eglentyne's name has fallen into disfavor, but the evidence adduced here from Joret shows that it need not have. For more on the spiritual (and secular) uses of the thorned rose see Barbara Seward, *The Symbolic Rose*, (New York, 1960), pp. 18–27.
6. "Literature in the Reader: Affective Stylistics," *New Literary History*, 2 (1970), 124; "*Making* Sense: Readers as Writers," lecture at McMaster University, 24 November 1975. For a less sophisticated statement of the reader's temporal approach to a text see Roman Ingarden, *The Cognition of the Literary Work of Art* (Evanston, Ill., 1973), p. 227.
7. John Livingston Lowes, *Convention and Revolt in Poetry* (New York, 1919), p. 60; Kemp Malone, *Chapters on Chaucer* (Baltimore, 1951), p. 181.
8. *Chaucer and Medieval Estates Satire* (Cambridge, 1973), p. 130.
9. Ibid.
10. *The Major Latin Works of John Gower*, trans. Eric W. Stockton (Seattle, 1962), p. 181. I have used this translation for easier accessibility.
11. *The Ancrene Riwle: The Corpus MS; Ancrene Wisse*, trans. M. B. Salu (Notre Dame, 1956), pp. 1–2. The translation is used for clarity.
12. D. W. Robertson, Jr., *A Preface to Chaucer* (Princeton, 1962), pp. 244–46.
13. R. E. Kaske, "Chaucer and Medieval Allegory," *ELH*, 30 (1963), 175–92.
14. Robertson, *Preface*, pp. 244–46; John M. Steadman, "The Prioress' Dogs and Benedictine Discipline," *Modern Philology*, 54 (1956), 1–6.
15. Lowes, *Convention and Revolt*, pp. 62–64; Muriel Bowden, *A Commentary on the General Prologue to "The Canterbury Tales"* (New York, 1967), pp. 96–97.
16. C. M. Drennan, "Chaucer's Prioress, *CT*, Prol. 136: 'Ful semely after hir mete she raughte,'" *Notes and Queries*, ser. 11, 9 (1914), 365.
17. *General Prologue to "The Canterbury Tales*," ed. Phyllis Hodgson (London, 1969), p. 81. Hodgson's excellent notes anticipate several of the comments made here, as does the fine article by Alan T. Gaylord, "The Unconquered Tale of the

Prioress," *Papers of the Michigan Academy of Science, Arts, and Letters*, 47 (1962), 613–36.

18. Ll. A 525–28. For a different interpretation see D. Biggins, "A Chaucerian Crux: *Spiced Conscience*," *English Studies*, 47 (1966), 169–80.

19. *Ancrene Riwle*, p. 184. The Benedictine Rule also enjoins monastics to keep aloof from worldly actions. On this and other cruxes see Rita Dandridge Simons, "The Prioress's Disobedience of the Benedictine Rule," *College Language Association Journal*, 12 (1968), 77–83.

20. Eileen Power, *Medieval English Nunneries* (Cambridge, 1922), p. 69.

21. Steadman, "Prioress' Dogs," pp. 1–6; Bowden, *General Prologue*, pp. 98–99.

22. Lowes, *Convention and Revolt*, p. 65; Kevin S. Kiernan, "The Art of the Descending Catalogue, and a Fresh Look at Alisoun," *Chaucer Review*, 10 (1975), 8–10.

23. G. J. Engelhardt, "The Ecclesiastical Pilgrims of the *Canterbury Tales*: A Study in Ethology," *Mediaeval Studies*, 37 (1975), 291.

24. The boldest statements in this vein—if somewhat uncertain at that—are by Gordon H. Harper, "Chaucer's Big Prioress," *Philological Quarterly*, 12 (1933), 308–10, who states that she "was in fact fat" (p. 308) but also that she was "possibly fat" (p. 309). See also S. T. Knight, "Almost a Spanne Brood," *Neophilologus*, 52 (1968), 178–80.

25. "The Prioress's Beads 'Of Smal Coral,'" *Medium Ævum*, 39 (1970), 301–05.

26. Only in Elizabethan times does someone give Chaucer a red and black string of beads. See M. H. Spielmann, *The Portraits of Chaucer*, The Chaucer Society, ser. 2, 31 (London, 1900), p. 12.

27. This does not occur in all MSS and is not in the translation by Salu. See, however, *The English Text of the Ancrene Riwle*, ed. Mabel Day, EETS. O.S. 225 (Oxford, 1952), p. 19, and *The Nun's Rule*, trans. James Morton (London, 1907), p. 35.

28. Lowes, *Convention and Revolt*, p. 66.

29. John Livingston Lowes, "The Date of Chaucer's *Troilus and Criseyde*," *PMLA*, 23 (1908), 297 (n. 2); Sister M. Madeleva, C.S.C., *A Lost Language and Other Essays on Chaucer* (New York, 1951), p. 43.

30. "Simple and Coy: A Note on Fourteenth Century Poetic Diction," *Anglia*, 33 (1910), 442.

31. On monastic rules see Robert B. White, Jr., "Chaucer's Daun Piers and the Rule of St. Benedict: The Failure of an Ideal," *JEGP*, 70 (1971), 13–30.

32. Ridley, *The Prioress and the Critics*, p. 25; Peter S. Taitt, *Incubus and Ideal: Ecclesiastical Figures in Chaucer and Langland* (Salzburg, 1975), p. 58.

33. "Chaucer's Daun Piers," 13–30.

34. E. Talbot Donaldson, *Speaking of Chaucer* (London, 1970), p. 11.

Resurrection as Dramatic Icon   GAIL McMURRAY GIBSON
in the Shipman's Tale

1. *Etymologiarum sive originum*, 1.37.22–23, ed. W. M. Lindsay (1911; rpt. Oxford, 1971):

Allegoria est alieniloquium. . . . Huius tropi plures sunt species, ex quibus eminent septem: ironia, antiphrasis, aenigma, charientismos, paroemia, sarcasmos, astysmos. Ironia est sententia per pronuntiationem contrarium habens intellectum.

2. See V. A. Kolve, *The Play Called Corpus Christi* (Stanford, 1966), pp. 145–51, and Kelsie B. Harder, "Chaucer's Use of the Mystery Plays in the *Miller's Tale*," *Modern Language Quarterly*, 17 (1956), 193–98.

3. See, for example, Bertrand H. Bronson, "Chaucer's Art in Relation to his Audience," University of California Publications in English 8 (1940), 11 (n. 8): "The art of oral narrative resembles music in this, that its points must in the main carry their own significance as they advance, and cannot await interpretation in the light of later developments. Their significance may be clarified and deepened by subsequent revelation; but if it is to have its due effect, the meaning must have been already suggested."

4. Jean Leclercq, *The Love of Learning and the Desire for God*, trans. Catharine Misrahi (New York, 1961), pp. 78–79:

> What results [from the oral reading of the Scripture] is a muscular memory of the words pronounced and an aural memory of the words heard. The *meditatio* consists in applying oneself with attention to this exercise in total memorization; it is, therefore, inseparable from the *lectio*. It is what inscribes, so to speak, the sacred text in the body and in the soul. . . . It is this deep impregnation with the words of Scripture that explains the extremely important phenomenon of reminiscence whereby the verbal echoes so excite the memory that a mere allusion will spontaneously evoke whole quotations and, in turn, a scriptural phrase will suggest quite naturally allusions elsewhere in the sacred books.

5. *The Art of Memory* (Chicago, 1966), esp. pp. 50–104.

6. *From Script to Print: An Introduction to Medieval Literature* (Cambridge, 1945), p. 10.

7. Saint Augustine, *On Christian Doctrine*, trans. D. W. Robertson, Jr. (Indianapolis, 1958), p. 38: "No one doubts that things are perceived more readily through similitudes and that what is sought with difficulty is discovered with more pleasure."

8. "Chaucer and the Visual Arts," in *Geoffrey Chaucer*, ed. Derek Brewer (Athens, Ohio, 1975), p. 309.

9. Ibid. See also D. W. Robertson, *A Preface to Chaucer* (Princeton, 1962), pp. 253–55 for the horse as symbol of lust in Chaucer's portrait of the Monk.

10. Donald R. Howard, *The Idea of the Canterbury Tales* (Berkeley, 1976), p. 276.

11. See *The Works of Geoffrey Chaucer*, ed. F. N. Robinson, 2d ed. (Boston, 1957), p. 732 (all citations from Chaucer refer to this volume). See also William W. Lawrence, "Chaucer's Shipman's Tale," *Speculum*, 33 (1958), 56–68.

12. The word *array* appears seven times in both the Shipman's Tale and the Parson's Tale; thirteen times in the Clerk's Tale. The Clerk's Tale also five times uses the word *arrayed*. See *A Concordance to the Complete Works of Geoffrey Chaucer*, ed. John S. P. Tatlock and Arthur G. Kennedy (Concord, Massachusetts, 1927), p. 43.

13. Augustine, *Confessions*, trans. R. S. Pine-Coffin (Baltimore, 1961), p. 178. Cf. the account of St. Augustine's conversion in *The Golden Legend of Jacobus de Voragine*, trans. Granger Ryan and Helmut Ripperger (1941; rpt. New York, 1969), p. 489:

And when he had sobbed and wept bitterly, he heard a voice saying to him: "Take and read, take and read!" Quickly he opened the book of the apostles, and at the first page whereon his eyes fell he read: "Put ye on the Lord Jesus Christ, and make not provision for the flesh in its concupiscences," and straightway every shadow of doubt fell away from him.

14. *The Towneley Plays,* ed. George England and Alfred W. Pollard, EETS, e.s. 71 (1897; rpt. London, 1966), p. 351. Cf. the speech by Quartus apostolus in the Thomas play in which the human flesh of Christ is referred to as a garment abandoned at the Resurrection:

QUARTUS APOSTOLUS. The holy gost in marye light / and in hir maydynhede
Goddis son she held and dight / and cled hym in manhede;
ffor luf he wentt as he had hight / to fight withoutten drede;
when he had termynd that fight / he skypt outt of his wede.

(ll. 204–07)

15. *Old English Homilies of the Twelfth Century,* ed. R. Morris, EETS, o.s. 53 (London, 1873), pp. 99–101.

16. *Mirk's Festial: A Collection of Homilies,* ed. Theodor Erbe, EETS, e.s. 96 (London, 1905), p. 131.

17. See, for example, the thirteenth-century lyric "Nou goth sonne vnder wode" (in *English Lyrics before 1500,* ed. Theodore Silverstein [Evanston, Illinois 1971], p. 15), and *A Critical Edition of John Lydgate's Life of Our Lady,* ed. Joseph A. Lauritis, Ralph A. Klinefelter, and Vernon F. Gallagher, Duquesne Studies, Philological Series 2 (Pittsburgh, 1961), p. 344.

18. See John V. Fleming's interesting essay "Toward an Iconography of Medieval Poetic Forms," *Studies in Iconography* 2 (1976), 3–10 for a discussion of *double entendre* use of the Vulgate word *surgere* in medieval Advent sermons and dawn songs.

19. See Karl Young's chapter entitled "The Visit to the Sepulchre, Third State" in *The Drama of the Medieval Church* (Oxford, 1933), vol. 1, 369–410.

20. *Chaucer Life Records,* ed. Martin M. Crow and Clair C. Olson (Oxford, 1966), p. 546.

21. E. Catherine Dunn, "Popular Devotion in the Vernacular Drama of Medieval England," *Medievalia et Humanistica,* n.s. 4 (1973), 59.

22. See Helen Meredith Garth, *Saint Mary Magdalen in Medieval Literature* (Baltimore, 1950), pp. 87–88, and a forthcoming article by V. A. Kolve entitled "God's Spade: Christ as Gardener in Medieval English Drama and the Visual Arts." The commentaries of Augustine and Gregory were popularized in vernacular texts like the *Mirrour of the Blessed Lyf of Jesu Christ* (a free translation of the Pseudo-Bonaventura's *Meditationes,* ed. Lawrence F. Powell [Oxford, 1908]) written by Nicholas Love in 1410:

and thouȝ oure lorde was not bodily / as sche supposed / a gardyner, neuertheless / as the same clerk seint Gregory seith / he was so in sooth goostly to hir; for he it was that planted in the gardyn / of hir herte the plantes of vertues and of trewe loues.

(p. 268)

and thou oure lorde was not bodily / as sche supposed / a gardyner, neuertheless /

23. *"Mary Magdalen* from the Digby MS" in *Medieval Drama,* ed. David Bevington (Boston, 1975), p. 723.

24. Saint Augustine, *The City of God,* 22. 15, trans. Marcus Dods (New York, 1950), p. 838.

25. There is no agreement in the Gospel accounts of the Resurrection about the number of the Marys at the sepulchre. Matthew 28:1 says "Mary Magdalen and the other Mary" went to anoint Jesus' dead body, but in Mark 16:1 we are told that three Marys—Mary Magdalen, Mary the mother of James, and Mary Salome—went to the tomb. Luke 24:10 says that Mary Magdalen, Joanna, Mary of James, and "the other women that were with them" went to the tomb; John (20:1) mentions only Mary Magdalen. A confusion about the number is frequent in the liturgical plays; sometimes two Marys are mentioned in the introductory antiphon although three actually appear in the play. See Young, *Drama of the Medieval Church,* vol. 1, p. 389.

26. Translated by David Bevington in *Medieval Drama,* p. 206,

> Mundi delectatio   dulcis est et grata,
> Eius conversatio   suavis et ornata.
> Mundi sunt deliciae,   quibus aestuare
> Volo, nec lasciviam   eius devitare.
>
> Pro mundano gaudio   vitam terminabo;
> Bonis temporalibus   ego militabo
> Nil curans de ceteris   corpus procurabo,
> Variis coloribus   illud perornabo.
>
> (23–30)

27. Ibid., p. 209: "Tunc deponat vestimenta secularia et induat nigrum pallium; et amator recedat, et diabolus." It was presumably because of this important and emblematic change of garments at Mary Magdalen's conversion that David Bevington rendered the *varii colores* of the scarlet woman as "array of brilliant finery" rather than as "cosmetics," which is its strictest meaning.

28. See M. D. Anderson, *Drama and Imagery in English Medieval Churches* (Cambridge, 1963), pp. 112, 152, 217 for examples in Norwich, Lincoln, and Windsor churches and on an alabaster relief in the Victoria and Albert Museum.

29. John 20:17; *Towneley Plays,* p. 324; *York Plays,* ed. Lucy Toulmin Smith (Oxford, 1885), p. 424; *The Chester Mystery Cycle,* ed. R. M. Lumiansky and David Mills, EETS, s.s. 3 (London, 1974), p. 487; *Ludus Coventriae or the Plaie Called Corpus Christi,* ed. K. S. Block, EETS, e.s. 120 (1922, rpt. London, 1960), p. 335.

30. See *Towneley Plays,* pp. 130, 133. On the sacral parody of the "Second Shepherd's Play" see Margery M. Morgan, "High Fraud: Paradox and Double-Plot in the English Shepherd's Plays," *Speculum,* 39 (1964), 678–89.

31. See *The Complete Works of Geoffrey Chaucer,* ed. Rev. Walter W. Skeat (Oxford, 1894), vol. 5, p. 172.

32. *The Southern Passion,* ed. Beatrice Daw Brown, EETS, o.s. 169 (London, 1927), p. 67.

33. *Chester Mystery Cycle,* p. 488; *Ludus Coventriae,* p. 336; *Towneley Plays,* p. 324.

34. Cf. John 20:2–5.

35. *Towneley Plays,* p. 367.

Grateful acknowledgment is made to V. A. Kolve, Robert P. Miller, and D. W. Robertson, Jr. for helpful criticism of this essay. A special debt of thanks is due to Edmund Reiss in whose classroom I first read the Shipman's Tale.

The Book of the Duchess: JAMES I. WIMSATT
Secular Elegy or Religious Vision?

1. For discussion of the place of *BD* in a tradition of secular consolations, see, for instance, my essay, "Machaut's *Lay de confort* and Chaucer's *Book of the Duchess*," in *Chaucer at Albany,* ed. Rossell Hope Robbins (New York, 1975), pp. 11–26. Compare the exposition of the poem's religious significance in my article, "The Apotheosis of Blanche in *The Book of the Duchess,*" *JEGP*, 66 (1967), 26–44.

2. E. D. Hirsch, Jr., *Validity in Interpretation* (New Haven, 1967), pp. 78–79.

3. F. N. Robinson, ed., *The Works of Geoffrey Chaucer*, 2d. ed. (Boston, 1957), ll. 39–40. Subsequent citations refer to this edition.

4. This ambiguity is noted in Bernard F. Huppé and D. W. Robertson, Jr., *Fruyt and Chaf* (Princeton, 1963), p. 33.

5. For the hunt-of-love tradition, see my *Chaucer and the French Love Poets,* Univ. of North Carolina Studies in Comp. Lit., 43 (Chapel Hill, 1968), pp. 39–47; and Marcelle Thiebaux, *The Stag of Love: The Chase in Medieval Literature* (Ithaca, N.Y., 1974).

6. For Octavian as Christ, see Edmund Reiss, "Chaucer's Parodies of Love," in *Chaucer the Love Poet,* ed. Jerome Mitchell and William Provost (Athens, Ga., 1973), pp. 33–34. For Christ as hart, see the commentators on the Canticle of Canticles 2:9, where the bridegroom is seen as "like a hart." In the popular legend of Saint Eustace the crucified Christ appears between the horns of a deer. And in Malory's story of the Grail quest (*The Works of Thomas Malory,* ed. Eugene Vinaver [Oxford, 1947], 2:1000), a hermit states that a hart that has appeared signifies Christ, noting, "Oftyntymes or thys hath oure Lord shewed Hym unto god men and to god knyghtes in lyknesse of an herte."

7. Ll. 888–90. Cf. Matt. 21:16, Mark 10:31, Luke 13:30.

8. Hirsch, *Validity in Interpretation,* p. 76.

9. For a chart of the borrowings, see my *Chaucer and the French Love Poets,* pp. 155–62.

10. See E. G. Sandras, *Étude sur G. Chaucer* (Paris, 1859), p. 95.

11. See my *Chaucer and the French Love Poets,* pp. 103–50.

12. See my "The *Dit dou Bleu Chevalier:* Froissart's Imitation of Chaucer," *Mediaeval Studies,* 34 (1972), 388–400.

13. *A Literary History of England,* ed. Albert C. Baugh (New York, 1948), p. 486.

14. See, for example, Machaut's *Remede de Fortune* (an important source of *BD*), ll. 1467–69, *Oeuvres de Guillaume de Machaut,* Société des anciens textes français, 3 vols. (Paris, 1908–21). Subsequent references to Machaut are to this edition.

15. Cf. another major source for *BD*, Machaut's *Jugement dou Roy de Behaingne*, ll. 557, 650.

16. Bertrand H. Bronson, "*The Book of the Duchess* Reopened," *Chaucer: Modern Essays in Criticism,* ed. Edward Wagenknecht (New York, 1959), p. 293.

17. See the discussion of "fruyt and chaf" and comparable terms, Huppé and Robertson, *Fruyt and Chaf*, esp. pp. 2–7.

18. *Le Roman de la Rose*, ed. Félix Lecoy, Classiques français du moyen âge, 3 vols. (Paris, 1966–70), ll. 659–66. Subsequent references to the *Roman* are to this edition.

19. Robinson's note to *BD* 311, p. 774, suggests that Tunis is chosen only for rime, but this is to ignore the rich history of the city.

20. See Huppé and Robertson, *Fruyt and Chaf*, p. 46.

21. Cf. esp. *BD* 335–43 with *Behaingne* 13–24.

22. Full documentation of the variants that show J to be the closest of the *JRB* MSS to the one Chaucer read and used will be presented in my edition of selected poems of Machaut for the Chaucer Library. The evidence is pervasive and cumulative rather than isolated and striking. An example of the evidence for J may be found in the readings of *JRB* 1074, in which Fortune is described as ever changing, in J to be "or au feu, or a table." Most other MSS read "or au feu, a la table." Chaucer in *BD* 646 says that Fortune is "Now by the fire, now at table." As in J, "now" ("or") is repeated, and the definite article before "table" is omitted. Further details for the readings of this line may be found in Hoepffner's edition.

23. Psalms 32:3, 39:4, 95:1, 97:1, 143:9, 149:1; Isaiah 42:10; Apoc. 5:9, 14:3. References to the Bible are to Jerome's Vulgate version and the Douay-Rheims translation of it.

24. Ll. 879, 883. Citations of *Pearl* are from E. V. Gordon, ed., *Pearl* (Oxford, 1953). Cf. also Chaucer's Prioress' Tale, B² 1774.

25. I quote the comment of the *Glossa ordinaria* on Psalm 32:3, *PL* 113, 888: "Canticum Novum. De incarnatione, de qua mundus exsultat, de qua Angeli cantaverunt." Many exegetes follow Augustine, *Enarrationes in Psalmos*, *PL* 36–37, in equating the New Song with the New Testament. The New Testament, of course, is the story of the Incarnation. For examples of others who state that the New Song is of the Incarnation, see Cassiodorus, *Expositio in Psalterium*, *PL* 70, 226 and 1048; and Haymo of Halberstadt, *Expositio in Apocalypsin*, *PL* 117, 1020.

26. *Opera*, 2 (Venice, 1732), f. 251: "Hoc autem Canticum novum quid aliud est quam desiderium Incarnationis futurae, vel exultatio, et laus jam exhibitae? Unde liber qui incipit: Osculetur me osculo oris sui, in quo desiderium Incarnationis exprimitur, dicitur Canticum canticorum." Hugh further states, 2: f. 79v, that the New Song concerns the new king of Canticles 3:11, whom the "daughters of Sion are called to see, and who has just been crowned by his mother 'diademate humanitatis.'"

Note also the association in Alan of Lille, *Distinctiones theologicalium*, *PL* 210, 730, s.v. "canticum": "Dicitur exsultatio aeternae beatudinis, unde in Apoc: Cantabunt sancti canticum novum in conspectu agni. Quandoque, antonomastice, Cantica canticorum, scilicet epithalamium Salomoni quod canit de ineffabili conjunctione Christi et Ecclesiae."

27. "Traces of the *Canticum* and of Boethius' *De consolatione philosophiae* in Chaucer's *Book of the Duchess*," *MLN*, 12 (1897), 378–80.

28. For further discussion of these parallels see my "Apotheosis of Blanche," pp. 35–37.

29. Rodney Delasanta, "Christian Affirmation in *The Book of the Duchess*," *PMLA*, 84 (1969), 251.

30. The connection between the bridegroom of Canticles and Psalm 18 is frequently made by exegetes. See, e.g., the comment on Cant. 2:8 by Gregory the Great, *Excerpta ex libris S. Gregorii Papae super Cantica Canticorum, PL* 180, 451: "Ecce, ut nos post se currere faceret, quosdam pro nobis saltus manifestata per carnem Veritas dedit, quia *exultavit ut gigas ad currendam viam.*"

31. The chess game in *BD* suggests especially Apoc. 12, in which the woman clothed with the sun, often interpreted as Mary, is pursued by the "serpent," usually seen as Satan, with whom the Virgin has a traditional enmity. In Chaucer's poem the description of Fortune has Satanic implications, notably in the characterization of her as a scorpion, which is directly based on a description of Lucifer in Machaut's Motet 9, 45–47 (*Poésies lyriques de Guillaume de Machaut*, 2 vols. [Paris, 1909]). At the same time, the medieval chess piece known as the "fers" (also called the "queen" in Chaucer's time and after), which Fortune opposes in *BD*, was commonly called "fierge" in French and was generally associated with the "vierge," Mary. See Henry Adams, *Mont-Saint-Michel and Chartres* (Boston, 1913), pp. 204–05; and H. J. R. Murray, *A History of Chess* (Oxford, 1913), pp. 423–34. Machaut's Motet 9 directly concerns the enmity of the Virgin and Lucifer.

32. *Fruyt and Chaf,* pp. 91–92.

33. "St. Augustine's Three Visions and the Structure of the *Commedia*," *MLN*, 82 (1967), 59.

34. See ibid., pp. 59–61, and the extensive references in his notes.

35. The popular characterization of Canticles by Isidore of Seville, *In libros Veteris ac Novi Testamenti proemia, PL* 83, 164–65, sees it as on the one hand passing over *visibilia* completely, and on the other finding the divine in the semblance ("sub specie") of the *sponsus* and *sponsa*. Jean Gerson, *Opusculum super Cantica Canticorum* (Nuremburg, 1470), pp. 5v–6, speaks of Canticles as providing "anagogic similes" which assist in attaining mystical experience, but he does not explain how these similes operate. Such description is highly equivocal, suggesting that in Saint Augustine's terms the mode of perception involved in Canticles is both spiritual and intellectual—but at the same time neither one.

36. Cited in Henri de Lubac, *Exégèse médiévale*, pt. 1 (Paris, 1959), 2:449–50.

37. Quoted by John Fleming, *The Roman de la Rose* (Princeton, 1969), p. 64n.

38. For these echoes of the Apocalypse and Canticles see Dante Alighieri, *The Divine Comedy*, ed. and trans. Charles S. Singleton, Bollingen Series 80, *Purgatorio, 2: Commentary* (Princeton, 1973), pp. 705–19.

39. See esp. the refrains on "wythouten spot" in section 1, and "maskelleȝ" in section 13. The nuptial imagery also depends on Canticles, sometimes with verbal echoes, as when the dreamer speaks of the Maiden, "To Krysteȝ chambre þat art ichose" (904).

40. "Apotheosis of Blanche," pp. 26–44; "Beatrice as a Figure for Mary," *Traditio*, 33 (1977), 402–14.

41. "Consolation on the Death of Valentinian," trans. Roy J. Deferrari, in *Funeral Orations by St. Gregory Nazianzen and St. Ambrose* (New York, 1953), pp. 294–96.

42. "Epistola CVIII, Ad Eustochium virginem," *PL* 22, 904. Alcuin employs Canticles in consoling Charlemagne on the death of the "femina nobilis" Luitgard; and the biblical poem became something of a standard item in hagio-

graphical descriptions of the ascending soul. For the references to Alcuin and relevant saints' lives see Rosemarie Herde, *Das Hohelied in der lateinischen Literatur des Mittelalters bis zum 12. Jahrhundert*, Münchener Beiträge zur Mediävistik und Renaissance Forschung, 3 (Spoleto, 1968), pp. 992, 1006–07, 1010, 1014.

43. *A Right Christian Treatise, Entituled St. Augustine's Praiers* (London, 1581), pp. 90–92. For the Latin original see *Liber meditationum, PL* 40, 918.

44. Marjorie Anderson, "Blanche, Duchess of Lancaster," *Modern Philology,* 45 (1947–48), 152. The account of her father Henry's benefactions presented by Kenneth Fowler, *The King's Lieutenant: Henry of Grosmont, First Duke of Lancaster* (New York, 1969), pp. 188–91, suggests that he too had a special devotion to the Virgin.

45. The Carmelites considered their order to be "divinely instituted in honor of the glorious and blessed Virgin Mary," and all of their abbey churches were named for Mary (Élisée de la Nativité, O.C.D., "La Vie Mariale au Carmel," *Maria II,* ed. Hubert du Manoir, S.J. [Paris, 1952], pp. 835, 847). The Assumption was the "annual feast *par excellence* of the order" (Archdale A. King, *Liturgies of the Religious Orders* [London, 1955], p. 275).

46. Eleanor P. Hammond, *Chaucer: A Bibliographical Manual* (1908; rpt. New York, 1933), p. 126.

47. For the pre-Reformation Sarum liturgy, see J. Wickham Legg, ed., *The Sarum Missal* (Oxford, 1916); and Francis Proctor and Christopher Wordsworth, *Breviarium ad usum insignis ecclesiae Sarum,* 3 vols. (Cambridge, 1879–86).

48. See Friedrich Ohly, *Hohelied-Studien: Grundzüge einer Geschichte der Hoheliedauslegung des Abendlandes bis um 1200* (Wiesbaden, 1958), pp. 145–46.

49. *Exposé sur le Cantique des Cantiques*, Sources chrétiennes, 82 (Paris, 1962), pp. 82, 100, 104, 306–08.

50. Of the numerous prominent medieval interpreters of Canticles only Honorius of Autun accepts Solomon as the literal *sponsus* and builds an interpretation on such a premise. See his *Expositio in Cantica Canticorum, PL* 172, 351–52. Implicit recognition of the carnal reference, though, can be found even in the most spiritually minded commentators like Bernard of Clairvaux and Gregory the Great.

51. See Sidney Armitage-Smith, *John of Gaunt* (1904; rpt. New York, 1964), pp. 75–78.

52. "Medieval and Modern in Chaucer's *Troilus and Criseyde,*" *PMLA,* 92 (1977), 203–16.

From Cleopatra to Alceste: V. A. KOLVE
An Iconographic Study of
The Legend of Good Women

1. The quotation from Chaucer (like all subsequent quotations) is from F. N. Robinson, ed., *The Works of Geoffrey Chaucer,* 2d ed. (Boston, 1957). Boccaccio, in *De claris mulieribus*, worked under a more capacious rubric, as he is careful to point out in his Preface: "Nor do I want the reader to think it out of place if together with Penelope, Lucretia, and Sulpicia, who were very chaste matrons, they find Medea, Flora, and Sempronia, who happened to have very strong but destructive characters. For it is not my intention to give the word 'famous' so

strict a meaning that it will always seem to signify 'virtuous,' but rather to give it a wider sense, if the reader will forgive me, and to consider as famous those women whom I know to have become renowned to the world through any sort of deed." Giovanni Boccaccio, *Concerning Famous Women*, trans. Guido A. Guarino (New Brunswick, N.J., 1963), pp. xxxvii–viii. The work lacks a modern edition; Guarino translates from that of Mathias Apiarius (Berne, 1539).

2. The reasons for this neglect can be briefly stated: though the Prologue is found charming, the Legends have not appealed, and it has been customarily assumed (partly because the poem is incomplete, partly because of explicit comments made by its narrator) that they did not appeal to Chaucer either. The best writing on the Prologue, that of Robert O. Payne, *The Key of Remembrance: A Study of Chaucer's Poetics* (New Haven, 1963), ch. 3, dismisses "the legends themselves, which follow the brilliant Prologue" as "flat, more or less unrelieved failures" (p. 111); his more recent essay, "Making His Own Myth: The Prologue to Chaucer's *Legend of Good Women*," *Chaucer Review*, 9 (1975), 197–211, is similar in focus. Insofar as the poem has been considered as a whole, it has customarily been described as a royal commission uncongenial to the poet, or more recently, in a useful book by Robert Worth Frank, Jr., *Chaucer and "The Legend of Good Women"* (Cambridge, Mass., 1972), as a set of exploratory exercises in the art of short narrative, imperfectly achieved in the *Legend* but mastered in *The Canterbury Tales*. Frank's book considers the Legends one at a time, with learning and often with critical acumen, but without any compelling vision of what they were meant to amount to as a whole.

3. Beverly Taylor, "The Medieval Cleopatra: The Classical and Medieval Tradition of Chaucer's *Legend of Cleopatra*," *Journal of Medieval and Renaissance Studies*, 7 (1977), 249–69, offers a condensed but very learned survey of the tradition; it should be supplemented by Ilse Becher, *Das Bild der Kleopatra in der griechischen und lateinischen Literatur* (Berlin, 1966), which provides an exhaustive study of the classical sources. Pages 151–73 concern Cleopatra's death. On the question of Chaucer's immediate source or sources, see W. K. Wimsatt, Jr., "Vincent of Beauvais and Chaucer's Cleopatra and Croesus," *Speculum*, 12 (1937), 375–81, and Pauline Aiken, "Chaucer's *Legend of Cleopatra* and the *Speculum Historiale*," *Speculum*, 13 (1938), 232–36.

4. Taylor suggests these changes are meant to invoke the Cleopatra one finds in other books, with Chaucer's omissions and discrepancies establishing a comic, ironic intention for the *Legend* as a whole: "Chaucer depicts subjects who illustrate the most perfidious and destructive—or in some instances, the most ludicrous—aspects of worldly love," and begins with Cleopatra in order to establish this "ironic principle" with particular clarity (p. 250). In my view, Taylor's essay fails to recognize the real materials out of which Chaucer invented Cleopatra's death, and substitutes for the poem he actually wrote a modern scholar's knowledge of the Cleopatra tradition—an enormous compilation of texts few of which could have been known to Chaucer or to his original audiences, but knowledge of which is essential to her interpretation of the poem.

5. Donald R. Howard, *The Idea of the Canterbury Tales* (Berkeley, 1976), ch. 1: "The Idea of an Idea."

6. I argue the historical justification for such an approach to Chaucer's fiction at greater length and with a great deal of pictorial evidence in my book, *Narrative*

Imagery in the Canterbury Tales, chs. 1 and 2. For a brief account of these ideas, see my essay, "Chaucer and the Visual Arts," in *Geoffrey Chaucer* (Writers and Their Background), ed. Derek Brewer (Athens, Ohio, 1974), pp. 290–320. Note that, in our present poem, *The Legend of Philomela* explicitly describes the experience of literature as a visual event: the story of Tereus infects with venom the eyes of anyone who would "behold" it (2238–43), and Philomela weaves her story in pictures and letters together (2350–65).

7. Florus, *Epitome of Roman History*, ed. and trans. E. S. Forster, Loeb Classical Library (London, 1929), p. 327.

8. Ch. 86 (trans. Guarino, p. 196). Boccaccio continues, "In this sleep the wretched woman put an end to her greed, her concupiscence, and her life." Chaucer's version could not conceivably yield such a moral.

9. Giovanni Boccaccio, *The Fates of Illustrious Men*, trans. Louis Brewer Hall (New York, 1965), p. 174 (a partial translation of the Latin text as published by Gourmont and Petit in Paris, 1520). Boccaccio again concludes with a moral: "Her body, softened with the greatest delicacies, used to the most tender embraces, was at last embraced by serpents while she was still sensitive to sight and touch. And the poison nourished the same blood that had been nourished by wines. The beauty she displayed with her feminine vanity, she buried alive. . . . And she who had yearned for great power, finished her life in a mausoleum."

10. Figure 1: see Adam von Bartsch, *Le Pientre-Graveur*, 21 vols. (Vienna, 1803–21), 8.88.12. Other impressions date the engraving 1524. (Photos for figures 1–4 have been supplied by the Warburg Institute, London.)

11. Figure 2: Bartsch, 9.172.5.

12. Figure 3: Bartsch, 8.147.77. For another engraving by the same artist, likewise set in prison, see Bartsch, 8.146.76; it is dated 1529.

13. Figure 4: Bartsch, 14.161.198. See also 14.162–64.199–200.

14. Figure 5: London, Brit. Lib. MS Royal 14 E. v, fol. 339, a copy of the second translation (1409) by Laurent de Premierfait, freer than the version he had made in 1400. Figure 6: London, Brit. Lib. MS Royal 18 E. v, fol. 363v; the MS is Flemish. The third miniature I refer to above (Munich, Bayerische Staatsbibliothek MS gall. 6, made in the workshop of Jean Fouquet) also illustrates the *De casibus:* it allows Cleopatra to meet her death totally naked, with serpents at her breasts. But that is just one event, barely visible in the middle distance, in a picture that also shows Anthony's cavalry victory over Octavius, the sea-battle at Actium, and (far more prominent) Anthony stabbing himself in a room filled with tombs and funeral effigies. It has been reproduced by Paul Durrieu, *Le Boccace de Munich* (Munich, 1909), pl. 20. On the French tradition of illustrations to the Boccaccio texts, see Carla Bozzolo, *Manuscrits des Traductions Françaises d'Oeuvres de Boccace, XV Siècle* (Padua, 1973), and *Boccace en France: De l'Humanisme à l'Erotisme*, catalogue of an exhibition at the Bibliothèque Nationale (Paris, 1975), compiled by Florence Callu and Francois Avril, esp. pp. 53–58. Though the *De casibus* text on its own is enough to explain the nakedness and serpents, these two instances may bear some kinship to a twelfth-century French tradition in stone carving, represented at Moissac, Vézelay, and Charlieu, that depicts Lust *(Luxuria)* as a naked woman with two serpents at her breast. On this tradition, see Emile Mâle, *Religious Art in France: The Twelfth Century*, ed. Harry Bober (Princeton, 1978), pp. 373–76, and figs. 17, 264, 265, and further refer-

ences there. The Boccaccio text can readily support such an identification; Chaucer's text does not.

15. Figure 7: Paris, Bibl. Natl. ms fr. 12420, fol. 129v, illustrating the French translation made in 1401 (the attribution to Laurent de Premierfait has been questioned) variously titled *Des Femmes Nobles et Renomées* or *Des Cleres et Nobles Femmes;* the present ms was presented to Philippe le Hardi in 1403.

16. Figure 8: Paris, Bibl. Natl. ms fr. 598, fol. 128v (a ms presented to the Duke of Berry in 1404). Its illuminations bear a family relationship to those of ms fr. 12420 above. For a detailed account, see *Boccace en France,* pp. 53–54, and Millard Meiss, *French Painting in the Time of Jean de Berry: The Limbourgs and Their Contemporaries,* 2 vols. (New York, 1974), 1:287–90. Two other versions of Cleopatra's death are of interest. London, Brit. Lib. ms Royal 16 G. v, fol. 101, shows her royally dressed with two dragons crouching beside her, catching in their mouths the blood that spurts from her arms. This interpretation of the serpents is without textual precedent, though another ms (London, Brit. Lib. ms Royal 20 C. v, fol. 131v) copies this picture. The image is bland and without expressive force, but its rendering of the customary serpents as dragons may be meant to move her death into a context of sin and its affiliations: perhaps her blood feeds dragons to signify that even in her death the devil is served. Compare Boccaccio's text (n. 8 above) in its medieval French translation: Cleopatra thus "print fin de avarice de vie et de plaisance charnele" (fol. 104). The picture is reproduced by Patricia Gathercole, *Tension in Boccaccio: Boccaccio and the Fine Arts,* Romance Monographs 14 (University, Miss., 1975), fig. 6, though she does not identify the creatures as dragons—describing them merely as "two strange animals" (p. 60)—and offers no guess as to their meaning. *Boccaccios Buch von dem fürnembsten Weibern,* ed. Kurt Pfister (Potsdam, 1924), a facsimile of a German translation of this work published at Ulm in 1473, reproduces on p. 233 its woodcut illustration of the lovers' death (a serpent at each of Cleopatra's arms), juxtaposed to a scene of the lovers feasting, with a servant attending them at table. The traditional moral association of gluttony with lechery may be the explanation of this double scene.

17. Figure 9: Paris, Bibl. de l'Arsenal ms 5193, fol. 272v. The ms was first owned by Jean sans Peur, Duke of Burgundy; its illuminations were published by Henry Martin, *Le Boccace de Jean sans Peur* (Brussels, 1911). On it see *Boccace en France,* p. 56, and Millard Meiss, *French Painting in the Time of Jean de Berry: The Boucicaut Master* (London, 1968), pp. 35, 47, 50, 54. That the snakes are shown *within* the tomb oddly—though fortuitously—suggests what Chaucer had already made of this event.

18. Figure 10: New York, Coll. Francis Kettaneh, likewise illustrating Laurent's *Des Cas des Nobles Hommes et Femmes* in its second translation, 6:15 (the ms is not foliated). See Meiss, *Boucicaut Master,* p. 50, for a description of this miniature (which he reproduces in color as figure 392) and pp. 102–04, for a description of the ms as a whole.

19. Figure 11: Paris, Bibl. Natl. ms fr. 226, fol. 183v. Millard Meiss, *French Painting in the Time of Jean de Berry: The Late Fourteenth Century and the Patronage of the Duke,* 2 vols. (London, 1967), 1: 93, 318, describes this ms; see too his *French Painting . . . The Limbourgs and their Contemporaries,* 1: 259, 261–62, 367, 378.

Meiss dates the MS ca. 1415, and attributes its illuminations to the Rohan work-shop. Callu and Avril, *Boccace en France*, p. 57, date the MS ca. 1420.

20. In the early decades of this century, when the search for sources and analogues dominated Chaucer studies, certain parallels were adduced, among them the fact that serpents are included in the punishments of hell, and that confinement in a serpent pit occurs within certain medieval romances and in certain medieval saints' lives. Griffith suggested that Chaucer may have invented such torture as a justification for thinking of Cleopatra as a martyr; Tatlock suggested that Chaucer may have known of serpent-pits in contemporary Africa, an idea which brings Robinson's note on the matter to an end: "This would be," he writes, "one of the most striking cases of [Chaucer's] use of local color." (See Robinson's note for the relevant bibliography.) All these explanations are defi-cient in one important respect: they cannot explain what Cleopatra intends by the action. Since she invents her own death, it must make some sense from within her story—from within the range of hypotheses concerning life and death avail-able to her. Professor Frank judges her Legend an artistic failure, and thinks it altogether "an odd choice and what seems on several counts an unfortunate choice" as the opening legend of the poem; he suggests that Anthony's tomb and Cleopatra's death are best seen as "acts of devotion" whose "appeal is their exoticism, their suggestion of opulence and passion" (pp. 37, 44). Taylor believes the death is a case study in immoderation: "Even her manner of committing suicide may be seen as partaking of this excess, for Chaucer's queen is content not with an asp or a few serpents, but with nothing less than a pit filled with 'alle the serpentes that she myghte have,'" (p. 261). One wonders what the appropri-ate number would be.

21. See the *OED.* evidence for *pit*, sense I.3, and, e.g., *English Lyrics of the XIIIth Century*, ed. Carleton Brown (Oxford, 1932), AE 13 (6–7); *Religious Lyrics of the XIVth Century*, ed. Carleton Brown, 2d ed. rev. G. V. Smithers (Oxford, 1952), AE 117 (20); and the lyric quoted by Rosemary Woolf, *The English Religious Lyric in the Middle Ages* (Oxford, 1968), p. 88 ("þync on me her in þys pet!"). Cf. old January in the Merchant's Tale (E 1400–1401): "Freendes, I am hoor and oold, / And almoost, God woot, on my pittes brynke." See also the *OED.* evidence for *worm*, senses I.1, 2, 6, and, e.g., *English Lyrics of the XIIIth Century*, #20 (21), #29 (31), #51 (48); *Religious Lyrics of the XIVth Century*, #100 (65), #134 (33), #135 (7, 15, 31); Woolf, *English Religious Lyric*, p. 88 ("Her sal I dwellen wermes to fede"); *St. Erkenwald*, ed. Ruth Morse (Cambridge, 1975), p. 62; *Ludus Coventriae*, ed. K. S. Block, EETS, e.s. 120 (London, 1922), p. 177 (the death of Herod). *English Lyrics of the XIIIth Century*, #29 (47) and #30 (2, 4) refer to worms and pit together. Woolf, *English Religious Lyric*, chs. 3 and 9, offers a magisterial study of medieval lyrics on death and their backgrounds. Douglas Gray, *Themes and Images in the Medieval English Religious Lyric* (London, 1972), ch. 10, is also valuable. For the burial rites accorded several of Chaucer's friends or associates, see Edith Rickert, *Chaucer's World*, ed. Clair C. Olson and Martin M. Crow (London, 1948), pp. 401 ff.

22. *The Bestiary: A Book of Beasts, Being a Translation from a Latin Bestiary of the Twelfth Century*, trans. T. H. White (London, 1954), pp. 190–91. Woolf, *English Religious Lyric*, p. 318, quotes an unedited lyric from the first half of the fifteenth

century that preserves this idea, though she does not remark upon it: "In mi riggeboon brediþ an addir kene." White's bestiary identifies the hypnale (a species of asp) as the snake that caused Cleopatra's death, p. 174, and describes the dragon as "the biggest of all serpents," p. 165.

23. Figure 12: Bartsch, 8.116–17.6; it copies a print made by his brother Barthel Beham, and is in the Potter Palmer Collection (21.316) of the Art Institute of Chicago. The engraving is fully described in *Images of Love and Death in Late Medieval and Renaissance Art*, a catalogue by William R. Levin for an exhibition at the University of Michigan Museum of Art, 1975, pp. 71–72, and reproduced there as pl. 51 (fig. 30). Plates 67 (fig. 88) and 68 (fig. 42) are also of interest. Oxford, Balliol College MS 238, a *Fontis memorabilium universi* (German, 1445–48), fol. 65, depicts a living woman whose body is filled with snakes, bones, and a skull, as an image of Bodily Corruption—of what the body will become.

24. The first is quoted from *English Lyrics of the XIIIth Century*, #10-B (34), the second from John Lydgate's translation of the *Dance Macabre*, in *The Dance of Death*, ed. Florence Warren, EETS, o.s. 181 (London, 1931), p. 74 (640).

25. This is so in fourteen out of the twenty-one medieval wall-paintings of this subject still clearly visible in English churches. See Philippa Tristram, *Figures of Life and Death in Medieval English Literature* (London, 1976), p. 234 (n. 60); for her general discussion of the theme, see pp. 162–67 and fig. 25. Woolf, *English Religious Lyric*, pp. 344–47, and Kathleen Cohen, *Metamorphosis of a Death Symbol: The Transi Tomb in the Late Middle Ages and the Renaissance* (Berkeley, 1973), pp. 33–38, offer useful discussion and bibliography.

26. Figure 13: London, Brit. Lib. MS Arundel 83, fol. 127. I quote the English phrases inscribed above the illumination; the full dialogue (which begins beneath) is in Anglo-Norman verse. The cadavers mirror to some extent the postures of their living counterparts.

27. Figures 14, 15: London, Brit. Lib. MS 37049, fol. 33, and fol. 32v. The verses under figure 15 serve as a kind of preface to the debate poem itself, which is formally begun (with a title) on fol. 33. The preface reads:

> Take hede vn to my fygure here abowne
> And se how sumtyme I was fressche and gay
> Now turned to wormes mete and corrupcoun
> Bot fowle erth and stynkyng slyme and clay
> Attende þerfore to þis disputacion written here
> And writte it wysely in þi herte fre
> At þerat sum wisdom þou may lere
> To se what þou art and here aftyr sal be.
> When þou leste wenes. venit mors te superare
> When þi grafe grenes, bonum est mortis meditari.

I quote from the edition by Karl Brunner, "Mittelenglische Todesgedichte," *Archiv für das Studium der neuren Sprachen*, 167 (1935), 30–35; the debate poem itself consists of thirty-one seven-line stanzas. For commentary on it, see Woolf, *English Religious Lyric*, pp. 313–14, 328–30, and Cohen, *Metamorphosis*, pp. 29–30. Both term it a picture of a double *transi* tomb, but Ralph E. Giesey, in a review of Cohen's book, *Speculum*, 52 (1977), 537–41, perhaps describes it more accurately: "Clearly the cadaver is not a picture of a sculpted *transi* that a spectator at the tomb could see, but rather a picture of the corpse itself decaying in the coffin. . . . The tomb [is] levitated to reveal the worm-eaten corpse" (p. 639). He regards the poem as a commentary upon (and explanation of) the double tombs already in existence rather than as a literary representation of them.

28. Brunner, "Todesgedichte," p. 31 (v. 5).

29. Ibid., p. 32 (vv. 13, 14). Note the thematic relation of this last catalogue to Chaucer's *Legend of Good Women.*

30. Verse 16 offers a comprehensive list of all the "venomos wormes" that eat the corpse; it corroborates the evidence cited in note 21 above. In v. 19 (p. 33) the worms explain to the cadaver that the lice and nits and stomach worms that tormented her (as they do all human beings) all her life long were sent as their messengers, to warn her to make ready.

31. Figure 16: MS cit., fol. 35.

32. Figure 17: MS cit., fol. 87 (the story is told on fols. 86v–87). The text has not been published. Woolf, *English Religious Lyric,* pp. 312–13, describes several variant versions and their provenance, and Gray reproduces this picture (his pl. 8) and summarizes the plot, pp. 206–07; both reprint the concluding verses. Woolf, Appendix H, surveys "The History of the Warning from the Dead"; it is of great antiquity.

33. Cohen, *Metamorphosis,* offers a comprehensive study of the *transi* tomb, exhaustively researched, beautifully written, and richly illustrated, with an appendix that lists all known examples by both country and type. The English examples are listed on pp. 192–94. The style develops late; only five examples date from the fourteenth century, while seventy-five date from the fifteenth. England furnishes more examples than any other country, by a vast proportion (p. 194), but it favored the emaciated *transi,* whereas France provides most of the examples riddled with worms, and Germany and Austria most of the examples of a corpse covered with frogs and snakes (p. 2). Only three *transis* in England are covered with snakes or frogs, and they are relatively late in date (ca. 1510–30)— see p. 78 (n. 102)—whereas France provides thirteen *transis* with worms, and Germany most of the twenty *transis* that are covered with snakes or other reptiles (p. 195). Cohen is careful to emphasize that the *transi* represents "a specific dead individual and not Death itself"; the word is derived from *transire,* and signifies one who has "gone across," "passed over," "passed away"; the noun is first recorded in a sixteenth-century tomb contract in France ("la portraiture d'un transsy et mort d'environ huit jours"), but the verb *transir* in the sense of "to die" had been common in French from the twelfth century (p. 10). Cohen notes that the first men to commission *transi* tombs—cardinals and archbishops—were churchmen famous for their power, political acumen, and worldliness, and that these tombs, while serving the traditional purpose of expressing hope for the salvation of the deceased (pp. 3–4, 62), also represent an attempt "to alleviate some of the anxiety felt by these men as a result of the conflict between their own pride and the traditional religious demand for humility" (p. 7). Erwin Panofsky, *Tomb Sculpture,* ed. H. W. Janson (New York, 1964), pp. 63–66 and figs. 256–71, locates the form within a history of tomb sculpture from ancient Egypt to Bernini.

34. Figure 18: the tomb was constructed in the church of St. Martial, Avignon; this fragment (all that survives) is now in the Musée Calvet of that city.

Cohen, *Metamorphosis*, fig. 3, reproduces a seventeenth-century drawing of the full tomb, and writes about it, pp. 12–14; I quote her translation of the Latin epitaph, p. 13. In his will, Lagrange requested that his bones be boiled and buried in Amiens, and that his flesh and entrails be buried under his *transi* in Avignon. The latter city was, of course, the seat of the French papacy. See Arne McGee Morganstern, "The La Grange Tomb and Choir: A Monument of the Great Schism of the West," *Speculum*, 48 (1973), 52–69.

35. Figure 19: Chichele's tomb was built in connection with a chantry chapel, and was in place by 1425; in 1437, he founded All Souls' College, Oxford; in 1443, he died. On this tomb, and for his epitaph, see Cohen, *Metamorphosis*, pp. 15–16.

36. Figure 20: Fleming was Bishop of Lincoln; this tomb, too, is part of a chantry chapel. Cohen describes it, ibid., pp. 17–18, and prints his vivid epitaph, probably composed by Fleming himself. Cf. the tomb of John Fitzalan (died 1435), in Arundel, Sussex, reproduced by Tristram, *Figures of Life and Death*, fig. 32.

37. Figures 21, 22: on this tomb, see Cohen, *Metamorphosis*, pp. 77–83. The chapel that houses it in the village church at La Sarraz was built in 1360, and Herbert Reiners would indeed date the tomb ca. 1360; Erwin Panofsky and Ernst Kantorowicz suggest a date nearer to 1370; Raoul Nicolas argues for the late 1390s. (See Cohen, pp. 77–78 [nn. 100, 101]; Cohen accepts Nicholas's dating.) On p. 83 Cohen develops an elaborate interpretation of this effigy, in which the frogs at the mouth represent unclean spirits expelled by the deceased's confession of his sins, the snakes represent his contrition (the gnawing pangs of conscience), and the scallop shells on his pillow and carved into his chest his hope of eternal life. I think the first part of this reading unlikely; on p. 93 Cohen admits later sculptors show no evidence of having understood it so. The Wakefield play of *Lazarus*, for instance, includes a first-hand account of all those creatures at work in the grave: see *The Towneley Plays*, ed. George England and Alfred W. Pollard, EETS, e.s. 71 (London, 1897; rpt. 1952), pp. 390–91. Like Cohen, I take the scallop shells to be an image of hope and faith, but set in juxtaposition to imagery of the body's corruption.

38. Manuscripts get lost, wear out, rot, burn, are eaten by worms, and sometimes are willfully destroyed. On the systematic destruction of religious art and sculpture in England during the Reformation, see John Phillips, *The Reformation of Images: Destruction of Art in England, 1535–1660* (Berkeley, 1973).

39. Book 3, ch. 1, quoted by Cohen, *Metamorphosis*, p. 43. Chaucer's translation has been lost, though he tells us he translated the work in the G version of the Prologue to our present poem (414–15).

40. Figures 23, 24: the tomb has been briefly described by T. S. R. Boase, "King Death. Mortality, Judgment and Remembrance," ch. 6 of *The Flowering of the Middle Ages*, ed. Joan Evans (London, 1966), pp. 220 (fig. 34) and 240; it is treated more extensively by Arthur Bolton, *Guide to St. Mary's Church, Ewelme, and to the Almshouse and the School*, rev. by K. St. C. Thomas (Ewelme: printed for the church, 1967), pp. 12–13. Russell Krauss, "Chaucerian Problems: Especially the Petherton Forestership and the Question of Thomas Chaucer," in *Three Chaucer Studies*, ed. Carleton Brown (New York, 1932), suggested that the rise of

Thomas Chaucer to great riches and power may imply that he was the illegiti-
mate son of John of Gaunt by Chaucer's wife Philippa, born during Chaucer's
absence from England in 1372–73. Though this is the purest conjecture, it could
also explain the high marriage(s) and elevation to the peerage of Thomas's
daughter, Alice, buried in the tomb described above. The idea has been given
renewed currency by John H. Fisher, ed., *The Complete Poetry and Prose of Geoffrey
Chaucer* (New York, 1977), p. 958, as well as by John Gardner, *The Life and Times
of Chaucer* (New York, 1977), pp. 158–62.

41. Brunner, "Todesgedichte," p. 30 (prefatory verses). Cf. the epitaph from
a woman's tomb in Picardy, quoted by Cohen, *Metamorphosis*, p. 74: "Celle qui dit
ces vers / Est mangie des vers / Et serez-vous" [She who speaks these verses is
eaten by worms: you will be too].

42. Book 7, chs. 9–15 and ff., in *The Complete Works of John Gower*, ed. G. C.
Macaulay, 4 vols. (Oxford, 1899–1902), 4:291–96; trans. Eric W. Stockton, *The
Major Latin Works of John Gower* (Seattle, 1962), pp. 270–74 ff. Each of the Deadly
Sins is shown to corrupt the dead body in its own particular way. I am grateful to
Patricia J. Eberle for calling my attention to this passage.

43. See the concluding pages of this essay, and the passage quoted above in
note 1.

44. Because the Legend of Hypermnestra is unfinished, it by chance
epitomizes the larger poem as we have it: its last line, which is also the last line of
the collection as a whole, begins a new sentence—"This tale is seyd for this
conclusion" (2723)—and ends in silence.

45. Figure 25: London, Brit. Lib. MS Add. 35321, fol. 43. An illumination in
Paris, Bibl. Natl. MS 12420, fol. 61v *(Des Cleres et Nobles Femmes)* likewise depicts
her death as isolated and distant; it was made between 1401 and 1403. Figure 26:
London, Brit. Lib. MS Royal 14 E v, fol. 77v *(Des Cas des Nobles Hommes et Femmes)*,
made ca. 1470–83.

46. Figure 27: from the latter MS, fol. 121v. On the iconography of Despair
[*Desperatio*], see Adolf Katzenellenbogen, *Allegories of the Virtues and Vices in
Mediaeval Art*, trans. Alan J. P. Crick (1939; rpt. New York, 1964), pp. 76–81, figs.
72(b), 76, and pp. 13 (n. 1), 59 (n. 3), 83 (n. 1).

47. Leroy P. Percy, when he was my student, first taught me to read the
Physician's Tale of Virginius and Virginia in such a way. *The Legend of Lucrece*
offers a partial exception to the generalization I make above, for Lucrece is
innocent victim, and Augustine (the poet tells us) felt compassion for her (1690);
she became "a seynt" among the Romans (1870). Indeed Chaucer concludes his
praise of her by recalling Christ's statement that He had found no faithfulness
greater than He had found in a woman. But Chaucer knew Augustine had also
condemned Lucrece for her suicide (Christianity cannot convert such a death
into a virtuous act), and he makes it clear that the only consequence of her death
was oblique and political: It brought down a corrupt dynasty. Though her history is noble, it is irredeemably tragic.

48. The idea is doubtless borrowed from Boccaccio, *De casibus*, where count-
less persons who fell from Fortune's favor are imagined as crowding the author's
study, hoping to have their stories told; in *The Fates of Illustrious Men*, trans. Hall,
see for instance pp. 9, 156, 168, 226, 241. That throng of self-mourners, only

some of whom get their histories narrated, is often shown in deluxe manuscripts of the poem: *Boccace en France*, p. 50, reproduces in color the opening illumination of the famous Munich MS.

49. Frank writes well on this, *Chaucer and "The Legend of Good Women,"* pp. 148–49.

50. D. W. Robertson, Jr., *A Preface to Chaucer: Studies in Medieval Perspectives* (Princeton, 1963), pp. 378–79; see pp. 141–42 on the Christian assimiliation of the Hercules myth.

51. See Franz Cumont, *Recherches sur le Symbolisme Funéraire des Romains* (Paris, 1942), pp. 30 (n. 4), 499 (add. n. 4); Hellmut Sichtermann and Guntram Koch, *Griechische Mythen auf römischen Sarkophagen* (Tübingen, 1975), pp. 20–22, pls. 17–19; and Carl Robert, *Die antiken Sarkophag-Reliefs*, 3.1 (Berlin, 1890–1919, rpt. Rome, 1969), pp. 25–38, pl. 6. Marcel Simon, *Hercule et le Christianisme* (Paris, 1955), offers an extensive study of the larger myth that brought Alceste into early Christian art. André Grabar, *Christian Iconography: A Study of Its Origins* (Princeton, 1968), pt. 1, contributes a masterly introduction to this subject. Though the earliest sources of the Alceste tradition are without direct medieval consequence, it is in Euripides' *Alcestis* that she finds her fullest and most memorable life; it was written in 438 B.C. She is praised in Plato's *Symposium* 179 B–C as an example of the sacrifice a lover will make for the beloved, and of the reward granted by the gods for such a deed; at 208 D it is suggested instead that she died for the sake of immortal renown. Her story and that of Admetus are narrated with extreme brevity in the *Fabulae* of Hyginus, a Latin work written sometime shortly before the year 207, which John of Salisbury clearly knew and which Chaucer may have known; it has been edited and translated by Mary Grant as *The Myths of Hyginus* (Lawrence, Kansas, 1960), p. 58 (#50, #51). Macrobius, *Saturnalia*, 5.19.3–5, briefly quotes and comments on a passage from Euripides' play; it is of no relevance here. Among Chaucer's English contemporaries only Gower tells Alceste's story, probably in imitation of Chaucer. In book 7 of the *Confessio amantis*—the book that summarizes the education given Alexander by Aristotle—she is included as exemplary proof that women can be "goode and kinde" (ll. 1917–49). Gower briefly narrates her decision to die so that her husband might live, but says nothing of her resurrection. He mentions her again among the company of lovers that he sees in a dream (8.2640–46) when he senses himself growing old and is led to renounce the adventure of love (8.2440 ff.). The lovers include Cleopatra, Dido, Phyllis, Penelope, Lucrece, and many others as well—a group that might have wandered in from the pages of *The Legend of Good Women*. It is at the least a literary allusion, and very likely a literary debt.

52. The paintings have been published by Antonio Ferrua, *Le Pitture della Nuova Catacomba di Via Latina* (Vatican City, 1960); see esp. pls. 75, 76, 79 (our figure 28), 80, 81, and (in color) 111, 112; these paintings are described on pp. 77–78; Grabar writes about them, *Christian Iconography*, p. 15, and in his *The Beginnings of Christian Art: 200–398* (London, 1967), p. 225 ff; on p. 228 he reproduces in color our figure 28. In Room E of this same catacomb there is a painting of the death of Cleopatra with an asp at her breast and a halo around her head (see Ferrua, pl. 102 and p. 61). Ferrua offers no guess as to the logic of her presence there, nor can I; see Grabar, *Christian Iconography*, p. 9, on the

frequency with which early Christian imagery eludes any confident interpretation.

53. *Mythologiae*, 1.22. I quote from the translation of Leslie George Whitbread, *Fulgentius the Mythographer* (Columbus, Ohio, 1971), p. 63.

54. *Scriptores rerum mythicarum Latini tres Romae nuper reperti*, ed. George Henry Bode, 2 vols. (Celle, 1834; rpt. Hildesheim, 1968), 1: 31, 128–29, 247–48. Fulgentius discovered in the name Admetus the word for "mind" [*mens, mentis*], and the phrase *adire metus* ["as one whom fear could seize upon"]. Alcestis he derived from the Greek *alce*, glossed as *praesumptio* by him and by the Vatican mythographers after him. The latter word is difficult to translate confidently in this context (Whitbread's "succour" seems a curious choice): in biblical usage, *praesumptio* means simply "opinion" or "thought" (Alexander Souter, ed., *A Glossary of Later Latin to 600 A.D.* [Oxford, 1949; corr. 1957]); in many medieval contexts it retains its original sense of "preconception, supposition, presumption"; but the Third Vatican Mythographer glosses it as *animositas* (op. cit., p. 247), probably in the sense of "boldness, confidence, or fearlessness of spirit." Only the identification of the yoked beasts with the strengths of mind and body, and of the gods who assist Admetus as standing for wisdom (Apollo) and strength (Hercules) makes the point of the marriage clear, even in the pages of the mythographers. Boccaccio, *Genealogie deorum gentilium libri*, 13.1, ed. Vincenzo Romano, 2 vols. (Bari, 1951), 2:642, offers essentially the same reading, and then one other in which Admetus stands for the rational soul, Alcestis for *virtus*, and the winning of her in marriage for a bridling of the irascible and concupiscent appetites. Such virtue or strength, he continues, can oppose our passionate desires for our soul's sake and, if we fall, can raise us up again.

55. Pierre Bersuire, *Ovidius moralizatus*, ed. F. Ghisalberti, *Studi Romanzi*, 23, 101; I quote Robertson's translation, *Preface to Chaucer*, p. 378. Bersuire's notice concludes: "Hercules igitur i. Christus istas de inferno eripit, et ad gloriam secum ducit. Psalmus: propter te mortificamur tota die."

56. Figure 29: Rome, Vatican MS Reg. Lat. 1290, fol. 5a v, Northern Italian. On this text, and on the present MS, see Jean Seznec, *The Survival of the Pagan Gods*, trans. Barbara F. Sessions (1953; rpt. New York, 1961), pp. 170–79. The text above the picture states that reason and strength of mind [*ratio et virtus animi*] vanquish all cupidinous desires and earthly vices, especially the vice of gluttony, whose three heads demand abundance (in terms of quantity), delicacy (in terms of quality), and steady attention (in terms of time): strength [*virtus*] overcomes all of these. And if anything were to be overcome through weakness of mind, that too it draws back [*abstrahit*] from hell. The text is printed by Hans Liebeschütz, *Fulgentius metaforalis* (Leipzig, 1926), p. 125. The picture bears a clear iconographic similarity to late-medieval representations of Orpheus, that other great (though unsuccessful) harrower of hell, as my colleague Hoyt N. Duggan has suggested to me; Orpheus too was read as a Christ-figure. See John Block Friedman, *Orpheus in the Middle Ages* (Cambridge, Mass., 1970), esp. figs. 23 (from this same MS), 27, 29, and Penelope B. R. Doob, *Nebuchadnezzar's Children: Conventions of Madness in Middle English Literature* (New Haven, 1974), pp. 164–207.

57. Figure 30: Rome, Vatican MS Palat. 1066, fol. 228, dated 1420. The *Fulgentius metaforalis* was written by John Ridevall, an English Franciscan, sometime

before 1333; on it see Beryl Smalley, *English Friars and Antiquity in the Early Fourteenth Century* (Oxford, 1960), pp. 110–15. The illustrations to this MS, for all their graphic power, are often difficult to interpret; they have even been presented as covert illustrations of alchemical mysteries, by Stanislas Klossowski de Rola, *Alchemy: The Secret Art* (New York, 1973), figs. 53–62. Though de Rola's alchemical interpretations wholly ignore the written text, his reproductions from this MS are of the highest quality (Cerberus is also shown in figs. 56 and 62). Unfortunately he does not reproduce our figure 30, which I describe above in only a provisional way. One other reading seems possible: the seated figures may be Alcestis and her father, in which case the figure riding the two beasts is probably Admetus, winning her as bride. But it is unlikely the father and daughter would be shown holding hands in that fashion, and the club used to discipline and direct the beasts belongs by iconographical tradition to Hercules (no such club is mentioned in the text). In Hyginus's fable, only Apollo aids Admetus in his assigned task, but in Fulgentius and the Vatican mythographers, Hercules and Apollo together harness the lion and the boar. Since Hercules is the strong man of the pair, he is also more than likely the figure shown here. A Troyes MS contains a memorial reduction of the legend: "A rege postulata, regi copulata, precio donata, facie venundata, infernis allata, Hercule salutata" (Liebeschütz, *Fulgentius metaforalis*, p. 116). Coluccio Salutati commented on the myth in *De laboribus Herculis*, written ca. 1378–81, expanded and revised in 1391, 1398, 1400; see the edition by Berthold L. Ullman, 2 vols. (Zurich, 1951), 1:612–13, and 2: 486, 526. But as Ullman makes clear, the work was virtually unknown in its own time; see his *The Humanism of Coluccio Salutati* (Padua, 1963), esp. pp. 21–26. On Renaissance interpretations of the myth, see Don Cameron Allen, *Mysteriously Meant* (Baltimore, 1970), pp. 59, 267.

58. Lisa J. Kiser, "In Service of the Flower: Chaucer and the *Legend of Good Women*," a Ph.D. thesis written under my direction at the University of Virginia in 1977, argues that Alceste stands for poetry itself—an art whose "figures" (images, fables, rhetorical devices) mediate between our limited human capacities (Chaucer, the offending poet) and the awesome nature of divine truth (the poem's God of Love). The argument is rich and complex; it deserves wide audience.

59. *Disteyne* can mean simply "stain" (the prefix intensive in force); it does so in *Troilus* 2.840. But Chaucer's example of the sun and the fire makes clear that the prefix is here privative in function. It means "de-stain," i.e., deprive of hue, or (following Skeat, Robinson, Baugh, and Fisher) "bedim," "dull," "outshine," "make pale." There is almost certainly a pun on "disdain" as well—the more expected word and a close homophone—but (as we learn when we discover more about this lady) an action not suited to Alceste's nature. She outshines rather than disdains.

60. Ll. F 490–91. This characterization of the poem's narrator is made even more emphatic in the G version of the Prologue, where the God of Love describes Chaucer as one grown too old for love's adventure [G 258–63], and who characteristically slanders love as a result: "thow reneyed hast my lay, / As othere olde foles many a day" (G 314–15).

61. Figure 31: London, Brit. Lib. MS Add. 5141, fol. 1; the MS is sixteenth century, and probably a copy (at one or more removes) of the so-called "Hoccleve

Portrait"; Roger Sherman Loomis, *A Mirror of Chaucer's World* (Princeton, 1965), figs. 2, 3, reproduces both with commentary. In the portrait before us, Chaucer's death is mistakenly dated 1402. The English daisy *(Bellis perennis)* has a yellow crown and white petals tinged with pink: "thise floures white and rede, / Swiche as men callen daysyes in our toun" (F 42–43).

62. John Livingston Lowes, "The Prologue to the *Legend of Good Women* as Related to the French *Marguerite* Poems, and the *Filostrato*," *PMLA*, 19 (1904), 593–683, remains an essential study. More recently, James Wimsatt has begun a scrupulous reassessment of Chaucer's debt to the French tradition in his early poetry; see his *Chaucer and the French Love Poets: The Literary Background of the "Book of the Duchess"* (Chapel Hill, North Carolina, 1968), along with his monograph, *The Marguerite Poetry of Guillaume de Machaut,* Univ. of North Carolina Studies in the Romance Languages and Literatures, 87 (Chapel Hill, North Carolina, 1970), and his essay, "Chaucer and French Poetry," in *Geoffrey Chaucer* (Writers and Their Background), ed. Derek Brewer, pp. 109–36, esp. pp. 127, 134.

63. Ll. F 195–96. On this ritualized courtly contest, and for the text of a poem that enshrines it, long attributed to Chaucer but now thought to have been written in the third quarter of the fifteenth century, see *"The Floure and the Leafe" and "The Assembly of Ladies,"* ed. D. A. Pearsall (Edinburgh, 1962), pp. 20–52 (a remarkable introduction) and 85–102.

64. *Concerning Famous Women,* trans. Guarino, pp. xxxiv, xxxviii.

65. There is, I think, no need to document the *topos* which declares the flesh is like a flower: it is found everywhere. But let me call attention to a fine poem by John Lydgate, a *balade* of 136 lines whose stanzas end in the refrain, "That now is heye some tyme was gras." It uses a brilliant nature poetry to talk about the world's and mankind's mutability, and includes a catalogue of famous women in its lament. The catalogue is indebted both in personage and in language to Chaucer's *Legend:*

> Whilome full feyre was Polixene,
> So was Creseyde; so was Helene
> Dido also of Cartage quene,
> Whos beaute made many one pleyne;
> But dethe came laste and can dysteyne
> Their fresheness, and made them full base,
> Your remembraunce let not disdeyne,
> That now is heye some tyme was gras.
>
> (49–56)

(In the next stanza, he goes on to name Esther and Griselda as further examples.) In Lydgate's poem it is Death that "dysteynes" (deprives of color) all these famous women, some good, some bad. Although Alceste is unmentioned in it, the poem ends with a description of the Celestial City which answers to the corruption of flesh and flower just as does the costume she wears in Chaucer's Prologue: the walls of the city, like the crown of Alceste, are made of precious stones. See John Lydgate, *The Minor Poems,* ed. Henry Noble MacCracken, 2 vols., EETS, e.s. 107, o.s. 192 (London, 1911, 1934), 2:809–13.

The Unlikely Narrator: The Narrative   BERNARD F. HUPPÉ
Strategy of the *Troilus*

1. Citations are to *The Works of Geoffrey Chaucer*, ed. F. N. Robinson (Boston, 1957).
2. This is similar to the incongruity which Boccaccio fully exploited in the *Teseide*.
3. *The Divine Comedy*, trans. H. R. Huse (New York, 1964).
4. *De doctrina*, 2.28.44.
5. Aldo Bernardo and I are presently collaborating on a study of Boccaccio's auctorial personae, particularly in the *Filostrato* and *Teseide*, by way of comparison with Chaucer's narrative persona.
6. *The Consolation of Philosophy*, trans. Richard Green (Indianapolis, 1962), p. 74.

Appendix A
The Structure of *Troilus*

BOOK 1

Proem:	The narrator as servant of lovers	1–57
Prologue:	The war setting	58–154
Scene I:	The temple	155–321
Scene II:	Troilus's chamber	322–435
·Interlude:	Explication of the course of Troilus's love	436–546
Scene III:	Troilus's chamber	547–1064
Coda:	Explication of Troilus's cupidinous conversion	1065–1085
Conclusion:	Formal transition	1086–1092

BOOK 2

Proem:	The narrator as rhetorical literalist	1–49
Prologue:	The awakening of Pandarus	50–77
Scene I:	Criseyde's palace	78–594
Scene II:	Criseyde's chamber	595–931
Scene III:	Troilus's chamber	932–1092
Scene IV:	Criseyde's palace	1093–1302
Scene V:	Troilus's chamber	1303–1400
Scene VI:	Deiphebus's palace	1401–1460
Scene VII:	Criseyde's palace	1461–1491
Scene VIII:	Troilus's chamber	1492–1540
Scene IX:	Deiphebus's palace	1541–1750
Conclusion:	Rhetorical transition	1751–1757

BOOK 3

Proem:	The rhetorician's celebration of love	1–49
Scene I:	Chamber in Deiphebus's palace	50–441
Scene II:	Pandarus's palace and chamber	442–1533
Scene IV:	Troilus's chamber	1534–1547

Appendix B

Translation
Book 1: 133–34, 141–47, 159, 393–99, 492–97
Book 2: 699–700, 1219–20
Book 3: 449–50, 501–04, 575–76, 1191–97, 1198–1200, 1324–38, 1576–79
Book 4: 1415–1421
Book 5: 19–21, 799–805, 806–25, 826–40, 1051–53, 1094–99, 1562–65, 1653–54, 1751–54
Explication and commentary
Book 1: 138–140, 449–51,
Book 2: 450–51, 561, 621–22, 666–86, 905, 965–66, 1261–74, 1331–37, 1561, 1564–68, 1595–96, 1723
Book 3: 442–48, 477–483, 918–24, 967–71, 1714–15
Book 4: 152–53, 185–86, 428, 935–55
Book 5: 89–90, 946–47, 1432–35, 1541–54, 1566–75
Interpolation and Apostrophe

Book 1: 211–224, 225–266, 308, 436
Book 2: None
Book 3: 617–623, 1204, 1212–19, 1223–25, 1310–23, 1373–93
Book 4: 197–203
Book 5: 267–273, 1748–50

Tabulation of subjects of the three types
by book and number of occurrences in each book

	Translation					Explication					Interpolation					Totals
	1	2	3	4	5	1	2	3	4	5	1	2	3	4	5	
Criseyde	2	2	3	1	4		3	3					1			19
Troilus	1		1		4	1	2	1	2	2					1	15
Pandarus							2	1								3
Diomede					1					2						3
Destiny						1	1	1	1	1	1		1		1	8
Love											3		4			7
Rhetoric	1		3				4									8
Pagan rite	1															1
Unruly mob														1		1
Total	5	2	7	1	9	2	12	5	4	5	4		6	1	2	65

Signs, Symbols, and Cancellations   JOHN GARDNER

1. "Simple Signs from Everyday Life in Chaucer," pp. 17–19.

2. Ibid., p. 19–20.

3. Ibid., p. 24.

4. F. N. Robinson, ed., *The Works of Geoffrey Chaucer* (Boston, 1957), is the source here and hereafter for the quotations from Chaucer.

5. Joseph E. Grennen, "Saint Cecilia's 'Chemical Wedding': The Unity of the *Canterbury Tales*, Fragment VIII," *JEGP*, 65 (1966), 466–81.

6. Bruce A. Rosenberg, "The Contrary Tales of the Second Nun and the Canon's Yeoman," *Chaucer Review*, 2 (1968), 291.

7. Paul M. Clogan, "The Figural Style and Meaning of the *Second Nun's Prologue* and *Tale*," *Medievalia et Humanistica*, N.S. 3 (1972), 215–18.

8. On translation in the Second Nun's Tale see Russell A. Peck, "The Ideas of 'Entente' and Translation in Chaucer's *Second Nun's Tale*," *AnM*, 8 (1967), 17–37. For my reading of *The House of Fame* see *The Poetry of Chaucer* (Carbondale, 1977), pp. 148–90.

9. Clogan, "Style and Meaning," pp. 224–25.

CONTRIBUTORS

DAVID CHAMBERLAIN is Professor of English at the University of Iowa. He received his M.A. from the University of Oxford and his Ph.D. from Princeton University, and has contributed articles on medieval literature to *Manuscripta*, *Modern Philology*, *Mediæval Studies*, *Speculum*, and *Chaucer Review*.

JOHN GARDNER is Writer-in-Residence at the State University of New York, Binghamton. After receiving his Ph.D. from the University of Iowa, he taught medieval literature and creative writing at Oberlin, Skidmore, San Francisco State, and Southern Illinois. In addition to his novels *Grendel*, *The Sunlight Dialogues*, *Nickel Mountain*, *October Light*, and *Freddy's Book*, the epic poem *Jason and Medeia*, and two opera libretti, he has published *The Complete Works of the Gawain Poet*, *The Alliterative Morte Arthure*, *The Construction of Christian Poetry in Old English*, *The Construction of the Wakefield Cycle*, *The Life and Times of Chaucer*, and *The Poetry of Chaucer*.

GAIL MCMURRAY GIBSON is Assistant Professor of English at Princeton University. She received her M.A. from Duke University, where she studied with Edmund Reiss, and her Ph.D. from the University of Virginia, where she wrote a dissertation under the supervision of V. A. Kolve. She has recently published articles in the *Keats-Shelley Journal*, *Journal of Medieval and Renaissance Studies*, and *Speculum*, and is currently at work on a study of medieval drama.

BERNARD F. HUPPÉ is Distinguished Service Professor of English at the State University of New York, Binghamton, and Director of the Center for Medieval and Early Renaissance Studies. He received his Ph.D. from New York University, and has taught at Duke, the University of Vienna, and Princeton. He is the author of *Piers Plowman and Scriptural Tradition* (with D. W. Robertson, Jr.), *Fruyt and Chaf* (with D. W. Robertson, Jr.), *Doctrine and Poetry*, *A Reading of the Canterbury Tales*, *Web of Words*, and *The Old English Homily and Its Backgrounds* (with Paul Szarmach), as well as articles in *ELH*, *PMLA*, *Studies in Philology*, *Modern Language Notes*, *Modern Language Review*, and *Journal of English and Germanic Philology*.

V. A. KOLVE is Professor of English at the University of Virginia. He received the D.Phil. from the University of Oxford, and previously taught at Stanford University. He is the author of *The Play Called Corpus Christi*, co-editor of the Norton Critical Edition of *Nine Canterbury Tales and the General Prologue*, wrote the chapter on "Chaucer and the Visual Arts" in *Chaucer (Writers and Their Backgrounds)*, ed. Derek Brewer, and is currently working on a book entitled *Narrative Imagery and The Canterbury Tales.* He has been resident scholar at the Villa Serbelloni Research Center of the Rockefeller Foundation (Belaggio, Italy), and has received fellowships from the Guggenheim Foundation and the Center for Advanced Studies of the University of Virginia.

EDMUND REISS is Professor of English at Duke University and Senior Fellow of the Southeastern Institute of Medieval and Renaissance Studies. After receiving his doctorate from Harvard University, he taught at Suffolk, Western Reserve, Penn State, Columbia, and Harvard. He has published books on *Sir Thomas Malory, William Dunbar,* and *The Art of the Middle English Lyric,* is editing the Shipman's Tale for *The Variorum Chaucer* and the Toronto bibliography on *Arthurian Legend and Romance,* and is co-editor of *The Complete Poetry of John Skelton.* He has written articles for *Annuale Mediæval, Papers on Language and Literature, Chaucer Review, Modern Language Notes, Studies in Philology, PMLA, Journal of English and Germanic Philology,* and *Medievalia et Humanistica,* as well as numerous chapters in collections and festschriften. He serves as Medieval Latin section head for the *MLA International Bibliography,* as well as on the editorial boards of *Studies in Iconography, Journal of Medieval and Renaissance Studies,* and *Chaucer Review,* and has held fellowships from the American Council of Learned Societies and the American Philosophical Society.

D. W. ROBERTSON, JR., is Murray Professor of English at Princeton University. After receiving his Ph.D. from the University of North Carolina, he taught at Maryland, North Carolina, and Yale. He has published *Piers Plowman and Scriptural Tradition* (with Bernard F. Huppé), *Fruyt and Chaf* (with Bernard F. Huppé), *A Preface to Chaucer,* and *Chaucer's London.* He has also edited *The Literature of Medieval England,* translated St. Augustine's *On Christian Doctrine,* and contributed articles to *Speculum, Studies in Philology, ELH, Modern Language Notes,* and *Philological Quarterly.* He has held fellowships from the American Council of Learned Societies and the Guggenheim Foundation, and was awarded an honorary D. Litt. from Villanova University for his contributions to the study of medieval literature and culture.

JAMES I. WIMSATT is Professor of English at the University of Texas. He received his Ph.D. from Duke University, and has taught at the University of Tennessee at Knoxville, Texas Christian University, and the University of North Carolina at Greensboro. He is editor of *Selected Poems of Guillaume de Machaut* for The Chaucer Library and The Book of the Duchess for *The Variorum Chaucer.* He is the author of *Chaucer and the French Love Poets, The Marguerite Poetry of Guillaume de Machaut,* and *Allegory and Mirror,* as well as articles in *Journal of English and Germanic Philology, Mediæval Studies, Modern Philology, Medium Aevum, PMLA, Traditio,* and *Chaucer Review,* and has received American Council of Learned Societies and Huntington Library fellowships.

CHAUNCEY WOOD is Professor of English at McMaster University. After receiving his Ph.D. from Princeton University, he taught at Hollins, Cincinnati, and Wisconsin. He is the author of *Chaucer and the Country of the Stars,* the chapter on "Chaucer and Astrology" in *A Companion to Chaucer Studies,* ed. Beryl Rowland, as well as articles in *Texas Studies in Language and Literature, Chaucer Review, English Studies, Modern Language Quarterly, Traditio, English Language Notes,* and *Philological Quarterly.* He has been awarded research fellowships by the Canada Council, the American Council of Learned Societies, and the Institute for Research in the Humanities of the University of Wisconsin.

INDEXES

Chaucer Index

General Index